Islamic technology
An illustrated history

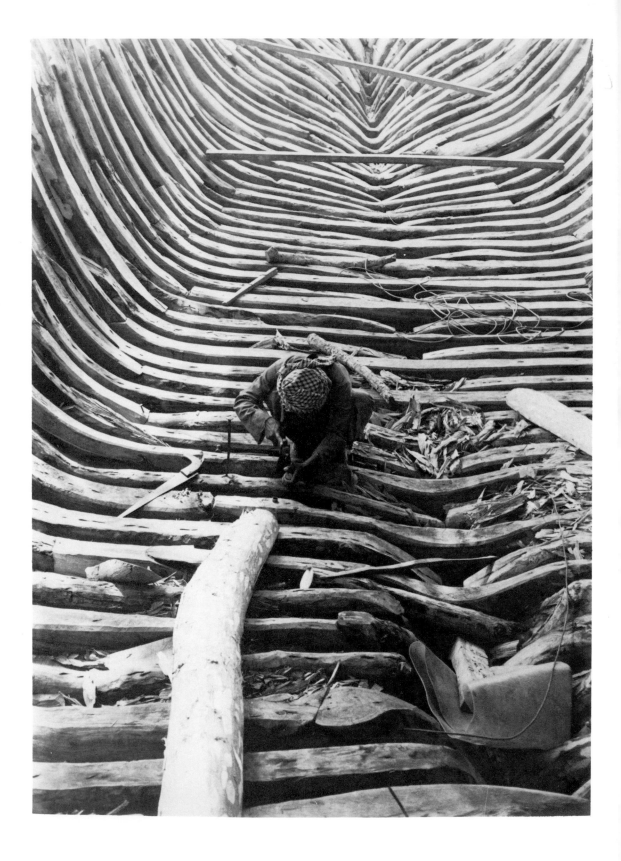

Islamic technology

An illustrated history

Ahmad Y. al-Hassan
Donald R. Hill

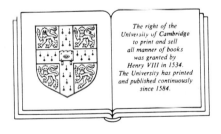

The right of the
University of Cambridge
to print and sell
all manner of books
was granted by
Henry VIII in 1534.
The University has printed
and published continuously
since 1584.

Cambridge University Press

Cambridge
New York   Port Chester
Melbourne   Sydney

Unesco

Paris

First published 1986
by the United Nations Educational,
Scientific and Cultural Organization,
7 Place de Fontenoy, 75700 Paris, France
and
The Press Syndicate of the University of Cambridge
The Pitt Building, Trumpington Street, Cambridge CB2 1RP
40 West 20th Street, New York, NY 10011-4211, USA
10 Stamford Road, Oakleigh, Victoria 3166, Australia

Printed in Great Britain by BAS Printers Ltd., Over Wallop, Hants.

British Library cataloguing in publication data
al-Hassan, Ahmad Y.
Islamic technology: an illustrated history.
1. Technology – Islamic countries – History
I. Title   II. Hill, D. R.
609'17'671   T27.3

Library of Congress cagaloguing in publication data
Hassan, Ahmad Yusuf.
Islamic technology.
Bibliography.
Includes index.
1. Technology – Islamic Empire – History.
I. Hill, Donald Routledge.   II. Title.
T27.3I75H37   1986   609.17'671   86–6069

Unesco ISBN 92 3 102294 6 hardback
        ISBN 92 3 102733 6 paperback
Cambridge University Press ISBN 0 521 26333 6 hardback
                           ISBN 0 521 42239 6 paperback

BO

Contents

Illustrations

viii

Unesco Preface

The need to promote the development of endogenous technologies has been expressed at various international meetings organised by Unesco; and it was emphasised at the Arab regional level during the Conference of Ministers of Arab States Responsible for the Application of Science and Technology to Development (CASTARAB) convened by Unesco in Rabat in August 1976.

Moreover, the shortage was felt of adequate reference material for use by engineering educators and students in the region involved in introductory courses dealing with the history of science and technology and the contribution of earlier Arab and Islamic civilisations thereto.

For these reasons, Unesco's Programme and Budget for 1979–1980 foresaw the compilation of inventories of endogenous technology within the general programme objective number 2/4.3/06, and it was decided that one such survey would deal in particular with the contributions of earlier Arab and Moslem civilisations to the progress of technology. The project was also incorporated within the framework of Unesco's participation in the celebrations of the Moslem World in commemoration of the fifteenth centenary of the Hegira.

The preparation of the study was entrusted to Professor Ahmed Yousif Al-Hassan who, although being a mechanical engineer by profession, was for some time the Director of the Institute of Islamic Science, Aleppo, and has, therefore, a great deal of knowledge of the history of science and technology in the Arab region. In preparing this work, he has drawn upon the expertise of many of his colleagues in the Arab region and elsewhere and was able to obtain the assistance of Dr Donald Hill, the co-author of the present work.

It is very much hoped that the book will be of use to those studying the history of science and technology and in particular those who are interested in the study of the contribution of the Islamic world in technological progress. Certain parts may also be useful as teaching material for engineering educators in the Arab region. The book has the great merit of drawing together information from a wide variety of sources, and therefore presents a balanced view of the subject.

Unesco extends its thanks to the authors and to all those who have assisted in one way or the other in accomplishing this task.

Finally, it should be noted that the opinions expressed in this book are those of the authors and do not necessarily represent the views of Unesco. The designations employed and the presentation of the material do not imply the expression of any opinion whatsoever on the part of the Organisation concerning the legal status of any country or territory, or of its authorities, or concerning the frontiers of any country or territory.

Preface and acknowledgements

Technology is the tool of civilisation, and for Islamic civilisation to have been such a leading force for several centuries, clearly it must have been based on important technological achievements.

No single synthetic work has been written until now on Islamic technology, for it seems that there was insufficient published research to enable writers to undertake such a venture. Even the leading published general histories of technology have no chapter devoted to Islamic technology, or if they have, the exposition has been written by an author with little affection for Islamic civilisation.

We were asked by Unesco to write this book on the occasion of the fifteenth century of Hijra. But to write a concise book on a vast subject in the absence of sufficient research is a very difficult task. It is also a distraction from one's own research programme.

We felt, however, that we must accept Unesco's request, and called on many academic organisations which are interested in the subject to co-operate. It was not possible in practice, in view of the short time and the limited number of words allowed, to organise a wide circle of contributors. The text was written, therefore, solely by us.

Because of the lack of published material, it was necessary to search out primary sources, especially Arabic manuscripts. In consequence some results are published here for the first time.

This book is only a concise introduction to the subject. Even so it is the first attempt to put together the story of Islamic technology. It also raises several critical issues but being a concise book intended for a wide circulation, and not a research monograph, we do not usually cite the relevant literature in footnotes. The selected bibliography will be sufficient to guide the interested reader to other sources.

Credit for initiating this book goes to Unesco and we should like to record our thanks for the support which it provided.

We should also like to thank Aleppo University, which

enabled one of us to devote time and effort to the project, supplied us through the Institute for the History of Arabic Science with a huge mass of literature and copies of manuscripts, and allocated the time of several assistants to this task.

In addition we wish to thank University College London and the Department of History and Philosophy of Science, which provided the opportunity to work in London near the marvellous research libraries.

An extensive literature search has been undertaken by collaborators in Aleppo, London and Paris, without which this work would have taken much longer to complete. We give special thanks to Mrs Dorriyyah al Khatib, Miss Safa Masallati, Mr Mustafa Mawaldi, Mr Samir Qamand, Mr Riad Sammani, and Miss Rene Shami, all of the Institute for the History of Arabic Science, Aleppo University, Syria; Mr Noman Haq, of University College London; and Mrs Simone Zakri, of the University of Paris.

Ahmed Y. al-Hassan was primarily responsible for Chapters 1.2 and 5; 2.6; 4.8; 6; 7; 8; 9; and 10. Donald R. Hill was primarily responsible for chapters 1.1, 3, 4 and 6; 2.1 to 5; 3; 4.1 to 7; and 5.

Mr Colin Ronan, the writer and historian of science, undertook a full editorial role in revising and preparing the typescript for publication. Ms Charlotte Deane undertook the picture research and completed the group of illustrations used in this book.

Grateful acknowledgement is due to those who have granted permission for the reproduction of illustrations.

Ahmad Y. al-Hassan
Donald R. Hill.

فقال الله للبق راجواز ربيع وللصق فحقب بن ريح انه بقوم لبحيكم ولد اليوم قال فكان الجماعة

ابن ربيع وقره واب نصركوره وكنون في افكارهم ما حي وفط لما يبطن من استنكام وحاذران

ثم قال ايه واه لا نصر واشاه لقول الله لبطر ان علطمنة الجوهر

الشك قدني بطماح من لزمان عبد لا يمكر يكم ارحل اويان

1 *Introduction*

1.1 BRIEF REVIEW OF PRE-ISLAMIC SCIENCE AND TECHNOLOGY

It would obviously be impossible in the space available here to discuss the development of science and technology from the rise of the ancient civilisations of Egypt, Sumeria and China up to the advent of Islam. In any case, it is more relevant to consider the state of knowledge on the eve of Islam in the countries that were about to be transformed into the Muslim world. These comprised the present-day Arabic-speaking countries, together with Iran, parts of Central Asia, the Iberian peninsula, and most of the Mediterranean islands (see the map on pp. 2–3). In many ways this area was a cultural entity, and its culture was the predominating influence upon the foundation and early development of Islamic science and technology.

In technology, apart from the works of a few writers such as Philon of Byzantium (third century BC) and Heron of Alexandria (first century AD), the main impetus for the growth of Muslim technology was to come from skilled technologists and from the examples provided by their works, such as irrigation systems and textile factories. In the case of science, however, the transmission was largely by means of written material and we have therefore to consider the works of the so-called Hellenistic period, which lasted from 323 BC until the advent of Islam.

Hellenistic science incorporated the works of Greek scientists of the classical period, while itself also making considerable advances in theory and practice. It embraced almost the entire corpus of scientific knowledge available because Greek science had itself embodied the results obtained by Babylonian, Egyptian and Indian scientists. It is significant that the centre of this intellectual activity was Alexandria, with daughter establishments in such places as Syracuse in Sicily, Antioch in Syria and Pergamon in Asia Minor. And though the language of learning was Greek, scientists came from all the countries of the Near East and the eastern Mediterranean. A common feature in the lives of most of them was that they lived either in

1.1 A public library near Baghdad, from a manuscript of the *Maqamat* by al-Hariri. Thirteenth century AD. Bibliothèque Nationale, Paris.

1

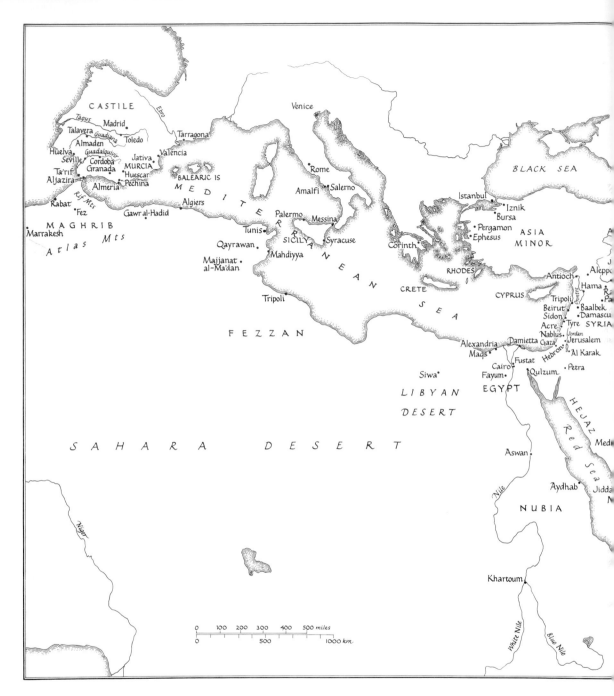

Alexandria or spent a period of learning and research in that city. Another centre of learning, not directly connected with Alexandria, flourished in the city of Jundaysabur in southern Iran. It was founded in Sassanid times (third century AD onwards) by the Nestorian Christians fleeing from Byzantine persecution, and was particularly renowned for its medical school, though other sciences were also studied there. Part of its importance lay in its assimilation of Indian scientific ideas.

We shall now give a very brief summary of the state of science and technology in the Mediterranean Middle East area on the eve of Islam.

1.1.1 Science

Scientific activity in Alexandria centred upon the Museum and Library, both founded towards the close of the fourth century BC. Members of the Museum were provided with free board and lodging, received salaries, and were aided in their research by the resources of the incomparable Library, containing more than 700 000 volumes. The predominant influence of the Alexandrian school was that of Aristotle, although its practitioners arrived at many conclusions diametrically opposed to those of the master. Science came to be considered as being independent of, though not necessarily opposed to, the metaphysical concerns of philosophers; Hellenistic science, being essentially practical, concentrated on the study of natural phenomena and their mathematical interpretation. Facts were no longer made to fit theories conceived in the abstract.

Hellenistic mathematics had a number of great exponents, including Euclid (first half of the third century BC), Archimedes (d. 212 BC), and Apollonios of Perga, who lived at Alexandria, Ephesus and Pergamos from the middle of the third century BC to the beginning of the second. This mathematics was strongly geometrical in tendency and usually expressed results in geometrical terms, even in subjects such as arithmetic and algebra. Euclid's *Elements* was the foundation of systematic geometry and remained the cornerstone for the teaching of the subject until recent times. It dealt exhaustively with plane geometry, but also included a general theory of ratios, as well as a study of straight lines for which no simple ratios existed, and a treatise on the basic solid figures, the sphere, the cone and the cylinder.

Archimedes carried out a number of brilliant studies of plane and solid figures, basing his theories upon mechanical rather than mathematical considerations. Later, however, he was able to provide a rigorous synthesis of these partly intuitive methods – a clear proof of his genius. The high point of the study of conic sections was reached, however, with the work of Apollonios, who introduced the terms 'ellipse', 'parabola' and 'hyperbola', and showed that the three curves can be obtained by cutting a cone in different directions.

A later Hellenistic mathematician was Diophantos. His approach marked a departure from previous mathematical trends, and it has been shown recently that he was indebted to Babylonian mathematicians, though his work goes beyond what they achieved. Instead of being geometrical in outlook, it was essentially algebraic, albeit that its method of writing the results was rudimentary compared with what we are accustomed to nowadays. However, this did not stop Diophantos from tackling some very difficult problems, from which later mathematicians were to derive much benefit. Another mathematical subject was trigonometry; it is exemplified in the work of the astronomer Ptolemy and is based upon a study of chords drawn across curves in order to calculate the angles involved in astronomical observations. From the theorem which bears his name, Ptolemy showed how to calculate the chord of the difference or sum of two arcs, the chords of each of which were known individually. He was thus able to draw up a table of chords that was of immense importance in astronomical computation.

The astronomical works of Ptolemy, who flourished at Alexandria between AD 127 and 151, were to become the standard treatises on the subject for the next fourteen centuries, although they were considerably modified by Muslim astronomers. Ptolemy certainly based his work on that of his predecessors, notably Hipparchos, who made most of his observations in Rhodes and Alexandria between 161 and 127 BC. Nevertheless, Ptolemy's *Mathematical Treatise* (*al-Majisti* in Arabic, *Almagest* in medieval Latin) is the most complete account of the geocentric system, which places the Earth at the centre of the Universe. However, to explain the motions of the Sun, Moon and planets as precisely as possible, he found it necessary to assume, first, that they move in circles whose centres are slightly displaced from the centre of the Earth and secondly, that these orbiting points themselves acted as centres of small circles – 'epicycles' – around the circumferences of which Sun, Moon and planets were carried. By rigorous demonstrations, countless observations and ingenious mathematical arguments, Ptolemy was able to construct a model of the Solar System that agreed, in general, with the actual behaviour of all orbiting celestial bodies.

Ptolemy also wrote a work on optics, in which he accepted Euclid's mistaken idea that the eye emitted visual rays, though both realised that light was propagated with great speed in straight lines. Ptolemy also studied reflection and refraction through transparent media such as air and water, formulating laws in an attempt to explain his observations.

Hellenistic achievements in mechanics and hydrostatics are impressive, particularly as evinced in the works of Archimedes and Heron. As is well known, Archimedes solved the hydrostatic problem which bears his name, as is related in the famous account of the way he assessed the purity of King Hieron's crown, weighing it first in air and then in water and comparing his results with equivalent amounts of gold and silver weighed in a similar manner. He also made notable contributions to the study of the specific gravity of bodies and to mechanics. Heron, for his part, gave practical demonstrations of the principles of aerostatics, hydrostatics and dynamics. These he described in his *Pneumatics* and *Mechanics*, which also have a considerable engineering content.

A number of chemical processes used in manufacturing industries were described by classical and Hellenistic writers. Chemical phenomena were never studied for their inherent interest, however, but rather were used to illustrate philosophical speculations. Bolos of Mendes, an Egyptian who lived at the beginning of the second century BC, wrote a treatise in which he combined ancient Egyptian alchemical practices with Greek metaphysical and physical conceptions; he may therefore be regarded as the father of alchemy. Although it is the task of specialists to disentangle the mystical elements of alchemy from the practical, there can be no doubt that this science was to play an important role in the development of chemistry and chemical technology.

After the end of the third century AD there was a falling off in original scientific work in the Hellenistic world. Emphasis shifted to writing commentaries and elucidating the works of the great scientists of earlier centuries. Nevertheless, the corpus of written material from the classical and Hellenistic period was kept in being in the libraries at various centres of learning, and became available for translation and study after the advent of Islam.

1.1.2 Technology

In his *de Architectura*, Vitruvius (first century BC) described a number of techniques and machines used in mechanical and civil engineering, and in building construction. He also mentioned several Hellenistic engineers, including Ctesibios (first half of the third century BC) and his contemporary Philon. Ctesibios constructed elaborate water-clocks and other devices, but we only know of his work from the descriptions of Vitruvius. However, the writings of Philon and his successor Heron have come down to us in Arabic translations, and from these we find that both described ingenious devices which embodied the principles of mechanics, aerostatics and hydrostatics. Vitruvius himself also described a number of machines, including a water-mill with a vertical undershot wheel (illustrated in Fig. 2.9, below, p.51), several water-raising devices and machines for raising heavy weights. We know that the vertical undershot, overshot and horizontal water-wheels were all in use in the Middle East and Europe for grinding corn before the seventh century AD, but as yet we have no evidence for the application of water-power to other industrial uses.

Civil engineering is represented by the extensive irrigation systems of Egypt and Iraq, with their associated dams, sluices and weirs. Large masonry dams were also built by the Romans, Persians and the Arabs of the Yemen to impound the water of rivers or wadis, for use in irrigation and to increase the head of water above water-mills. The Romans were particularly conversant with questions of water supply; they built impressive aqueducts and used large lead pipes to carry the water in syphons through valley bottoms. In addition, the Romans, Byzantines and Sassanid Persians all built well-engineered road systems, often with masonry bridges at river crossings.

Cavalry was the most important corps of all military forces. They were armed with swords, lances and composite bows, yet only on the eve of Islam did the stirrup come into general use. The crossbow was known in Hellenistic times but does not seem to have been a common weapon in the Byzantine and Sassanid armies. Siege engines were familiar, however, and used the resilience of twisted fibres or wood to provide the energy for discharging their missiles. In addition, the Byzantines had a formidable fleet of warships and maintained large naval dockyards in Asia Minor, Syria and Egypt.

There were textile factories in many places in the Byzantine and Sassanid empires, where cloths were woven from wool, silk and cotton – although large-scale production of cotton did not take place until Islamic times. New weaving techniques were invented in Syria and Upper Mesopotamia during the second and third centuries AD to suit new fibres and changing tastes, while the allied industry of dyeing stimulated the rise of chemical technology. Glass-blowing was discovered in Syria in the first century BC, with the result that new shapes could be produced more cheaply, and vessels made of glass became common items of household equipment.

1.2 SOME FACTORS OF INNOVATION IN ISLAMIC TECHNOLOGY

The relationship between technology and the two main economic factors, agriculture and industry, are discussed throughout this book, so we can pass on now to mention some of the other factors which influenced Islamic technology. These include Islam as a religion and as a society, the science policy of the State, and the skills, actual and latent, inherited from pre-Islamic times.

1.2.1 Religion and the cultural unity of Islam

It would seem unnecessary to discuss an obvious factor such as the role played by the Islamic religion in the renaissance of

Arabic civilisation, since without Islam probably no such renaissance would have taken place. We demonstrate through-out this book some of the Islamic technological achievements in agriculture, industry, war and in all aspects of daily life. And if we wish to analyse the teachings of Islam, we shall find ample evidence to show that it was a positive force in all these achievements.

The blossoming of science and culture in Islamic civilisations was the result of the increasing quality of material life in Muslim cities. The urban life of these cities, the material prosperity, the varied local industries, the local and inter-national trade, and the flourishing science and culture, were all linked together, while none of the aspects of life in the cities would have flourished without a developing technology. And if Islam was the force behind the rise of cities, as is frequently asserted, then it was also the force behind all aspects of the prosperity of these cities and hence the technological efforts associated with urban life.

In addition to the positive effects of the ideology of Islam as a religion, Islam achieved a unique historical effect in the history of mankind. It united into one the civilisations of the vast expanse which lies between the borders of China and the Atlantic. This area comprised the lands of those ancient civilisations which were also the seat of later civilisations in the Near East, such as the Hellenistic. This vast region remained under one government during the first centuries of Islam. But the more important result, even after the rise of various dynasties, was the cultural unity of Muslim countries. Islam abolished the barriers which had isolated these countries from each other, so that the whole area now had one religion and one literary and scientific language. The cultural unity also ensured free passage and free trade with China in the east to Spain in the west. Scientists and men of letters were free to travel, and crossed vast distances to meet other scholars. Moreover, although the Umayyads in Spain did not acknowledge the Abbasid Caliphate in Baghdad, there always existed links between Spain and the East.

1.2.2 The State and its science policy

We are entitled to use the modern term 'science policy' when we speak about Islamic science and technology. It is an important fact in Muslim history that civilisation flourished only under a stable government with an enlightened science policy. Even in epochs when there were multitudes of smaller Islamic states, science and technology flourished whenever there was an independent government and a national army. The science policy of a Muslim state was behind the Arabicising and translation movement; the establishment of academies, observatories and libraries; the patronage of scientists and conduct of scientific and technological research; as well as the running of some state industries and projects. Throughout this book there are numerous examples of the role of the State in creating and maintaining projects. We can, therefore, move on to deal briefly with other aspects of innovation in Islamic technology.

1.2.3 Arabicising and the role of Arabic

When we speak about the achievements of Islamic civilisation, we think immediately of the huge written heritage which has come down to us in all branches of knowledge. It is estimated that there exist at the present day, in spite of destruction and many losses, nearly a quarter of a million manuscripts, mostly in Arabic, in the various libraries of the world. And this does not include unrecorded collections.

The Islamic religion and the Arabic language were the two unifying forces of the Islamic state. They were always interrelated. Arabic is the language of the Qur'an and hence it is held in respect as holy by all Muslims. But the real miracle of Islamic civilisation is that Arabic became the language of all the peoples who lived between Baghdad and Cordoba. It became both the language of daily life and the language of science and literature, replacing completely Coptic, Aramaic, Greek and Latin. Beyond Baghdad Islam and Arabic also had a great impact. Persian and Turkish developed into Islamic languages, and Arabic influenced the languages of other Islamic peoples. During the Hellenistic period, Greek did not succeed in becoming the language of the peoples of the Near East; it did become the literary and scientific language, but was used only in the scientific schools of Alexandria and other cities. The main national languages were Aramaic and Coptic. Craftsmen and ordinary people could neither read nor understand the Greek writings of the scholars. Under Roman rule the failure of Latin in the Near East was even greater. It did not even succeed in replacing Greek as the language of culture, and of course it was never the language of the populace. But under Islam the peoples of the ancient civilisations of the Near East and the Mediterranean spoke and wrote one common language for the first time in history.

Arabic played the key role in the rise of Islamic science and culture. As a basic part of their science policy, the Caliphs realised this from the early days of the Umayyads. The sciences of the Greeks, of the Near East (Hellenistic and Syriac), and of India were to be translated into Arabic, because it became apparent that it was not possible for a civilisation to flourish if the sciences were studied in a language limited only to very few scholars. With the translation of the sciences into Arabic the cultural barrier between the scholars and the people was removed, and learning came within the reach of all.

The admirable flexibility of the Arabic language enabled the Muslims to coin exact scientific and technological vocabularies capable of expressing the most complicated scientific and technical ideas. They did not hesitate also to borrow some terms from other languages. The technological books written by the Banu Musa brothers, al-Jazari, Ridwan, Taqi al-Din and others used simple Arabic, for all these engineers were practical men and their interest was confined to conveying exact meanings. We find in the language of the Banu Musa and al-Jazari many grammatical errors, but these did not affect the accuracy of their expression. We also observe that all these engineers used the same terms that were common currency among the craftsmen of the time, many of which have continued in use up to the present day. We do not find them in the classical dictionaries, but we come across them in technical books; a state of affairs that still obtains. The situation should of course be remedied for it is, surely, the task of lexicographers to keep in step with the progress of the language.

1.2.4 Academies, schools, observatories, and libraries

To help in implementing science policy, Islamic Caliphs and rulers established scientific academies, schools, libraries and observatories.

One such scientific institution was the *Bayt al-Hikma* (House of Wisdom) founded in Baghdad by al-Ma'mun, whose reign started in 198 AH/813AD. This academy rendered a great service by translating philosophical and scientific works into Arabic, and it exerted a considerable influence on the development of Islamic science and thought. Missions were sent to the country of Rum (Byzantium) to collect manuscripts. The academy, which included a staff of eminent scientists and translators, as well as copyists and binders, was extremely tolerant, and among its members were such famous men as the Islamic Banu Musa brothers, the Nestorian Christian Hunayn b. Ishaq, and Thabit b. Qurra, a member of the Sabean religion. Attached to the academy were two astronomical observatories, one in Baghdad and the other in

Damascus. *Bayt al-Hikma* was a natural development of the science policy which started with the Arabicisation movement. Before al-Ma'mun an important library called *Khizanat al-Hikma* (Library of Wisdom) had already been established by Harun al-Rashid (170–93 AH/AD 786–809) and the Barmakids; where a translation movement was already in progress.

Under the Fatimids (297–567 AH/AD 909–1171) the same policy was adopted. The palace housed a large library, and meetings were organised for men of learning. Soon, in 395 AH/AD 1004, al-Hakim established the *Dar al-Hikma* (House of Science), which was also housed in a part of the palace. It contained a library and a reading-room, and served as a meeting place for traditionists, jurists, grammarians, logicians, doctors, astronomers, and mathematicians. *Dar al-Hikma* was directed by an acknowledged scholar who used to invite scientists to regular seminars. The academy collected books on all subjects, produced a catalogue and was served by librarians, copyists and binders. Lecturers were provided to teach all scientific subjects and its facilities were free to the public, who were provided with ink, pens and paper. The *Dar al-Hikma* and *Khizanat al-Hikma* are typical of the names given to scientific institutions and libraries. Houses or libraries of science, on the model of the *Bayt al-Hikma* in Baghdad and the *Dar al-Hikma* in Cairo, became numerous. Some were established by public funds, others by individuals. Moreover, all large mosques had libraries attached, as many people donated their books to them. It was also the custom of Caliphs, kings, notables and scholars to establish large libraries. But such libraries were too numerous for us to be able to give information and reports about them here.

The mosque was always a centre of learning and in the early days lessons were given in the mosques themselves, with each teacher and his students occupying a corner or space by a pillar. From these beginnings the institution of the *madrasa* (school, *lit.* the place for lessons) came into being. Gradually teaching became more formal and special buildings were erected for such schools, with mosques attached to them. Similarly, the university, in which various subjects were taught, developed from the *madrasa*. The most important universities were at al-Azhar in Cairo (Fig. 1.2), the Zaytuniyya in Tunis and the Qarawiyyin in Fez (Fig. 1.3). In addition, medical schools were attached to hospitals, which therefore became institutions combining the function of healing with the teaching of medicine, pharmacology and allied subjects.

The observatory was a scientific institution in itself, carrying out both research and teaching. The observatories of the *Bayt al-Hikma* have already been mentioned, but gradually the Muslim observatory gained in importance so that the Maragha observatory, where Nasir al-Din al-Tusi worked, was a major scientific institution in which many scientists co-operated together. The observatories of Ulugh Beg in Samarqand and of Taqi al-Din in Istanbul (Figs. 1.4, 1.5) represented further developments, and in them Islamic observatories reached their peak. It was these last two that served as models for the early European observatories such as that of Tycho Brahe.

In addition, scientists and engineers were also educated in private circles under the guidance of well-known teachers. Such students met their teacher either at his house or at the house of one of his disciples. This was always a powerful and important means of instruction.

1.2.5 Patronage of scientists

The patronage of scientists and engineers was always a deliberate policy of state, as represented by the Caliph or the ruler. This tradition became adopted equally throughout the vast Islamic empire and by the smaller independent states. Whereas the Banu Musa brothers flourished in Baghdad in the golden days of the Empire (third century AH/ninth century AD), al-Jazari received no less patronage from the Artuqid kings of the small state of Amid three hundred years later. In all the academies, libraries, *madrasas*, hospitals and observatories, mentioned above, financial means were provided to enable scientists to devote all their time to study and research. They were paid salaries and granted pensions. What is more, this patronage was not confined to scholars within such institutions, but was also given in various other circumstances. The Caliph al-Mu'tadid (d. 290 AH/AD 902), for example, provided in his palace lodgings and rooms for all branches of science, and professors were paid salaries for teaching there.

1.2.6 Research, experiment and invention

The State enabled scientists and engineers to spend all their time on research, inventions and writing. In addition, the Caliphs used to form scientific missions to make observations, carry out measurements or report on natural phenomena, while some research was also undertaken for military purposes. There are reports explaining how the state took great interest in developing gunpowder and firearms, and we read in military treatises and histories reports about such experiments and their results.

1.2 A view of the courtyard of the university mosque of al-Azhar, Cairo, founded in the tenth century AD.

One can detect a real spirit of research and invention prevalent among scientists and engineers. Such invention and research would follow this sequence:

Crafts arose and developed because an original creator transmits to a successor what he had created earlier. This successor examines it critically and adds to it as far as he possibly can. This process continues until the craft achieves perfection.

The same author, Abu'l-Faraj 'Abd Allah b. al-Tayyib (d. 435 AH/AD 1043) described the stage when Muslim scientists started by studying the works of their predecessors:

In our studies we have followed in the footsteps of our predecessors and taken pains to understand their works well. We have also discovered, in connection with obscure statements and explanations of them, a number of ideas going beyond what they had said.

Taking the Banu Musa brothers as an example, we find that

1.3 A doorway of the Qarawiyyan university mosque, Fez. The mosque, mostly dating from the twelfth century AD, is at the centre of the university which was itself founded in the ninth century AD.

they lived during the initial stage of translation, but soon moved to a stage of research and innovation. As scientists and engineers they established an observatory at their own home and, in addition, the observatory of the *Bayt al-Hikma* was available to them. They carried our reliable observations, which were highly valued by later workers, studied atmospheric phenomena, and were members of several field missions. Their originality was expressed in their mathematical and engineering writings, and out of the hundred devices described in the *Kitab al-Hiyal* (Book of Ingenious Devices), about seventy five were of their own design. As is natural in the history of civilisation in general, Muslim scientists and engineers received the heritage of their predecessors, but this grew into their own science and technology through a continuous process of invention, research and development. As a result,

1.4 Part of the sextant of Ulugh Beg's observatory in Samarkand, built in the fifteenth century AD.

later generations of Muslim scientists and engineers studied the works of their predecessors more than anything else. Thus by the time of al-Jazari in the sixth century AH (twelfth century AD) the link with translated books had become weak; the sources al-Jazari used were mostly Islamic.

Neither the Banu Musa brothers nor al-Jazari, however, accepted the role of merely describing former designs. They were conscious of the importance of their own inventions, as we can sense from reading al-Jazari's statements in which he praises the Banu Musa brothers because they initiated the subject of ingenious machines, but declares he did not follow their ideas in his own designs. The title of al-Jazari's book, *A Compendium of the Theory and Practice of the Mechanical Arts*, itself reveals this attitude. He criticises those who wrote books without verifying the practicability of their designs, and says

1.5 Taqi al-Din and other astronomers in his observatory in
Istanbul. Miniature from a manuscript of the sixteenth century AD.
Istanbul Üniversitesi Kütüphanesi.

that any industrial science (*'ilm sina't*) that is not verified by
experiments is a doubtful science. In some places his book
gives unique descriptions of careful calibration procedures.
For example, when designing a flow regulator, he started by
checking experimentally three earlier designs. On finding
them unsatisfactory, he then produced his own and conducted
a series of experiments until he was able to reach his desired
objectives.

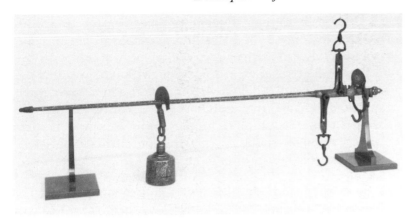

1.6 A steelyard from Egypt. It was probably used for weighing goods being traded in the Gulf area, for it is calibrated in the units of weight used in Basra as well as those of Egypt. Tenth to twelfth century AD. Science Museum, London, on loan from the Petrie Collection, University College, London.

Still later than al-Jazari, we find that Taqi al-Din was influenced both by al-Jazari as well as by his own immediate predecessors. He mentions clearly that the Greek books fell into disuse and disappeared because they were not related to practice, but he acknowledges the debt he owes to his own immediate teachers. In his books, Taqi al-Din always identifies his own designs in such words as 'this is one of the inventions of the present writer', or 'and the following is an invention of mine to achieve this purpose'.

1.2.7 International trade

In addition to agriculture and industry, international trade formed the third source of national income in the Islamic state. The strategic geographical position of Islamic countries between the East and the West, whereby they controlled important land and sea routes, enabled them to dominate international trade in the Middle Ages. This was aided by the appearance of the large cities of Islam, which gave rise to bourgeois merchants who were at one stage the dominant economic-social factor in the Muslim city.

The products which were traded at international level were varied. They included the products of Islamic lands themselves in addition to those of China and the Far East, and of Europe. As the historian Watt has written, 'In its specific character this trade between Europe and the Islamic world bore some resemblance to the colonial trade of the nineteenth and twentieth centuries, except that Europe was in the position of a colony. Its imports from the Islamic world consisted mainly of consumer goods, and in return it exported raw materials and slaves'.

Commercial methods and practices developed. Merchants

used their own capital and entered into partnership with others, increasing the total capital available to them. Conversely they invested their own capital with others with the object of diversifying their business activities and spreading the risk. They received goods on credit. Other sources of capital came from outside the merchant class, since all men of substance from the Caliph or Sultan downwards invested part of their capital in trade, just as the merchants themselves invested part of their profits in land.

Islamic currency was used in Europe. Scores of thousands of Islamic coins have been found in Scandinavia and in the Volga basin. These coins date from the first to fifth centuries AH (seventh to thirteenth centuries AD), which is the period of dominance of Muslim international trade, though the Islamic gold dinar continued in circulation in Europe for several centuries after this. The course of trade during this period 'brought Muslim gold into the great circuits of European commerce', and in turn 'brought it back to its country of origin – either directly or via Byzantium, which was a creditor to the West, but in debt to the East'. A milestone in European financial history occurred when Genoa minted its first gold currency at the close of this era.

The *Sarraf* or money-changer became an essential feature of every Muslim market. Banks with headquarters in Baghdad and branches in other cities are mentioned in Arabic sources. They carried on business through an elaborate system of cheques, letters of credit, etc., which was 'so developed that it was possible to draw a cheque in Baghdad and cash it in Morocco'. Indeed, it is reported that in Basra, the centre of trade with the East, each merchant had his own bank account; payments were effected in cheques and never in cash. It may be significant to mention that the word 'cheque' is derived from the Arabic word *sakk*.

This flourishing international trade had far-reaching effects. It was an important source of wealth and benefited the whole economy because merchants invested their surplus profits in agriculture, while the export of local goods caused industries to flourish. Moreover, merchants advanced capital to craftsmen to enable them to produce goods and raw materials which were not available in sufficient quantity from imports. In addition to all this, international trade was an effective means of communication among contemporary civilisations and was important for the transfer of technology. Thus, as Watt puts it, 'through trade contacts and through political presence in Spain and Sicily the superior culture of the Arabs gradually made its way into Western Europe'. This trade also had its direct effects on the technology of navigation, both in the construction of merchant navies and in the development of navigation techniques, as will become evident later.

1.3 DEVELOPMENT OF THE NATURAL SCIENCES IN ISLAM

1.3.1 The growth of Islamic science

We have so far seen how Islamic science, together with other types of intellectual activity, had its roots in the Hellenistic civilisation, whose main centre was at Alexandria, and how that civilisation in turn had been nourished by the earlier cultures of the Near East and the Mediterranean. We have also seen how scientific activity was fostered by the patronage and encouragement of enlightened princes and wealthy individuals, and how the founding of institutions such as academies, schools, libraries and observatories provided scientists with the means for pursuing their studies and passing on their knowledge. It will not have escaped notice, however, that the real beginnings of Islamic science did not occur until the start of the third century AH (ninth century AD), nearly two hundred years after the beginning of Islam.

The reasons for this interval are not difficult to identify. In the first two Muslim centuries men's thoughts and energies were directed towards establishing the new Islamic state. Not until about 100 AH/AD 728 were territorial limits reached with the addition of the Iberian peninsula and Central Asia. Even then, as with the conquest of every other region, there ensued a period of consolidation, during which the Muslim faith became predominant and the Arabic language gradually superseded the indigenous tongues. New legal systems were needed, and it was also a major task to reconcile existing fiscal arrangements with the precepts of Islam. At the same time, the Arabic language, ideally suited for coining new words, was adapted to meet the needs of the new society. By the end of the second and beginning of the third centuries AH (eighth to ninth centuries AD) some brilliant scholars such as Abu Zayd, Abu 'Ubayda and Al-Asma'i working in Basra completed the codification of the language and, by compiling a number of authoritative dictionaries and grammars, made it available to all educated Muslims as a vehicle for the expression of literary and scientific ideas. But the origins of Arabic writing in prose are earlier than this. We have the history of Ibn Ishaq (d. *c.* 86 AH/AD 705), which has come down to us in the recension of Ibn Hisham, and the works of historians such as Abu Mikhnaf and al-Mada'ini, whose works are quoted by al-Baladhuri and al-Tabari. The process of assimilation is exemplified by the writings of Ibn al-Muqaffa' (d. 138 AH/AD 756), who made a number of translations from Pahlevi into Arabic, notably the Indian fables of the *Kalila wa Dimna*, for which he used a Pahlavi version of the original. It has to be said, however, that we are insufficiently informed about science in the early Caliphate and Umayyad period; many works have been lost. We may conjecture, nevertheless, that the work of translation and original scientific writing had begun before the Abbasids assumed power, although it is unquestionably the Baghdad of the third century AH (ninth century AD) that witnessed the earliest, and one of the finest, flowerings of Islamic scientific activity. Over the next seven centuries, Muslim science flourished wherever and whenever conditions were propitious.

There can be no doubt that the institutions – academies, libraries, observatories, etc. – played a major role in the continuing vitality of Islamic science. These, together with the readiness of students to travel hundreds of miles to learn from acknowledged scholars, ensured that the whole corpus of knowledge was kept intact and transmitted from one place to another and from one generation to the next, with continual expansion and enrichment. There is ample confirmation of this, not least in the writings of the scientists themselves, who frequently refer to the works of their predecessors in such a manner as to leave no doubt that they were thoroughly familiar with them. It is therefore somewhat misleading to discuss science in, say, Fatimid Egypt or Umayyad Spain unless we make it clear that we are discussing two manifestations of the same phenomenon, since the same body of scientific knowledge, earlier and contemporary, was available to all Muslim scientists. Certainly, a great scientist could initiate a particular line of enquiry that would be followed by his successors, but this is characteristic of all good scientific work and is not limited by time or locality. Thus the line of astronomical research begun by Nasir al-Din al-Tusi at Maragha in the seventh century AH (thirteenth century AD) was completed by Ibn al-Shatir in Damascus a hundred years after. The work done by al-Biruni on specific weights in the fifth century AH (eleventh century AD) in Ghazna was continued by al-Khazini in Marw about a century later. Many other examples of this kind of continuity could be cited.

We give below brief details of a few great Islamic scientists, and equally brief discussions about four of the major branches of science. This is done in an effort to emphasise some of the high points of Muslim science. In the end, however, the Islamic contribution to physics, for example, can only be appreciated by a thorough study of Muslim physics, both separately and in comparison with its predecessors and successors. Such a task is clearly beyond the scope of this work. What we can say with certainty is that the most distinctive feature of Islamic science is its insistence on subjecting theories to every form of test – observational, mathematical and experimental.

1.3.2 Islamic science in general

Present state of research

In his monumental Introduction to the *History of Science*, George Sarton adopted the practice of dividing his work chronologically into chapters, giving each chapter the name of the most eminent scientist of the period in question. For the period from the middle of the second century AH (eighth century AD) to the middle of the fifth century AH (eleventh century AD), each fifty-year period carries the name of a Muslim scientist; there are seven in all. Thus we have the 'Time of al-Khwarizmi', the 'Time of al-Biruni', etc. Within these chapters we have the names of about one hundred important Islamic scientists and their main works. But although Sarton was one of the first historians to acknowledge the importance of the Muslim achievement, he has left the impression that there was a steep decline in Muslim scientific endeavour after the fifth century AH (eleventh century AD).

This was by no means the case. Anyone who leafs through the new volumes of F. Sezgin's history of Arabic literature will see not only the amount of material available from the first four centuries of Islam, but also that available from later centuries, which is considerably more. Moreover, the physical size of Sezgin's volumes on alchemy, medicine, astronomy and mathematics amounts to almost the total size of his volumes on the traditional Islamic sciences. Although this observation is not intended to imply that the total volume of scientific material approaches the volume of the available religious, historical or literary matter, it does illustrate the relative importance of science in medieval Islam. Yet books purporting to cover the whole field of Islamic culture are still being written with little or no mention of science. What is more, there is no satisfactory work on Islamic science as a whole, nor on any one of its branches.

There are hundreds of thousands of Islamic manuscripts in the world's libraries, most of them in Arabic, of which a large number deal with scientific subjects. Some collections have not been properly catalogued, and only a handful of the total number of manuscripts has been edited and published. Valuable work was done in the early years of this century by Eilhard Wiedemann, and recently a few dedicated scholars have devoted themselves to the tasks of cataloguing, describing and editing some of the mass of scientific material. However, only a co-ordinated international programme of research, sustained over many years, will ensure that the magnitude of the Islamic achievement is brought to the attention of the world. In view of the foregoing, it will be appreciated that singling out for mention a few Islamic scientists will to some extent lead to a distortion of the general picture, involving as it will the omission of many great names. Nevertheless, a brief discussion of some of the greatest scientists of Islam, provided it is not taken as implying any detraction from others of equal stature, may help to bring the Muslim achievement into focus.

Islamic scientists

The education of the Islamic scientist was broad enough to comprise most of the sciences of the day. But later in life each scientist became through his aptitude and interests an expert and a specialist in one or more of the sciences, such as medicine, engineering, mathematics, astronomy, and alchemy. From time to time scientists might be required to undertake projects at the request of a ruler, but in general they were provided with means for carrying out their work without undue interference from the state. And it should not be inferred, merely because they covered a range of subjects, that their approach was in any way superficial. They brought the full powers of their intellect to bear upon any subject on which they were engaged, and treated all subjects with equal seriousness. Though the scope and range of the topics covered by the great scientists excites our admiration, it should be remembered that in most cases we are judging them by only a small part of their total output, the greater part of their work having been lost.

Al-Kindi, Abu Yusuf Ya'qub (d. *c.* mid-third century AH/ ninth century AD) was one of the most original thinkers of Islam. Known as 'The Philosopher of the Arabs' he wrote upon a wide variety of subjects in addition to philosophy. He drew up a classification of the sciences and wrote two treatises on mineralogy as well as an important one on metallurgy and the art of making swords – the first of its kind in Arabic. He also wrote works on geology, physics, pharmacology and medicine, and was an accomplished physician. Al-Kindi warned against the mere reading of texts, which he considered an inadequate path to learning. We must, he said, 'follow along the paths of nature' to understand her.

Hunayn b. Ishaq (d. 260 AH/AD 873) may be taken as one of the best of the school of translator-scientists who worked in Baghdad in Abbasid times. From infancy he was bilingual in Arabic and Syriac, and he later became so astonishingly proficient in Greek that he was able to recite passages from Homer. He was chief physician to the court of the Caliph al-Mutawakkil, and most of his translations have high scientific value since he used to collect as many Greek manuscripts as possible of a given work and then collate them in order to get a sound textual basis for his translation. Besides his translations he composed numerous original works, mainly on medical subjects, though he also wrote on philosophical, geographical, meteorological, zoological, linguistic, and religious subjects.

Ibn al-Haytham, Abu 'Ali b. al-Hasan, (d. 430 AH/AD 1039) was one of the principal Muslim mathematicians and without any doubt the greatest physicist. The names of over a hundred of his works are known to us, and some nineteen of these, on mathematics, astronomy and physics, have been studied by modern scholars. His work exercised a profound influence on later scholars, both in Islam and the West, where he was known as Alhazen. One of his works on optics was translated into Latin in 1572. It includes a solution to a problem that still bears his name because of the mathematical genius he exhibited in resolving it. The demonstration, which is very complex, leads to an equation of the fourth degree (an equation involving x^4), which he solved geometrically by the intersection of an equilateral hyperbola with a circle.

Al-Biruni, Abu'l-Rayhan (d. after 442 AH/AD 1050), according to the historian D.J. Boilot, 'was one of the greatest scholars of medieval Islam, and certainly the most original and profound. He was equally well versed in the mathematics, astronomical, physical and natural sciences and also distinguished himself as a geographer and historian, chronologist and linguist, as well as an impartial observer of customs and creeds'. This is certainly an accurate description of this great scientist, one of the greatest of all time. He composed no less than 180 works embracing vast fields of knowledge. About forty of these have come down to us, a few of which have been edited, but there is no full edition of his extant works. A man well versed in several languages, al-Biruni was a careful scholar who always tested his conclusions by observation and experiment. He was also a competent instrument-maker and constructed astrolabes and a geared mechanical calendar. In this he did not differ from other Muslim scientists; indeed, the most highly-prized astrolabes were those made by astronomers.

Ibn al-Shatir (d. 777 AH/AD 1375), a Syrian and one of the most important of the later Islamic astronomers, was noted for his planetary theory and for inventing and constructing a number of astronomical instruments, both for observation and for computation. In planetary theory he followed Nasir al-Din al-Tusi, who had invented the 'Tusi couple' as a means for improving the Ptolemaic theory of planetary motion. Ptolemy had found that in order to account satisfactorily for observations of the motions of the outer planets – Mars, Jupiter and Saturn – he could not use the centre of the Earth as the centre of their circular motion, and had therefore devised the 'equant', a centre of rotation set a specific distance away from the centre of the Earth. Al-Tusi had proposed his 'couple' to restore uniform circular motion around the centre of the Earth for these planets. But it was only Ibn al-Shatir who was able to reach a satisfactory solution for the two most difficult orbiting bodies, Mercury and the Moon. Ibn al-Shatir's achievement shares many features with the models proposed by Copernicus over two centuries later, and there can be little doubt that Copernicus knew of Ibn al-Shatir's work.

1.4 ASPECTS OF ISLAMIC SCIENCE

In the space available it is only possible to mention some of the significant features of four sciences – mathematics, astronomy, physics, and chemistry.

1.4.1 Mathematics

The most important contribution of the Muslims in arithmetic was the introduction of the Indian system of reckoning, using the nine Arabic numerals, with a point for zero. The first manual of Indian reckoning, that of Muhammad b. Musa al-Khuwarizmi (c. 210 AH/AD 875) exists only in a number of Latin versions. Very significant innovations were introduced later, however, particularly by Abu'l-Hasan-al-Uqlidisi whose book *Kitab al-fusul fi'l-hisab al-hindi* (*Book of the parts of Indian arithmetic*) was composed in Damascus in 341 AH/AD 952–3. The most surprising feature of this book is the explanation and application of decimal fractions, an innovation which until recently had been attributed to Al-Kashi, five centuries later.

Al-Khuwarizmi, whose name has produced the word 'algorithm', was also responsible for laying the foundations of Islamic (and hence Western) algebra. 'Umar Khayyam (d. 526 AH/AD 1131), now more famous in the West as the poet 'Omar Khayyam', made considerable progress in this field. He classified equations of the third degree (those containing x^3) into 25 categories and then attempted to solve them, giving numerical solutions for equations of the first and second degrees (i.e. those with x and with x^2), and geometrical solutions (by means of conic sections) for those of the third degree.

Islamic geometry was founded on a deep study of Greek works, and was also influenced by the Indian *Siddhanta* (*Final Conclusion*). Of particular interest is the use of conic sections to solve problems and make calculations. Geometry was applied successfully in the fields of surveying and the construction of machines, including siege engines. And there is no doubt but that the Muslims were the inventors of plane and spherical trigonometry. The Greeks had calculated tables of chords, but with the Muslims the functions of the now familiar sine, cosine, and tangent became explicit. In spherical trigonometry al-Battani (d. 317 AH/AD 929) presented an important formula involving three sides and one angle of a spherical triangle, which has no equivalent in Ptolemy. Abu'l-Wafa (d. 388 AH/ AD 998), one of the greatest Muslim mathematicians, made further advances. He was probably the first to demonstrate the sine theorem for the general spherical triangle and proposed a new technique for the construction of sine tables. He also invented the trigonometrical quantities secant and cosecant.

1.4.2. Astronomy

The first impulse for the study of mathematical astronomy in Islam came from the translation of the Indian treatise, the *Siddhanta*. This occurred in Baghdad in 155 AH/AD 771. In the same period other Indian works became available and very shortly after, early in the third century AH (ninth century AD), an Arabic translation was made of a Pahlavi work, the *Astronomical Table of the King*, which had been produced in the last years of the Sassanids. But the most important sources of all, which were translated at the beginning of the third century AH, were the Greek works of the school of Alexandria. By far the most important of these was Ptolemy, whose major work, *Almagest*, was the greatest influence in the Middle Ages, both in Islam and in the West. Ptolemy's astronomy was, of course, Earth-centred or geocentric, but this poses no problems from a practical and computational point of view either for the fixed stars or, for a limited span of years, for the Sun. It does, however, render the explanation of planetary motion extremely difficult, and Ptolemy was obliged to introduce geometrical constructions involving eccentric circles and epicycles to account for these motions. Even so, Ptolemy's solutions were not wholly satisfactory even within his own premises and, as we have seen, the contradictions were only finally resolved by Ibn al-Shatir in the eighth century AH (fourteenth century AD).

The main astronomical achievement of the Muslims lay in the fields of observation, instrumentation, and in the development of spherical trigonometry for the solutions of problems in astronomical mathematics. They were able to correct many of the Hellenistic numerical values for astronomical quantities, including the obliquity of the ecliptic (i.e. the angle between the Sun's apparent path – the ecliptic – and the celestial equator, the other great reference circle in the sky). These new values proved equally valid when the heliocentric or Sun-centred system replaced the geocentric view of the universe. Muslim astronomers also applied themselves to a number of practical problems including the calendar, time-keeping and the *qibla* (the direction of Mecca from a given locality). The last is a special case of a general problem – the determination of the azimuth of one place relative to another when the latitudes and longitudes of both places are known. From the third to the eighth centuries AH (ninth to fourteenth centuries AD) the solutions to the *qibla* problem became increasingly more accurate as trigonometrical and computational techniques improved. The culmination of these efforts is represented by the very accurate *qibla* tables of the Syrian astronomer al-Khalili (eighth century AH/fourteenth century AD).

1.4.3 Physics

As already mentioned, the work of Ibn al-Haytham on optics was outstanding in this field. His *Kitab al-manazir* (*Book on Optics*) was translated into Latin and exercised a profound influence in the Middle Ages, inspiring the studies of Roger Bacon and Witelo. In this and other works he studied mirrors and lenses, and the nature of light. Like Ibn Sina and al-Biruni, he established that rays of light start from the object and travel towards the eye, not the reverse as the Greeks had believed. He established that astronomical twilight began or finished when the Sun was actually 19 degrees below the horizon and realised that this was due to refraction by the atmosphere; proceeding from there, he fixed the height of the atmosphere at 52 000 paces. He also correctly explained refraction by the Earth's atmosphere as the cause of elevating the apparent positions of celestial bodies above the horizon, and the enlargement of the apparent diameters of the Sun and Moon when they are near the horizon. Ibn al-Haytham also discovered spherical aberration (the failure of a lens to bring rays passing close to its edge to focus at the same point as those passing through its central regions), and was the first to describe the camera obscura.

In his *Kitab Mizan al-Hikma* (*Book of the Balance of Wisdom*) completed in 515 AH (AD 1121–2), al-Khazini based his work on specific gravity on the conclusions of al-Biruni, but the book is not confined to this topic. One of the most remarkable books on mechanics, hydrostatics, and physics of the Middle Ages, it contains a history of the subjects dealt with; these include a discussion on obtaining specific gravities, together with tables giving values for many liquids and solids; a theory of gravity, which is identified as a central force directed towards the centre of the Universe (i.e. the Earth); a theory of solids; the weight of air; observations of the rise of liquids up narrow tubes (capillarity); the use of an aerometer to measure the densities and give an appreciation of the temperatures of liquids; the theory of the lever; the application of the balance to levelling and to the measurement of time using water-clocks. The work is distinguished by accuracy of observation, scrupulous use of evidence, and a wholly 'modern' preference for experimentation. Foremost among those who demonstrated the application of physics to construction were the Banu Musa brothers, whose work is discussed in the next chapter.

1.4.4 Chemistry

No real differentiation was made by the Muslims between chemistry, alchemy and chemical technology. A number of matters relevant to Muslim achievements will therefore be found in Chapter 6, Chemical technology, in particular with regard to chemical processes and laboratory apparatus. Perhaps the two most influential of the Muslim chemists were Jabir b. Hayyan (second century AH eighth century AD) and Abu Bakr al-Razi (d. 313 AH/AD 925). The works of both men were known to the medieval Latins, by whom they were called Geber and Rhazes, respectively. Both were practical men who preferred the positive work of the laboratory to theoretical speculation. Jabir divided minerals into three groups: spirits, which became volatile when heated; metals; and non-malleable substances which could be reduced to powder. He mentioned nitric acid and described many processes for the industrial application of chemistry. Al-Razi was perhaps the greatest clinical doctor of Islam, but his work in chemistry is equally impressive. He has left us a valuable description of the equipment in his laboratory and of the chemical processes known to him. These include distillation, solution, calcination, evaporation, crystallisation, sublimation, filtration, amalgamation and ceration. He gave a systematic classification of mineral substances, to which he added a number of materials obtained artificially.

1.5 TECHNOLOGY FROM NON-ISLAMIC SOURCES

In this section we shall discuss briefly the transfer of technology into Islam from the first to the tenth centuries AH (seventh to sixteenth centuries AD). We have already seen how the basis for the advance and development of technologies in Islam was provided by the pre-Islamic civilisations of the Near East and eastern Mediterranean, and we know that technology transfer took place for long centuries before Islam between that area and other regions of the Old World. We are concerned here, however, only with the Islamic period. In the ensuing chapters, although we have of course devoted ourselves mainly to a description of Muslim technology in its own right, we have from time to time mentioned specific cases of transmission into and out of the Muslim world. This can only be done when the evidence points with reasonable probability to transmission in a given direction; there are very many subjects upon which the evidence is inconclusive. We shall therefore confine ourselves here to a general discussion of the interrelationships between Islam and other cultural areas, citing a few examples for which the evidence allows one to reach reasonably wellfounded conclusions.

In the next section we argue that, for the period in question, most transmission of technology took place from Islam to Europe and not in the reverse direction. The evidence of our research and the opinions of distinguished scholars both support this contention, which will be controversial only to those who have been conditioned to think Eurocentrically. This is not to imply that Europe lacked dynamism in this period, nor that it failed to develop a technology appropriate to its needs. It does not prompt us, however, to devote much space to considering cases of the transfer of technology from

Europe to Islam. In any case, some Western innovations were applicable only in northern Europe. The heavy wheeled plough, for example, is suitable only for the wet clayey soils of that region. One machine, the clock, provides us with a good example of that process of successive interdependent technological developments that we discussed in the second section of this chapter.

There were weight-driven clocks with mercury escapements in Islam not later than the fifth century AH (eleventh century AD); al-Muradi, also in the fifth century AH, incorporated complex gear trains with segmental and epicyclic gears in some of his machines, while the monumental water-clocks described by Ridwan and al-Jazari have elaborate displays of automata to mark the passage of the hours (see Chapter 11). The mechanical escapement for controlling the speed of a weight-driven clock was invented, probably, in northern Europe about the beginning of the eighth century AH (fourteenth century AD). The tower-clocks incorporating this mechanism, which spread over Europe in the eighth century AH, had gears in their going and striking trains, and they all had elaborate automata very similar to those of the Arabic water-clocks. This is an interesting case of technological interdependence. It would be difficult, however, to identify another case before AD 1500 where European technology introduced any significant addition to that of the Muslim world.

Islam's neighbour, the Byzantine Empire, had little more to offer. Byzantium and Islam were recipients of the same techniques from the Middle East. But 'Islam was advancing largely at the expense of Byzantium and was finally to absorb her, to surpass her in power and wealth' – and as a consequence in technology as well. The story of Callinicus, the Syrian architect from Baalbeck, who fled to Byzantium during the Umayyad period, taking with him the secret of a new military incendiary device, is told elsewhere in this book (p. 106). This helped the Byzantines to defend Constantinople (Istanbul) against Muslim attacks for a very long time. But these incendiary weapons were in continuous development in Islam. They affected the outcome of the Crusades, helped to repulse the Tartars, and culminated in the appearance of the cannon, which was a decisive weapon in the siege and fall of Constantinople in 857 AH/AD 1453.

Whereas Islam, Byzantium and Europe, despite their conflicts, formed one cultural area as regards science and technology, China and the Far East formed another. Because of the ideographic language, Chinese science penetrated little outside China, though several important Chinese technological achievements spread westwards to Muslim lands and ultimately reached Europe.

With the conquest of Transoxiana (an area roughly corresponding to the present Uzbek and Kazakh regions of the USSR) by the middle of the second century AH (eighth century AD), Islam stood face to face with the Chinese cultural area. In 134 AH/AD 751 Tashkent was taken, and in the same year the Arabs won a decisive victory over the Chinese at the Battle of the Talas River. Soon afterwards the Chinese withdrew from the whole of Turkestan, and after that no Arab army crossed the Chinese border.

Cultural contacts had already started, for several Chinese artisans taken prisoner at the Talas River settled in Samarqand and other Muslim cities. This is how the manufacture of paper began in the Islamic lands (see Chapter 8). Diplomatic relations with China started under the Umayyads, who sent an ambassador in 108 AH/AD 726, while commercial relations were established under the Abbasid Caliphate from 133 AH/AD 750 onwards, and in the event merchants played a more important role than diplomats. Since the overland routes were sometimes obstructed, the Muslims relied on sea routes to reach Canton (Khanfu). Islamic 'factories' and quarters were set up at the Chinese ports, and Arab and Persian merchants soon became powerful enough to revolt against the Chinese authorities in 141AH/AD 758. But Islamic–Chinese trade continued without interruption until the arrival of the Portuguese in the Indian Ocean in the late fifteenth century.

These encounters with China through trade, by land and sea, and the proximity of Transoxiana to China, resulted in a mutual transfer of technology between China and the Islamic world. The dates of some events in this transfer, such as that of paper manufacture, are known, but in some other cases, such as the invention of gunpowder and of the compass, though the transfer is established the dates are not exactly determined. The contributions of Chinese technology have been the subject of detailed study and research in the multi-volume *Science and Civilisation in China* written by Joseph Needham and his collaborators.

The remaining important civilisation with which there was a mutual transfer of technology with the Muslim world was that of India. Here Islam established a vast subcontinental empire. Muslims arrived on the coasts of Southern India as missionaries and merchants. In 93 AH/AD 711 the Umayyads annexed that part of India in the north now known as Sind (on the lower Indus), which therefore came into direct contact with the caliphate and was the main channel through which the ancient

Indian sciences passed to Baghdad. Islamic Sind was visited by al-Mas'udi, Ibn Hawqal and al-Istakhri, who left interesting accounts of it. The third wave of Muslim descent upon India was through the passes of Afghanistan. It began with the invasions of Mahmud of Ghazna (388–421 AH/988–1030 AD) and the establishment of Ghaznavid power in the Punjab. Successive Islamic states were created, but the Mughal Empire founded by Babur in 933 AH/AD 1526 marks the highest point of splendour in Islamic India.

Such, then, is a brief account of the contacts between the Islamic lands and the contemporary civilisations of China, India, Byzantium and Europe. Its brevity and generality were imposed by the fact that although in the last thirty years there have appeared comprehensive multi-volume histories of technology of the West such as that by Charles Singer and his associates and of the Chinese by Joseph Needham and his collaborators, the technology of Islam has received scarcely any attention. Indeed, the present short book is the first work to deal with Islamic technology as a whole. Furthermore, some of those who were commissioned to write on the subject in general histories, wrote in a spirit of belittlement and denigration, and it is therefore premature to attempt to discuss the transfer of technologies to Islamic lands from other contemporary civilisations. The first urgent task is to start comprehensive research into Muslim technology, together with the pre-Islamic technology of the same lands and their peoples. For example, a noria wheel for raising water that was first used on the River Orontes in Syria just before Islam should be part of the story of Muslim water-wheels. A comparative history of technology cannot be valid if we consider the pre-Islamic technology of Syria and Egypt as a Western heritage. Moreover, any comparative study of the history of technology in different cultures should use the same time scales.

1.6 TRANSFER OF TECHNOLOGY FROM THE ISLAMIC WORLD TO THE WEST

The traditional view of Western historians is that European culture is the direct descendant of the classical civilisations of Greece and Rome. According to this theory, the works of classical authors – mostly in Latin, but some in Greek – were preserved by the Church during the centuries that followed the fall of the Roman Empire, to re-emerge as a potent source of inspiration in the later Middle Ages and the Renaissance. Few would deny the strong influence of classical literature on European thought. Until recently the works of Homer,

Thucydides and the Greek dramatists, of Tacitus, Virgil and Horace, to name but a few, were part of the cultural background of every educated European. In science, however, the situation is very different. During the sixth century AH (twelfth century AD) the writings of such scholars as al-Farabi, al-Ghazali, al-Farghani, Ibn Sina and Ibn Rushd were translated into Latin, and became known and esteemed in the West. The works of Aristotle, soon to become a predominating influence on European thought, were translated from the Arabic together with the commentaries of Ibn Sina and Ibn Rushd (Avicenna and Averröes to the medieval Europeans). These commentaries were as important as the works of Aristotle himself in forming European scientific and philosophical thought. Many other scientific works, which had originally been translated from Greek into Arabic centuries earlier, were now translated into Latin. As we have seen, however, most of these were from the Hellenistic period, and though they were written in Greek, their authors came from all the countries of the Near East and eastern Mediterranean. It seems, therefore, that some European writers, being deeply appreciative of the *literary* masterpieces of Greece and Rome, have been led to believe that Western civilisation, *in all its aspects*, was based upon Greek and Roman foundations. This is not the case with science and technology.

Charles Singer, in the Epilogue to the second volume of *A History of Technology*, discussed some of the points already touched upon. To summarise, these are that the Graeco-Roman heritage was built upon the great civilisations of the Near East and, furthermore, that the major achievements in science and technology that are called Hellenistic and Roman were mainly Near Eastern achievements due to the scholars and artisans of Egypt and Syria. The pre-Islamic civilisations from Spain to Central Asia and northern India were inherited by Islam. Under the influence of Islam and of the Arabic language, the science and technology of these regions was developed and improved. Referring to the Eurocentrism of Western historians, Singer wrote: 'Europe, however, is but a small peninsula extending from the great land masses of Afrasia. This is indeed its geographical status and this, until at least the thirteenth century AD, was generally also its technological status.' In skill and inventiveness during most of the period AD 500 to 1500, Singer continues 'the Near East was superior to the West.... For nearly all branches of technology the best products available to the West were those of the Near

East . . . . Technologically, the West had little to bring to the East. The technological movement was in the other direction'. We shall now indicate how this technology transfer occurred, and give some examples of the transfer of ideas and techniques from Islam to the West. Other examples will be found in the ensuing chapters.

The adoption by Europe of Islamic techniques is reflected by the many words of Arabic derivation that have passed into the vocabularies of European languages. In English these words have often, but not always, entered the language from Italian or Spanish. To cite but a few examples: in textiles – muslin, sarsanet, damask, taffeta, tabby; in naval matters – arsenal, admiral; in chemical technology – alembic, alcohol, alkali; in paper – ream; in foodstuffs – alfalfa, sugar, syrup, sherbet; in dyestuffs – saffron, kermes; in leather-working – Cordovan and Morocco. As one would expect, Spanish is particularly rich in words of Arabic origin, especially in connection with agriculture and irrigation. We have, for example, *tahona* for a mill, *aceña* for a mill or water-wheel, *acequia* for an irrigation canal.

Many Arabic works on scientific subjects were translated into Latin in the later Middle Ages; the translation bureau in Toledo in the twelfth century AD, where hundreds of such works were rendered into Latin, is a notable example of this activity. There was, unfortunately, nothing comparable in the field of technology, in which direct translations from Arabic were extremely rare. About AD 1277, in the court of Alfonso X of Castile, a work in Spanish entitled *Libros del Saber de Astronomia* was compiled under the direction of the King, with the declared objective of making Arabic knowledge available to Spanish readers. It includes a section on timekeeping, which contains a weight-driven clock with a mercury escapement. We know from other sources that such clocks were constructed by Muslims in Spain in the eleventh century, hence about 250 years before the weight-driven clock appeared in northern Europe. We have cited such direct examples of technology transfer whenever we have found documentary evidence to support the case. For example, about AD 1277 the secrets of Syrian glass-making were communicated to Venice under the terms of a treaty made between Bohemond VII, titular prince of Antioch, and the Doge (see Chapter 6). Because the subject of Islamic technology is in the early stages of research, such direct evidence is still comparatively rare, but more will undoubtedly come to light as work proceeds. It is worth mentioning now that the present writers, while engaged on research for this book, have already uncovered a number of previously unknown cases of technology transfer.

For the moment, we can indicate several points in space and time where the exchange of ideas took place. Relations between Christian Europe and the Islamic World were not always hostile. Muslim rulers were often enlightened men and tolerant towards their Christian subjects, an attitude enjoined upon them by the precepts of the Holy Qur'an. Furthermore commercial considerations led to the establishment of communities of European merchants in Muslim cities, while groups of Muslim merchants settled in Byzantium, where they made contact with Swedish traders travelling down the Dnieper. There were particularly close commercial ties between Fatimid Egypt and the Italian town of Amalfi in the fourth and fifth centuries AH (tenth and eleventh centuries AD). The ogival arch, an essential element of Gothic architecture, entered Europe through Amalfi – the first church to incorporate such arches being built at Monte Casino in AD 1071. Some historians think that the influence of the Crusades on European culture has probably been exaggerated, but transmission certainly occurred, as we have seen in the case of Syrian glassmaking. Certainly, however, the most fruitful exchanges took place in the Iberian peninsula, where over many centuries the generally tolerant rule of the Umayyad Caliphs and their successors permitted friendly relationships between Muslims and Christians. Muslim operations in agriculture, irrigation, hydraulic engineering, and manufacture were an integral part of everyday life in the southern half of the peninsula, and many Muslim ideas in these three fields, and in others, passed from Spain into Italy and northern Europe. These transmissions were not checked by the Reconquista. Indeed, they were probably accelerated, since the Christians took over the Muslim installations and maintained them in running order in the ensuing centuries. The Muslim irrigation systems with their associated hydraulic works and water-raising machines (Fig. 1.7) remained as the basis for Spanish agriculture and were in due course transferred to the New World. Other installations passed into Christian hands. Industrial plants, such as the the paper mill at Jativa near Valencia, were taken over. Two large water-clocks on the banks of the Tagus at Toledo were found by the Christians when they entered the city in AD 1085, and they continued in operation for at least fifty years. These few examples serve only as indicators of the passage of Muslim ideas into Europe. Numerous other examples of technology

1.7 A noria for raising water in the Spanish province of Murcia, a relic of the Muslim period which ended there in the middle of the thirteenth century AD.

transfer are given throughout the pages of this book. As research proceeds, it should be possible to build up an integrated picture of the transfer of Muslim techology to the West.

2.1 Two *shadufs* being used to raise
water from a river in Egypt.

2 *Mechanical engineering*

2.1 WATER-RAISING MACHINES

The supply of water for irrigation, drinking, domestic and industrial purposes has always been a vital consideration in Muslim lands. The climatic and topographical conditions typical of northern Europe – heavy rainfall, abundant rivers and streams – do not occur in many Islamic countries. In medieval Islam only parts of Iran, Mesopotamia (the area between the upper reaches of the Tigris and Euphrates rivers), and some Mediterranean coastlands had sufficient rainfall to enable agriculture to be practised without irrigation. Although the boundaries of Islam have changed over the centuries the basic pattern remains the same, with irrigation and pastoral farming playing a predominant role compared with the cultivation of crops under rainfall. The problem has therefore always consisted of finding effective means of raising water from various sources for the needs of man. At its most basic – in desert or steppe lands – the problem resolves itself into drawing water from wells to supply the essentials, i.e. water for drinking and cooking. The simplest way of doing this is to tie a rope to a bucket and lower the bucket into the well. Somewhat more advanced is the well-head gear consisting of a drum upon which the rope is wound, and a windlass to turn the drum. With settled populations, however, the requirements for higher extraction rates made these methods inadequate and led to the introduction and spread of three machines.

The first machine is the *shaduf*, which was known in ancient times in Egypt and Assyria. It consists of two posts made from wood, masonry or other materials. Between them is a horizontal wooden bar which provides a fulcrum for the rotatable beam of the machine, dividing it approximately in a 2:1 ratio. At the end of its short arm is a counterweight made of stone or clay that raises the full bucket. The bucket is suspended by a rope or pole fixed to the end of the long arm of the beam. The operator bears down on the beam or the rope and lowers the bucket into the water; the counterweight then brings the bucket up, and its contents are tipped into a head tank or directly into an irrigation channel. It is not uncommon for two *shadufs* to be erected by the same source, one as a standby in case the other breaks down. When it is necessary to raise water to a considerable height, then a series of *shadufs* is erected in a line on a gradient leading from the source to the discharge point. The machine nearest the source discharges water into a tank, whence it is extracted by the second, and so on. The *shaduf*, which is cheap and reliable, is still in widespread use in Egypt.

The two other machines are the *saqiya* and the noria (*na'ura*), the one driven by animal power, the other by water. The problem of the terminology of water-wheels is practically insoluble. In some areas one generic term is used for all machines, irrespective of type, but elsewhere they are referred to in words of purely local usage. Only in Syria, where *saqiya* is used for the animal-powered machine, *na'ura* for the water-driven wheel, is there any consistency. For the remainder of this chapter the Syrian usage will be followed. The central mechanism of the *saqiya* consists of two gears meshing at right angles, a large vertical cogwheel and a large lantern pinion

2.2(*a*) A *saqiya* at Babraki, Pakistan. Water is being discharged from the pot-garland into a trough leading to a channel on the left.

2.2(*b*) The cogs of the gear wheel of another Pakistani *saqiya* meshing with the lantern pinion.

(Fig. 2.2(*a*) and (*b*)). As the name implies, the lantern pinion consists of two wooden disks held apart by spacer bars; the wooden teeth of the cogwheel enter the spaces between the bars. The vertical cogwheel is mounted on an axle over the source of the water, usually a well. On the other side of the cogwheel from the teeth is a drum for carrying a chain-of-pots or 'potgarland' – the pegs for carrying the potgarland are in fact the protruding ends of the cogs. Sometimes the potgarland is carried on a separate wheel on the same horizontal axle as the cogwheel. The potgarland consists of a number of earthenware pots secured between two ropes, each spliced to form a single long loop. (The ropes and pots may be replaced by chains and metal buckets.) The potgarland is slung over the pegs on the drum of the vertical wheel A draw-bar is slotted into the extension to the vertical axle of the lantern pinion and the animal – donkey, mule or camel – is tethered to this bar. As the animal walks in a circular path the lantern pinion turns the potgarland wheel and the chain of pots is in continuous motion. The pots dip into the water, are raised to the surface, and discharge into a head tank. Usually the water is led from this tank through a conduit under the animal's track to a main tank, typically of about 100 cubic metres capacity. A vital part of the larger *saqiyas* is the pawl, which rests in the cogs of the potgarland wheel. This is essential because the animal is subjected to a constant pull from the loaded pots. The pawl is activated in two cases – when the animal is unharnessed and in the event of the harness or the traces breaking. Without it the machine would turn backwards at great speed, the draw-bar would strike the animal on the head, killing or maiming it, and the machine would be damaged. Water for drinking and domestic use is drawn directly from the main tank; in the evening the sluices of the tank are opened and the water is conducted through irrigation channels to the fields. The efficiency of the *saqiya* has been estimated at 60 per cent, with a delivery of 4 cubic metres of water against a head of water of 4 metres.

The *saqiya* was known in Roman times, from about the start of the Christian era. It was in use in Egypt, Syria, and probably along the North African coast. At first it was a luxury article, used for supplying water to the houses of the wealthy. It became an appliance of wider application after the introduction of the pawl and earthenware pots in the fourth or fifth century AD. Almost certainly it was in use in Arabia before the advent of Islam, since by the time of the Prophet there was a special term (*nadih*) for a camel used for drawing water from wells. The machine was probably transmitted to Spain from Syria, when the Muslims introduced their irrigation methods to Spain. Writing at the close of the fifth century AH (eleventh century AD), Ibn Bassal described the *saqiya* as a standard machine for irrigation. It is still in limited use today in the Muslim world and in the Iberian peninsula and the Balearic islands. The machine may work on a 24-hour basis for 100 days at a time, and a stoppage of even a few days can ruin a crop. The mechanical pump has now replaced the *saqiya* almost completely in most areas, especially in the irrigated agriculture of cotton plantations.

The noria is a water-driven machine that is most suitable in areas where there are fast-flowing streams whose courses are some distance below the surrounding fields. Although the machine is now rarely used in practice, some fine examples can still be seen, notably on the River Orontes at Hama in Syria (Fig. 2.3). The wheels are mounted between piers which carry the bearings for the iron or wooden axle, around which is a framework of stout timbers to which the axle is secured by wedges. Radiating from this central framework are wooden spokes that carry the wooden rim of the wheel. The diameter of the largest wheel is about 20 metres, and there are 120 compartments in the rim; between each pair of compartments is a wooden paddle. The wheel is turned by the impact of the water on the paddles. The compartments dip into the water and are carried to the top of the wheel, where they discharge into a head tank connected to an aqueduct. In some norias, instead of compartments, earthenware pots are strapped to the rim of the wheel.

The noria was already in use in Roman times. It was described by Vitruvius, writing in the first century BC. Al-Muqaddasi (d. 390 AH/AD 1000) tells us that there were many norias on the river at Ahwaz in Iran. The water raised by them flowed through aqueducts into cisterns in the town, and also through irrigation channels to the orchards. Al-Idrisi, writing in 584 AH/AD 1154, described a noria that provided the water supply

2.3 A noria at Hama on the river Orontes in Syria. The water raised by the wheel flowed along the aqueduct seen to the left of it.

of Toledo. The wheel was 90 cubits (135 feet) in diameter, and it raised water from the River Tagus and delivered it into an aqueduct that led into the city. The installation was therefore very similar to the norias of Hama. A treatise written at the beginning of the fifth century AH (eleventh century AD) gives details of the construction of norias and of the amount of water that a noria would raise in an hour. This was in Iraq. The height of lift is not given, but if one assumes that it was 19 metres, then the output can be calculated at about 5.6 horsepower. References in the works of the Arab geographers show that norias were in use throughout the Muslim world, dams sometimes being built to increase the head of water above them (see chapter 3). The reason for the obsolescence of the noria is mainly that it was replaced by the centrifugal pump, while the recent construction of large dams such as those at Aswan in Egypt and at al-Thawra on the Euphrates in Syria, which supply water-power for electricity generation and for pumping irrigation water, has also made the noria redundant. But much earlier Muslim engineers were exploring new methods for increasing the effectiveness of water-raising machines, as we shall now see.

Al-Jazari and Taqi al-Din both described water-raising machines that show an awareness of the need to develop machines with a greater output than the traditional ones. The first machine described by al-Jazari (Fig. 2.4) was designed to operate a flume-beam swape, a device which is a modification of the *shaduf*. Instead of a pole, an open channel is connected to the scoop, which has its spout elongated into a flume; the scoop dips into the water, and when the beam rises the water runs back through the channel and discharges into the irrigation system. The swape is supported at the fulcrum near the open end of the channel. In the case of al-Jazari's machine the fulcrum was a long axle mounted on stanchions near the edge of the source of water. On this axle was a lantern-pinion meshing with a vertical segmental gear-wheel on a second horizontal axle, at the other end of which was a vertical gear wheel meshing with a horizontal gear wheel fixed to a vertical axle. At the top of this axle was a draw-bar to which a donkey was tethered. The animal walked in a circular path, as in the *saqiya*, turning the first pair of gears and hence the segmental gear wheel. The teeth of the latter entered the spaces between the bars of the lantern-pinion, and the swape was raised to discharge its contents. When the teeth disengaged the swape fell back into the water. And so on. Segmental gears first appeared in Europe in Giovanni de Dondi's intricate mech-

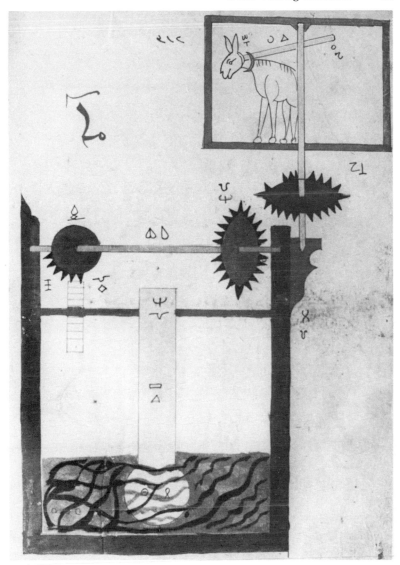

2.4 Al-Jazari's first water-raising machine using a flume-beam swape. Thirteenth century AD. Topkapi Sarayi Müzesi, Istanbul.

anical clock, completed in AD 1364, and later found a number of uses in modern machines. Al-Jazari's second machine was a quadrupled version of the first, with four lantern-pinions and four segmental gears. After pointing out that the output was increased fourfold, the author says that another advantage was that the operation was much smoother than in the first machine.

The third machine was a development of the *saqiya*, in which water power replaced animal power (Fig. 2.5). An elegant open structure was erected by an ornamental lake, its working parts visible to spectators. At the bottom of the structure was a tank

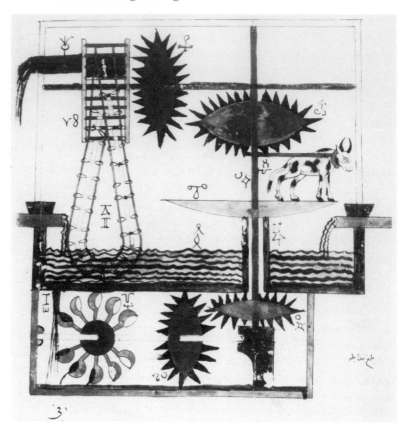

2.5 Al-Jazari's third machine for raising water, a *saqiya* producing a cascade of water at the side of an ornamental lake. The water-driven mechanism was hidden and the wheel appeared to be turned by a wooden model of a cow. Thirteenth century AD. Süleymaniye Kütüphanesi, Istanbul.

into which water was conducted through pipes from the lake. The chain-of-pots raised water from this tank. A smaller concealed tank that contained the machinery was below the floor. A horizontal axle was erected over the small tank and a scoop-wheel was fixed to it near one end. A hole in the floor of the upper tank discharged water into the scoops, so causing the wheel to rotate. At the other end of the axle was a vertical gear-wheel that meshed with a horizontal gear whose axle went up into the structure. At the top of this axle was another pair of gears, and the wheel carrying the chain-of-pots (al-Jazari calls it a Sindi wheel) was mounted on the horizontal axle of the second gear of this pair. A channel led from the Sindi wheel and discharged into the lake. As long as the pipe discharged on to the scoop-wheel, the chain-of-pots was in constant motion, and a cascade of water descended into the lake. On the visible part of the vertical axle a platform was erected, upon which was a wooden model of a cow; its feet did not touch the surface of the platform, and it was connected to the axle by a draw-bar. Clearly, the machine was intended as a decorative lakeside attraction with an element of mystification about it. It was, however, simply an elegant variation of a utilitarian machine that was used for supplying water for irrigation and domestic purposes.

One such machine was located on the River Yazid in Damascus, on a riverside path called 'Lane of the Norias' because of the number of norias and mills that used to line it (Fig 2.6). It was probably built prior to the death in 653 AH/AD 1254 of the Amir Sayf al-Din, and served the needs of a hospital. In 923 AH/AD 1516 a mosque was built in the vicinity and the appliance then served the requirements of both establishments. It continued in use for many centuries, being kept in working order by successive generations of curators, until it fell into disuse and disrepair about 1960. However, it was recently restored to working order by a project sponsored by Aleppo University. Instead of a scoop-wheel as in al-Jazari's machine, there was a paddle-wheel, also called a noria. The term is correct, because in addition to its main function it had buckets set into its rim for raising water for a short distance to supply nearby houses and gardens. Apart from this (and the omission of the model animal) the machine is a large-scale version of the one described by al-Jazari. The chain-of-pots raised the water to a height of 12 metres and discharged it into a channel that flowed into an aqueduct leading to the hospital and the mosque.

Al-Jazari's fourth machine (Fig. 2.7 (*a*) and (*b*)) again used a flume-beam swape, the upper end of which was pivoted on an axle mounted near the side of the water source, where the channel discharged into the supply system. Below the channel a long bar was fixed with a space between it and the underside of the channel. The lower horizontal arm of the crank was fixed to the centre of a vertical gear-wheel that meshed with a horizontal gear-wheel. The axle from this wheel was extended upwards through the floor of the 'engine-house' and a donkey was tethered to its upper end by a draw-bar. As the animal walked in a circular path, the crank rotated and its lower arm moved back and forth in the slot under the channel, causing the swape to rise and fall. This is the first known instance of the use of a crank as part of a machine. Manually operated cranks were known earlier, for example in hand-querns, and the Banu Musa brothers (third century AH/ninth century AD) used cranks in some of their devices, but these made only partial rotations and were lightly loaded. The earliest appearance in Europe of the crank as part of a machine occurred in the first half of the fifteenth century AD.

The fifth machine, a water-driven pump, is a complete

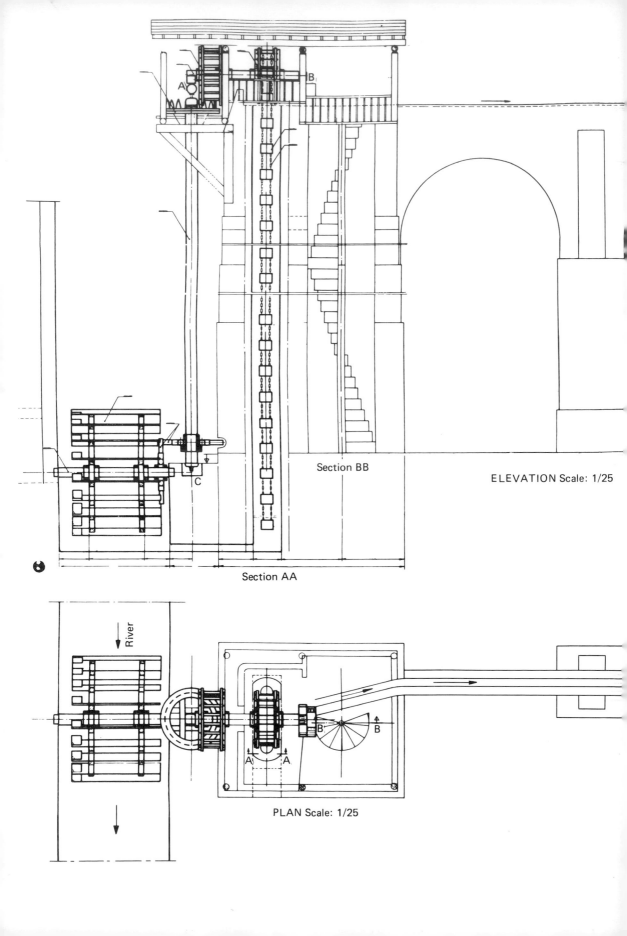

Section BB

ELEVATION Scale: 1/25

C

Section AA

River

A A

B B

PLAN Scale: 1/25

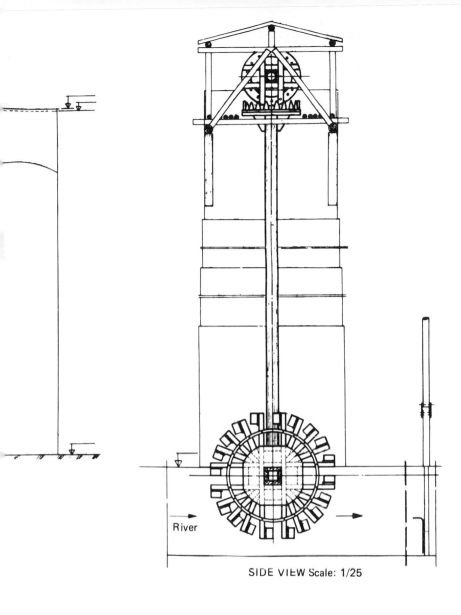

River

SIDE VIEW Scale: 1/25

2.6 A restored paddle-wheel driven *saqiya* on the river Yazid, Damascus, dating from the thirteenth century AD. It is very similar to al-Jazari's third water-raising machine.

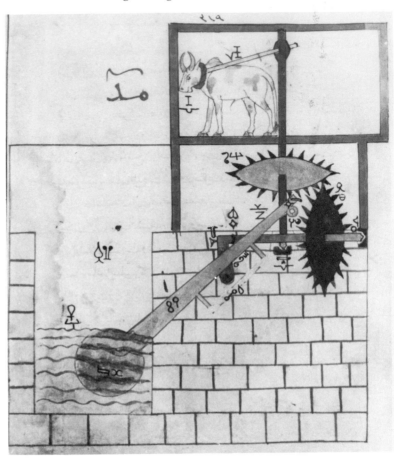

2.7(*a*) Al-Jazari's fourth water-
raising machine, an animal powered
flume-beam swape incorporating
the first known use of a crank in a
machine. Thirteenth century AD.
Topkapi Sarayi Müsezi, Istanbul.

departure from traditional designs. It could be constructed in
two versions, one driven by a vaned wheel, the other by a
vertical paddle-wheel. In the first version, the vertical shaft of
the wheel entered the pump chamber in which the machinery
was identical to that of the second design. A paddle-wheel was
erected over a flowing stream that provided the input power
for the pump. On the other end of the wheel's axle was a
vertical gear-wheel that meshed with a horizontal gear-wheel,
located inside the pump chamber. This consisted of a triangular
timber box, mounted over a sump that was kept full of water by
a channel leading from the stream. On the surface of the
horizontal gear-wheel, close to its perimeter, was a vertical peg
that entered a slot-rod. At one end of the slot-rod was a long
iron bar that was pivoted at one side of the box. At each side of
the slot-rod was a stout staple, which was entered by the ring at
the end of the connecting rod. The pistons were at the other
ends of the connecting rods, and these entered smooth copper
cylinders. The pistons were made from two copper discs, the

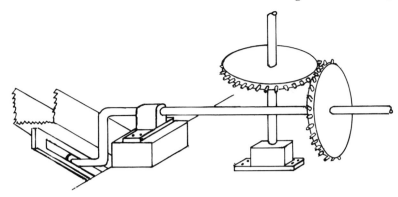

2.7(*b*) Diagram of the gears and crank of Fig. 2.7(*a*).

space between them being packed with hemp. The cylinders, says al-Jazari, were similar to but larger than those used for discharging *naft* fire – an incendiary substance. (This is one of the few clear indications we have of the design of the so-called 'Byzantine siphon'.) Each cylinder had a suction pipe and a delivery pipe; the ports between the pipes and the cylinders were fitted with non-return clack-valves, i.e. valves hinged at one end, but free to flap in one direction only. The suction pipes descended through the floor of the box into the sump. The delivery pipes were connected together in an inverted Y-joint above the machine to form a single outlet that discharged into the supply system about 12 metres above the installation. As the paddle-wheel turned, the vertical gear-wheel caused the horizontal gear-wheel to rotate, and the peg oscillated in the slot. The slot-rod moved from side to side, so that one piston was on the suction stroke while the other was delivering. This is therefore an early example of the double-acting principle, and the conversion of rotary to reciprocating motion. Another significant feature of the machine is the use of true suction pipes, albeit short ones. The force pumps known from classical sources, literary and archaeological, had no such pipes. The cylinders stood upright in the water, which entered them through plate-valves set in the bottoms of the cylinders. Al-Jazari's machine is clearly a successful attempt to provide a more efficient method of raising water than the noria. It would have been particularly useful in al-Jazari's homeland, the area between the upper reaches of the Tigris and the Euphrates, where the waterways are generally well below the level of the surrounding fields.

In his book on machines Taqi al-Din described a very similar pump to al-Jazari's, except that there was a scoop-wheel instead of a paddle-wheel, and the connecting rods were attached to an extension of the slot-rod, not at its centre line

(Fig. 2.8). Even more remarkable, however, is a six-cylinder 'monobloc' pump driven by water-power (Fig. 2.9). A scoop-wheel was erected over a running stream, at one end of a long horizontal axle, the bearings for which were supported on piers. The axle had six cams, spaced at equal distances along its length. Opposite each cam was a lever-arm supported at its centre on a fulcrum, and pin-jointed at the other end to a vertical piston rod. On the upper end of the rod was a lead weight, on the lower end was the piston that entered one of six

2.8 Opposed-cylinders pump described by Taqi al-Din. Sixteenth century AD.

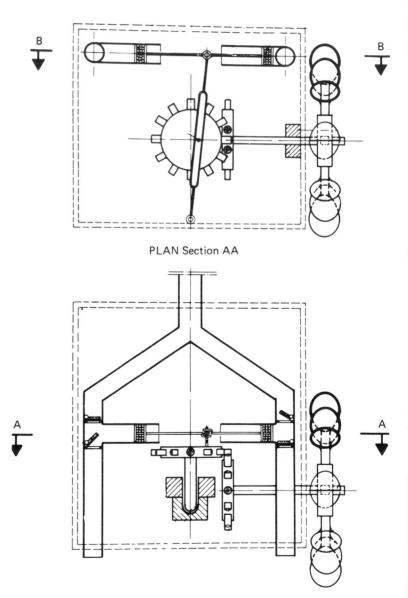

PLAN Section AA

ELEVATION Section BB

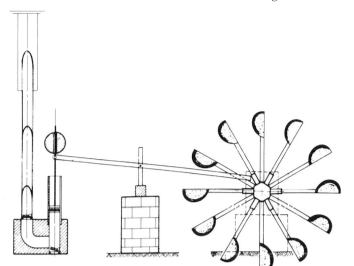

2.9 Six-cylinder 'monobloc' piston pump described by Taqi al-Din. It is driven by a water-powered scoop wheel. Sixteenth century AD.

ELEVATION Section AA

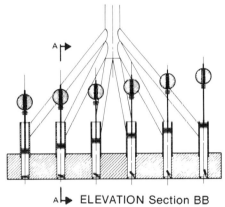

A ELEVATION Section BB

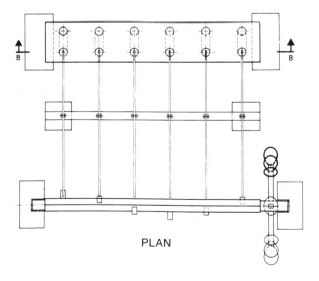

PLAN

cylinders set in a large block of timber. The block rested
directely in the water and at the bottom of each cylinder was a
non-return clack-valve. Delivery pipes led out from the
bottoms of the cylinders and were brought together above the
machine into a single delivery pipe. As the scoop-wheel rotated
the cams bore down in succession on the lever arms. When the
lever-arm was raised, water was drawn into its cylinder through
the non-return valve. When the lever-arm was released the
piston was forced down by the lead weight and water was
ejected through the delivery pipe. It is worthy of note that Taqi
al-Din's book, which also includes a steam-driven spit, ante-
dates the famous book of machines, *Le diverse et artificiose
machine* of Agostine Ramelli published in Paris in 1588.

2.2 POWER – WATER AND WIND

2.2.1 Water-power

There are three basic types of water-wheel. The first is the
undershot wheel (Fig. 2.10), often known as the Vitruvian
wheel because the earliest known description of it is in the
work of Vitruvius (first century BC). It is a paddle-wheel,
mounted on a horizontal axle over a running stream, and
driven by the velocity of the water. The second type is the
overshot wheel (Fig. 2.11), whose rim is divided into bucket-
like compartments into which water is directed from above,
turning the wheel by its weight rather than by its velocity. In
both types there is a vertical gear-wheel mounted on the axle of
the water-wheel, inside the millhouse. This engages a horizontal gear-wheel. The millstones are mounted on the vertical
axle of the second gear-wheel, in an upper chamber of the
millhouse. The third type is the horizontal water-wheel (Fig.
2.12), which consists of a number of propellers or vanes

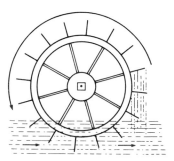

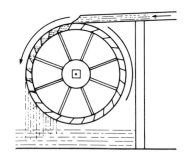

2.10 The undershot, or Vitruvian,
water-wheel. The wheel is turned
by the pressure of the moving
water on the paddles of the lower
part of the wheel.

2.11 The overshot water-wheel,
turned by the pressure of water
pouring from above into the
bucket-like compartments on its
rim.

radiating from a central hub fixed to a vertical axle. Normally the wheel is driven by a jet of water directed on to the vanes from a nozzle set in the bottom of a water tower. In the seventeenth century the so-called 'tub-wheel' came into use in Europe; in this case the wheel was mounted at the bottom of a cylinder into which water cascaded from above. In the first variety the flow was a combination of axial and radial components, in the second it was largely axial. The millstones were mounted directly on the axle of the horizontal wheel – there were no gears. We cannot enter here into a discussion of the origin and diffusion of the three basic types – in any case the problem has not yet been solved satisfactorily. We can, however, be sure of two things. The first is that there were mills in pre-Islamic times in countries that became part of the Muslim world, and the second is that all three types were known in medieval Islam. Writing in the third century AH (ninth century AD) the Banu Musa brothers described a horizontal wheel in one of their fountains. This was driven from below by a number of vertical jets of water, so it is clear that the principle of axial flow was known in Islam. Al-Muradi, who worked in Spain in the fifth century AH (eleventh century AD), mentioned the overshot wheel, without any suggestion that it was a novelty. Apart from the treatises on machines, however, there are many references to water-mills in the works of geographers and travellers, though there are very rarely any indications of the type of water-wheel referred to. Nevertheless, we can infer that undershot wheels were common; indeed it is almost impossible to imagine any other kind in a ship-mill (a mill mounted in a boat and driven by a river current – see below). Yet it is also very probable that the type of wheel used in a given locality depended upon the terrain, the hydraulic conditions, and the kind of building materials available.

Muslims were obviously very keen to exploit every possible water supply as a potential source of power for milling. They even gauged the flow of a stream by the number of mills it would turn – the stream was, as it were, so many 'mill-power'. Tidal mills were in use at Basra in the fourth century AH (eleventh century AD), whereas the earliest record of their use in Europe was a hundred years later. More usually, of course, mills were mounted on the banks of streams and rivers, and sometimes on the piers of bridges, to take advantage of the increased velocity of the water. There were mills in every province of the Muslim world from Spain and North Africa to Transoxiana. In many cases mills were installed to meet the

2.12 A horizontal water-wheel described by al-Jazari. The wheel is turned by a jet of water directed on to its vanes and so turns the millstone above it, which is on the same vertical axle.
Above Illustration from a manuscript of the thirteenth century AD. Bodleian Library, Oxford.
Below Elevation and plan.

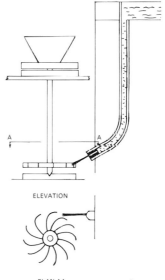

ELEVATION

PLAN AA

needs of a community, with no surplus for export, and until the later Middle Ages, this type of milling predominated in Europe. But the needs of the big Islamic cities made some form of large-scale milling of cereals essential. Thus there were 70 water-mills located near the city of Nishabur in Khurasan, and there was a series of mills on the river below Palermo in Sicily when the island was under Muslim rule. But the most remarkable example of this type of operation was the processing of cereals grown in Upper Mesopotamia, which was the granary for Baghdad. According to an account of the fourth century AH (tenth century AD), large ship-mills made of hardwood and iron were moored to the banks of the Tigris and Euphrates from Mosul and Raqqa down to Baghdad. Each mill had two pairs of stones and each pair, working day and night, ground 50 donkey loads of corn every day. Taking a load as 100 kg, this gives a daily production of 10 tonnes from each mill. Only certain types of stone are suitable for milling, and a town in Tunisia supplied millstones to the whole of North Africa, and the area around Amid provided Upper Mesopotamia and Iraq with theirs. Sometimes mills were state-owned, in other cases the state imposed taxes on their produce.

Paper mills were introduced to Samarqand in 134 AH/AD 751, and were erected soon after this in many parts of Islam. According to al-Biruni water power was used for driving the trip hammers in the mills in Samarqand (see Chapter 7). Water power was also used for the paper mills in Syria and at Jativa in Spain; in Baghdad floating paper-mills were to be found.

Recent archaeological work in Jordan has uncovered the remains of 32 water-mills used for processing sugar-cane in Ayyubid and Mamluk times. There is also a record of the use of water power for sawing timber. In some of al-Jazari's machines the axles of the water-wheels are extended and carry cams, an idea that he surely must have derived from his experience of industrial milling. Al-Biruni also described the use of water-driven trip-hammers for the crushing of gold ores, but only further extensive research will enable us to complete our account of industrial milling in Islam.

2.2.2 Wind-power

According to Joseph Needham 'the history of windmills really begins with Islamic culture, and in Iran.' Windmills were certainly mentioned in *Kitab al Hiyal* (*Book on Mechanical Devices*) by the Banu Musa brothers in the third century AH (ninth century AD). The book mentions wind-wheels 'which are customarily used by the people', while a century later windmills of Sistan were described by Muslim geographers. A detailed description of them occurs in *Kitab Nukhbat al-Dahr* (*Cosmography*) by al-Dimashqi, written about 700 AH/AD 1300 (Fig. 2.13 and see also Fig 8.13). From this we find that these windmills were of the horizontal type, and were enclosed in walls to shield them from the wind except on one side; here the wind entered to drive them in the fashion of a turbine.

The historian of technology, Robert Forbes, is of the opinion that the Islamic windmill was a local Persian adaptation of the horizontal water-mill to a region where there was no water but where steady winds prevailed. 'Subsequently the invention spread thoughout the Moslem world and beyond it to the Far East in the twelfth century after having been confined to Persia and Afghanistan. In China, India and the Moslem world they became important power resources used not only to grind corn and pump water, but also to crush sugar cane etc. As crushing mills they were a feature of the Egyptian sugar cane industry and thence travelled to the West Indies when Arabic experts from Egypt were lured there to help and establish the first sugar plantations.'

Needham says that by the sixteenth century the Islamic horizontal windmills had become well known in Europe, and designs based on them figured largely in *Machinae Novae . . .* (*New Machines . . .*) of 1615, the engineering book of the bishop and engineer Faustus Verantius. Needham thinks that 'this must surely have been a westward transmission from Iberian culture originally derived from Muslim Spain'. Windmills at Tarragona during the Muslim era were mentioned by Muslim authors (for instance in *Kitab al-Rawd al-Miᶜtar* [*The Book of the Fragrant Gardens*] written by al-Himyari in 661 AH/AD 1262). Needham refers also to the West Indian horizontal windmills working sugar-mills and to their Islamic origin.

It is assumed by several authorities that the vertical windmill which is used in Europe was an independent European invention. While maintaining that this European vertical mill was equally original, Needham thinks that it was also due to a stimulus from the Islamic windmill, but that it seems more likely to have derived from the *anemourion* (wind-vane) of Heron and from the vertical as well as the horizontal water-wheel.

2.13 Cross-section of a horizontal windmill from a manuscript of *Kitab nukhbat al-dahr* by al-Dimashqi. Fourteenth century AD. Bibliothèque Nationale, Paris.

2.3. WATER-CLOCKS AND MECHANICAL CLOCKS

2.3.1 Water-clocks

The outflow clepsydra, the simplest form of water-clock, was probably invented in Egypt about 1500 BC. This was a cone-shaped vessel narrowing towards the base, with a hole in its side near the base. As the water discharged from the hole, the drop of the water level in the vessel gave a measure of the passage of time. A later development was the inflow clepsydra: this consisted of an upper vessel with a hole, a constant supply of water, and an overflow. The hole discharged into a cylindrical container and, because the head of water in the upper vessel was kept constant, the water in the lower vessel rose at a steady rate. Various refinements of the inflow clepsydra were described by Vitruvius, some of them concerned with the operation of celestial and human automata. This type of clepsydra was introduced into China about 200 BC and remained a standard method of timekeeping there until the end of the Middle Ages. The crowning achievement of Chinese horology, however, was the monumental water-clock built by Su Song towards the close of the eleventh century AD. This was driven by a water-wheel some 3 metres in diameter, whose speed of rotation was controlled by an ingenious escapement that permitted the wheel to turn only in precise steps. An amillary sphere (a device depicting the sphere of the heavens and the reference circles on it), and various celestial and human automata, were also driven by the water-wheel through systems of gearing. The inspiration for the monumental water-clocks of Islam, however, came from a combination of Greek, Hellenistic and Iranian ideas. Ridwan tells us that the basic water-machinery was invented by Archimedes, together with a device for ejecting balls from the beak of a bird to mark the time. Improvements and additions were made to the basic design in Sassanid Iran, and this modified design was transmitted to Byzantium. The tradition for the construction of these clocks was continued in Syria in Islamic times. There is ample confirmation for Ridwan's statement. A monumental water-clock built at Gaza in the sixth centuty AD was described by Procopius, unfortunately without any details of its construction, and a century later a Chinese report mentions a steelyard clepsydra at Antioch. (This was a device in which a beam balance or steelyard marked the time, see next page.) More importantly, we still have a treatise, extant only in Arabic manuscripts, which is attributed to Archimedes. As it stands it is probably an amalgam of Greek, Iranian, Byzantine and Islamic ideas, though the first two sections, describing water-machinery and the discharge of a ball, may be the work of Archimedes himself. These manuscripts were referred to by Ibn al-Nadim, and acknowledged as a source by Ridwan and al-Jazari.

Too much emphasis, however, should not be placed upon

the origins of Islamic water-clocks. In range and inventiveness
al-Jazari's clocks go well beyond anything known from pre-
Islamic times, and in any case he had a number of illustrious
Muslim predecessors. There is a record of an elaborate water-
clock having been presented to Charlemagne by vassals of
Harun al-Rashid, and it is known that one was constructed by
the famous scientist Ibn al-Haytham (d. 430 AH/AD 1039). But
the earliest descriptions we have in Arabic of water-clocks
occur in the treatise on machines by al-Muradi, who worked in
Spain in the fifth century AH (eleventh century AD). Unfortunately, the only known manuscript of this work is badly
defaced and it is not possible to understand exactly how the
clocks worked. However, it is clear that their power came from
large outflow clepsydras provided with concentric siphons; this
power was transmitted to automata by very sophisticated
mechanisms which included segmental and epicyclic gears, and
the use of mercury. These are highly significant features: they
provide the first known examples of complex gearing used to
transmit high torque, while the adoption of mercury re-
appears in European clocks from the seventh century AH
(thirteenth century AD) onwards.

Also in the fifth century AH (eleventh century AD), al-
Zarqali built two large water-clocks on the banks of the River
Tagus at Toledo. These consisted of two vessels which
gradually filled while the moon was waxing, then gradually
emptied as the moon waned. These clocks were still in
operation when the Christians captured Toledo in 478 AH/AD
1085, and one of them was still working more than fifty years
later. Al-Khazini completed his great work on physics, *Kitab
Mizan al-Hikma* (*The Book of the Balance of Wisdom*) in 515 AH/AD
1121-2. The eighth treatise of this work described two
steelyard clepsydras. The main one, called the Universal
Balance, was designed for 24-hour operation, and consisted of
an iron beam divided into unequal arms by a fulcrum. An
outflow clepsydra equipped with a siphon was suspended on
the end of the short arm, and two movable weights, one large
and one small, were suspended from the long arm, which was
graduated into scales. As water discharged from the clepsydra,
the weights were moved along the scale to keep the beam in
balance. At any moment the hour of the day could be told from
the position of the large weight, its minutes from the position
of the small one.

Muhammad al-Sa'ati built a monumental clock at the Jayrun
Gate in Damascus about the middle of the sixth century AH
(twelfth century AD); the clock was described by his son

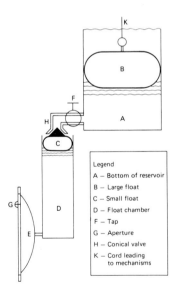

Ridwan in a treatise completed in 600 AH/AD 1203. The clock was very similar to the one described by al-Jazari in his first chapter, and Ridwan (and by implication his father) have always suffered in comparison with al-Jazari. This is not unjust; al-Jazari's design is better, his descriptions are clearer, and his illustrations superior. Nevertheless, al-Sa'ati's clock was a sound piece of engineering, and his son's treatise contains information not to be found in al-Jazari's. Because the latter was an accomplished engineer he omitted minor constructional details on the assumption that they were widely understood, whereas Ridwan, a layman, included such details.

Al-Jazari's treatise is the most important document on machines from ancient times until the Renaissance to come from any cultural area. It is therefore impossible, in the space available, to describe even a part of it adequately, and we shall therefore confine ourselves to a description of only one type of water-machinery. Figure 2.14 shows that incorporated in the clocks described in chapters 1 and 2 of Category I of the book. This was derived from the 'Archimedes' clock. Its operation was as follows: at daybreak (or nightfall) the tap F was opened and water flowed into the float-chamber D through the conical valve H. Float C rose and closed valve H momentarily; water flowed from the float-chamber into the flow regulator E, and the valve opened momentarily; and so on. A virtually constant head was therefore maintained in the float-chamber by feed-back control, and the discharge from the float-chamber did not vary. The flow regulator was necessary because the clock recorded the passage of temporal hours, i.e. the hours of daylight and darkness were divided by 12 to give 'hours' that varied in length from day to day as the comparative periods of daylight and darkness changed. This meant that the rate of flow, and hence the head of water, had to be changed daily. The calibrated orifice G was in a plate that could be rotated inside a ring, which was itself divided into the Zodiacal signs, each of which was subdivided into degrees. On a given day a pointer on the radius of the orifice was set to the correct degree. The graduation of the ring was done by painstaking empirical methods, and in the clocks of 'Archimedes' and al-Sa'ati the graduation was quite inaccurate. Cord K from float B operated some of the time-recording mechanisms – others were activated by the water discharging from the orifice.

Al-Jazari's clocks are full of ideas and techniques that are of importance in the history of machine design. Without attempting a comprehensive listing, we can mention some of the more significant of these: accurate calibration of small orifices;

Legend
A — Bottom of reservoir
B — Large float
C — Small float
D — Float chamber
F — Tap
G — Aperture
H — Conical valve
K — Cord leading
     to mechanisms

2.14 Regulator for a water clock described by al-Jazari.
Above Drawings of parts of the regulator, from a manuscrtip of the thirteenth century AD. Bodleian Library, Oxford.
Below Diagram of the regulator.

feed-back control methods; the use of paper models to establish intricate designs; the use of wooden templates; the static balancing of wheels; the use of laminated timber to minimise warping; one-way hinges; and tipping buckets. To these we should add the complex gears and the use of mercury in al-Muradi's clocks. The latter is of especial significance because a weight-driven clock with a mercury escapement appears in the *Libros del Saber*, a work written in Spanish at the court of Alfonso X of Castile about AD 1277 and consisting of translations and paraphrases of Arabic works.

2.3.2 Mechanical clocks

Several of Taqi al-Din's writings are concerned with time-keeping, and one of these, *The Brightest Stars for the Construction of Mechanical Clocks*, written about AD 1565, has been edited by Sevim Tekeli, with Turkish and English translations. In this he described the construction of a weight-driven clock with verge-and-foliot escapement, a striking train of gears, an alarm, and a representation of the moon's phases. He also described the manufacture of a spring-driven clock with a fusee drive (Fig. 2.15). He mentions several mechanisms invented by himself, including, for example a new system for the striking train of a clock. He is known to have constructed an observatory clock and mentions elsewhere in his writings the use of the pocket watch in Turkey. The weight-driven clock was not invented in Europe until about AD 1300, and the spring-driven clock only around 1430. The manufacture of watches began in Germany about 1525 and in England some time around 1580. Taqi al-Din's descriptions are lucid with clear illustrations, showing that he had mastered the art of horology. Clockmaking did not, however, become a viable indigenous industry and Turkey was soon being supplied with cheap clocks from Europe. Taqi al-Din himself commented on the low price of these European clocks, which entered Turkey, he said, from Holland, France, Hungary and Germany.

2.4 AUTOMATA, FOUNTAINS AND MECHANICAL TOYS

The Arabic word *hiyal* as applied to mechanics can denote almost any machine from a small toy to a siege engine. In the present section however, we shall be concerned only with those devices that were intended to provide amusement and aesthetic pleasure. Islamic courtly circles not only gave

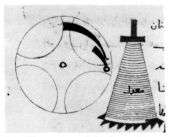

2.15 Illustration of the fusee drive (the conical cylinder) of a spring-driven mechanical clock, from a manuscript of Taqi al-Din. Sixteenth century AD. Bodleian Library, Oxford.

encouragement and assistance to writers and scientists, but also were most appreciative of the work of engineers, some of whom attained high status in urban society. Many of the devices contrived by these engineers could be dismissed as trivial, were it not for four important factors: first, there was a leisured class in Islam that took an interest in sophisticated mechanical effects; secondly, the engineers themseves took their work very seriously indeed; thirdly, many of the ideas and components embodied in the devices are relevant to the development of modern machine technology; fourthly, the pre-occupation of Muslim engineers in describing ingenious machines and devices does not reflect a lack of interest in the application of their skills for useful purposes. A study of what follows will make our point clear. In this connection, however, we must remind ourselves of an important aspect of all Arabic mechanical engineering books. No engineer ever described common or familiar everyday machinery; rather he recorded only ingenious and unfamiliar inventions.

Mention has already been made of the works of al-Muradi and al-Jazari, both of whom described the construction of ingenious devices (see below). Another important work on the same subject was the eighth chapter of *Mafatih al-'Ulum* (*The Keys of the Sciences*), written by Abu 'Abd Allah al-Khuwarizmi towards the end of the fourth century AH (tenth century AD). This is essentially a technical encyclopaedia which gives the names and etymology of various devices and components, together with information about their manufacture and use. Without question, however, the most important work on the subject was written by the Banu Musa brothers. Their work, and that of their successors, was certainly influenced by the writings of Hellenistic inventors, particularly Philon and Heron, whose books were rendered into Arabic in the third century AH (ninth century AD). But the Banu Musa's book, *Kitab al-Hiyal* (*The Book of Ingenious Devices*), displays notable advances on the works of their Hellenistic predecessors. These advances can be demonstrated by their masterly use of small variations in air pressure and water pressure, and by their frequent employment of conical valves as automatic regulators in flow systems. Indeed, their book is the earliest record we possess of the confident use of these valves as 'in-line' instruments. Another important innovation was the double concentric siphon; here, if the flow is interrupted, it cannot be resumed because the siphon produces an artificial air-lock. There are 103 models in the existing manuscripts of *Kitab al-Hiyal* of which 93 can confidently be attributed to the Banu Musa brothers, and of these 83 are trick vessels of various kinds, and 6 are fountains. The vessels demonstrate a bewildering variety of effects; for example, there are pitchers from which outpouring cannot be resumed once it has been interrupted; there are vessels that will replenish themselves if small quantities of liquid are removed from them but will not do so if a large quantity is extracted; and vessels into which a mixture of liquids is poured yet, when the outlets are opened, the liquids discharge separately. Here it is impossible to give even a summary of the various systems used to obtain these effects, for they had at their disposal a set of about 15 components from which, for a given device, they could select those which together would produce the desired result. These components included double and single concentric siphons, bent-tube siphons, conical valves, concealed air-holes, balances, pulleys, gears, miniature water and wind-wheels, floats and cranks. The cranks, however, did not perform a complete rotation, nor did they transmit much power though they are, nevertheless, the first known example of non-manual cranks. Figure 2.16 is a self-replenishing design that gives some idea of the Banu Musa brothers' methods. The container JDHT is divided into two chambers by the horizontal plate CK. Soldered to a hole in its centre is a bronze tube with conical valve seats at either end. The valve rod carrying the

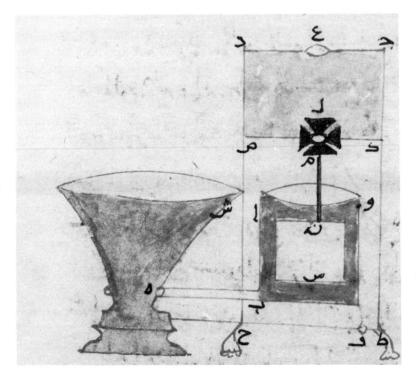

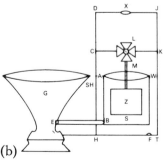

(b)

2.16 A self-replenishing vessel described in *Kitab al-hiyal* by the Banu Musa brothers.
Left Illustration from a manuscript. Ninth century AD. Topkapi Sarayi Müzesi, Istanbul.
Above Diagram

upper plug L and the lower plug M passes through the tube; its other end is soldered to the float Z, which is in the tank S. There is a concealed air-hole at F. A pipe BE connects the bottom of the tank S to the bottom of the exterior vessel G. The chamber JDCK is filled with liquid, the valve L being closed. A few litres of liquid are poured into the vessel G and flow through the pipe BE into the tank S. The float Z rises, valve L opens, and liquid flows into tank S, through the pipe BE and into the vessel G until the float Z rises far enough to close the valve M. When small amounts of liquid are taken from the vessel G, the tank S and vessel G are replenished through the valve M. If, however, a large amount is taken from the vessel all at once, the valve L closes and no replenishment can occur. This is the earliest example we have of a double-acting valve.

Each of the Banu Musa's devices is an automaton in itself. Other writers describe moving automata that are similar to those on water-clocks, but without precise timing. The first five of al-Muradi's machines are of this type. Power was supplied by water-wheels, which could be overshot or undershot; al-Muradi advised using the former if the flow was slight. Figure 2.17 is a photograph of a manuscript of one of al-Muradi's designs: the concentric circles to the left of the illustration represent the water-wheel. This drawing is for model 5, which had a number of doors that opened in succession to reveal figures. It can clearly be seen that a complex system of gearing was used to transmit power. The text is quite explicit that this included segmental gears, but because the relevant sections are badly defaced it has not been possible to ascertain whether there were also epicyclic ones, although these are indicated on the illustration. Nor has it been possible to discover whether the water-wheels incorporated some kind of escapement to control their speed. In a passage of al-Jazari's book describing musical automata in general, he suggests that he knew of such a mechanism. These first five machines of al-Muradi have great significance in the history of mechanical technology. Certainly, the earliest known example of really complex gearing occurs in an astronomical computer dated about 80 BC, discovered close to the Greek island of Antikythera. But this gearing did not transmit large forces, whereas al-Muradi's gears had to transmit high torque from the water-wheel. Moreover, the first known instance of the use of very sophisticated gearing in the West does not occur until the treatise written is AD 1365 by Giovanni di' Dondi, describing the weight-driven astronomical clock that he had constructed. Another important point is the use of water-wheels to drive the

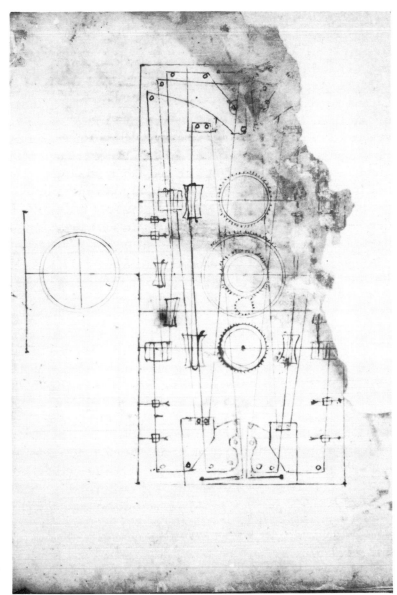

2.17 Drawing of al-Muradi's model 5 showing a complex system of gearing. The power was supplied from a water-wheel on the left. Eleventh century AD. Biblioteca Medicea Laurenziana, Florence.

machines. The same method, with an effective escapement, was used to drive the astronomical clock in China made by Su Sung, who flourished about AD 1090 and so was roughly contemporaneous with al-Muradi. In either case, of course, the idea may have been derived from earlier devices. We cannot now accept the probability of the transmission of this idea from China to Islam; on present evidence it could have been in either direction.

Al-Jazari's clocks and water-raising machines have already been discussed. The remainder of this book included liquid dispensers, blood-letting or phlebotomy measuring instruments, fountains and musical automata, and some miscellaneous items. The step-by-step instructions for manufacture and assembly, and the close attention to details of construction, give us a great deal of information about the skills of Islamic mechanical engineers. The vessels are similar to those of the Banu Musa brothers, but they rely more on direct mechanical and hydraulic transmissions and less upon subtle variations in pressure. A notable feature is the use of taps with multiple borings and of valves with inclined water passages. In one pitcher the hot chamber is separated from the cold by a partition consisting of two copper sheets with an air space between them – clearly a direct ancestor of the modern vacuum flask. The blood-letting devices worked on the principle of directing the blood into a cylinder in which there was a float. As the float rose, it caused pointers to move over a scale which recorded the volume of blood extracted. The cylinders were removable for cleaning. The fountains and musical automata all worked on similar principles. Figure 2.18 shows a typical example. The continuous water supply f flows into the funnel z, which is on top of the pipe jy. The pipe is balanced on a fulcrum; its end j discharges into the tank x, and its end y into tank h. The small pipes q and m discharge into tipping buckets a and t respectively. A wide pipe l leads from the bottom of tank x to a fountain head that emits several jets. A narrow pipe e leads from the bottom of tank h, passes through pipe l and its fountain head, and terminates above the latter. When the balanced pipe is discharging into tank h the water flows through the pipe e and emerges as a single jet n. When the tipping-bucket fills after one hour, it tilts and the projection on its rear inclines the balanced pipe towards tank x. The water now emerges as several jets. When tipping-bucket a is full, it tilts and inclines the balanced pipe back again, so that y discharges, h fills, and the single jet n again comes into action. The whole procedure is now repeated, and the cycle will continue as long as the water supply is uninterrupted.

2.5 INSTRUMENT MAKING

In this section we shall be concerned mainly with astronomical equipment used for observation and calculation, but we must first mention one or two other instruments. Prominent among these is the balance. Al-Khazini's work *Kitab Mizan al-Hikma* (*The Book of the Balance of Wisdom*), written it will be remembered at the beginning of the sixth century AH (twelfth century AD),

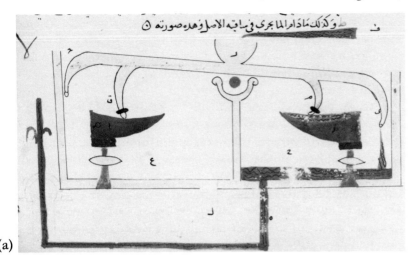

(a)

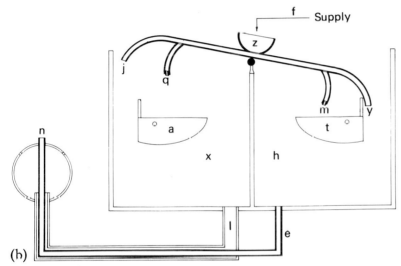

(b)

2.18 A fountain with automatically changing jets described by al-Jazari. *Above* Illustration from a manuscript. Thirteenth century AD. Bodleian Library, Oxford. *Below* Diagram.

represents the summit of Muslim skills in the construction and use of balances to determine the specific as well as the absolute weight of a body, and the proportion by weight of each substance in an alloy. Al-Khazini based his work on the writings of Archimedes and al-Biruni (d. after 442 AH/AD 1050), and describes a number of balances that enabled him to produce very accurate results. Small steelyard clepsydras, such as the two described by al-Khazini, were used for measuring short periods of time for astronomical purposes, or when constructing other water-clocks. The *tarjahar*, already mentioned in connection with the allocation of irrigation water, was also used for the same purpose. This was a brass bowl with a calibrated opening in its underside, which was placed on a water surface and sank in a given time.

The usual instruments were available for mathematical work and for technical drawing – the square, plumb-line, straight-edge, compasses etc. Al-Jazari also devised a special protractor for determining the centre between of three points on a spherical surface.

Already by the second and third centuries AH (eighth and ninth centuries AD) Muslim astronomers had prepared treatises on the armillary sphere, the flat or planispheric astrolabe (Fig. 2.19), the spherical astrolabe (Fig. 2.20), and the sun-dial; all were instruments of Hellenistic origin. But some of these early Islamic treatises also contain tables for marking the curves on astrolabes and sun-dials so that they could be used for observation from different latitudes. These tables present a purely Islamic development. The planispheric astrolabe, not only the earliest analogue computer but also a valuable observational instrument, was the most powerful tool available

2.19 A planispheric astrolabe made in Toledo in AD 1068. *Left* front, *Right* back. Museum of the History of Science, Oxford.

to astronomers before the advent of modern instruments, and is still useful for teaching the principles of spherical astronomy. With it one could determine the times of rising, setting, and southing or culmination of the Sun and the stars, or conversely find the position of a celestial body at a given time, as well as use it for a number of other astronomical problems. Astrolabes were made by craftsmen, scientists and astronomers; it was not unusual for the designation *al-Asturlabi* – 'The Astrolabist' – to be added to a man's name. Many modifications were made to the basic instrument by Muslim scholars, particularly a universal astrolabe which would serve all latitudes. New kinds of quadrants for observing the altitudes of celestial bodies, hemispherical and other unusual sundials were also developed. In addition, some specialised instruments are known to us, either from written or archaeological evidence, or from both. For instance, al-Biruni constructed a geared calendar, consisting

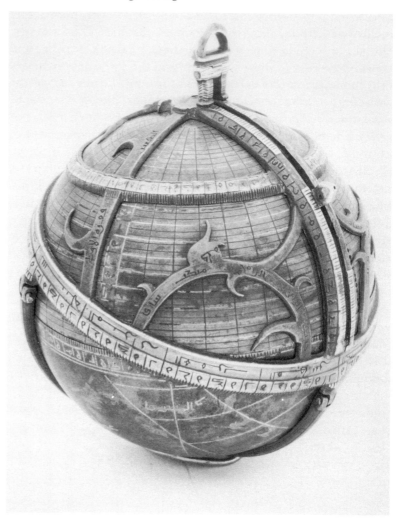

2.20 An eastern-Islamic spherical astrolabe made of brass and silver. Late fifteenth century AD. Museum of the History of Science, Oxford.

of a circular brass box inside which were eight gear-wheels of various sizes. A pointer on the lid was set to a point on a dial representing the Sun's position on a given day, whereupon a pointer on another dial showed the Moon's position, while its shape was displayed through an aperture in the lid. Another kind of instrument was the equatorium, which was designed to relieve the tedium of numerical computation of planetary positions; by mechanical means the celestial longitude of any one of the planets could be determined for any given time. The famous Andalusian astronomer al-Zarqali is known to have constructed one of these about 442 AH/AD 1050. An interesting instrument made in the eighth century AH (fourteenth century AD) in Syria by the celebrated astronomer Ibn al-Shatir is preserved in the Awqaf Library in Aleppo. This consists of two universal sun-dials, one polar, the other equatorial. The latter could be used to measure the hour-angle (the angle measured westwards between the meridian and a celestial body) of the sun and the stars. An important treatise written in the seventh century AH (thirteenth century AD) by the Cairo astronomer Abu 'Ali al-Marrakushi is a compendium of Islamic astronomical instruments.

One of the most important contributions of Islam to the study of astronomy was the establishment of observatories which were, of course, fully equipped with a wide range of instruments. Significant advances in astronomical theory were made at the observatory at Maragha, founded by Nasir al-Din al-Tusi in 657 AH/AD 1259. (It was al-Tusi, as we have seen earlier, who initiated valuable modifications to the system of Ptolemy.) A treatise describing all the instruments in the observatory was prepared by Mu'ayyad al-Din al-'Urdi (this has now been edited). The work of al-Tusi was continued at Tabriz and Damascus, but his most famous imitator was Ulugh Beg, who founded the observatory at Samarqand in 823 AH/AD 1420. The last important Muslim observatory was built for Taqi al-Din at Istanbul between 983–5 AH/AD 1575–7, and a surviving treatise that he wrote describes the instruments in use there. Several of the instruments and some of the organisational features of the Maragha, Samarqand and Istanbul observatories appeared again at the two observatories of the Danish astronomer Tycho Brahe which he founded on the island of Ven in the strait between Denmark and Sweden, Uraniborg (AD 1576) and Stjerneborg (AD 1584).

2.6 THE SEARCH FOR ENERGY

In an area which was the birthplace of the utilisation of water and wind-power and in which many types of hydraulic machinery were developed, attention had been turned to ingenious devices since pre-Islamic times. With the Islamic civilisation this activity reached its climax and the water-wheel became an integral part of Muslim culture. We have seen this represented in such books on ingenious devices and automata as those of the Banu Musa brothers and al-Jazari. Yet the Banu Musa and al-Jazari are separated by more than three centuries of progress and activity (third to sixth centuries AH/ninth to twelfth centuries AD). There must, surely, have been some treatises on machines in this period and the gap in our knowledge may be filled by future discoveries. Certainly al-Muradi's treatise (fifth century AH/eleventh century AD) is a promising one if a full version can be found. We also possess a chapter on water-wheels which is found in at least eight manuscripts which deserves our attention.

This chapter was included principally in a military manuscript called *Al-ḥiyal fi'l-ḥurub wa fath al-mada'in wa hifz al-durub* (*Stratagems in wars, the conquest of towns and the guarding of passes*), which was compiled in about the same period as al-Jazari's book. The author is unknown. Most copies are attributed to Alexander the Great, but this is only an example of customary practice in the case of such compilations, because Arab authors used to attribute them to pseudo-authors of great fame in order to give them some importance. The chapter on water-wheels was certainly not written by the compiler of the military treatise and it must have been copied from an original treatise which is at present unknown to us. We can tell, however, that this original was written between the third and sixth centuries AH (ninth to twelfth centuries AD). A feature of the chapter is that it does not describe the normal noria or the chain-of-pots wheels. Such ordinary wheels are also ignored by al-Jazari and Taqi al-Din, because the authors were concerned only with the innovative and ingenious; ordinary wheels were taken for granted and evoked no interest.

Taking the manuscripts together, they contain at least sixteen machines, all of which are different not only from the normal wheels but also from the water-raising machines of al-Jazari and Taqi al-Din. The main concern of the unknown author was to minimise energy input, a concern which is reflected in the fact that six of his machines are of the perpetual motion type. But the whole sixteen machines embody one philosophy and one motivating spirit and must be taken together in any serious analysis.

In comparison with the books of the Banu Musa brothers, al-Muradi, Ridwan, al-Jazari and Taqi al-Din, where the illustrations are usually clear and comprehensible, we find the illustrations in this chapter almost unintelligible. This is due to the copyist's ignorance of the subject and the long period of at least six centuries between the original copy and the surviving copies. With frequent copying by non-technical copyists drawings become distorted; indeed, this can be taken as an indicator when deciding the approximate date of a manuscript. For a distortion to reach such an extent as to render an illustration almost unintelligble, the last copy must have descended through the hands of several copyists.

Perpetual motion was a natural development in Islamic technology, and represents the ultimate concern for the utilisation of power. In India about AD 1150 Bhaskara described a perpetual motion wheel which resembles one of the six such wheels in the Arabic manuscripts, but the original Arabic text is of an earlier date. The Arabic technical descriptions, the illustrations, and the whole complex of the sixteen machines are quite elaborate and, as we have seen, constitute a single approach. The occurrence, therefore, of one or two perpetual-motion wheels in the Indian text does not imply a case of transmission from one culture to another, though there was an important transmission to the West. Indeed, perpetual-motion wheels attracted the attention of scientists and engineers in the West until the early part of this century; in fact the question was taken so seriously that it intrigued some eminent people, and even their governments.

A perpetual-motion machine is simply one which does useful work without an external source of energy; or it can be a machine in which the output is greater than the input. Figure 2.20 shows three such machines as described in Arabic manuscripts. In Fig. 2.21(*a*) closed pipes are partially filled with mercury. The pipes are not radial towards the centre but are inclined at an angle to the radial direction. As the wheel turns the mercury will move inside the pipes from one end to the other, and it was thought that this would exert a turning force. In Fig. 2.21(*b*) hinged mallets are used. In this figure some of the mallets are ascending and others are descending; there is an overbalance of one side compared with the other, and the wheel is supposed to turn indefinitely. In Fig. 2.21(*c*) the arms are multi-jointed and as the wheel turns they close up and wrap themselves around the wheel on one side and extend themselves on the other, thus creating an imbalance which is supposed to cause rotation. These designs and similar ones continued to be of interest in Europe until comparatively recently; indeed, this last principle was adopted by George Lipton in England only a hundred years ago.

(*a*)
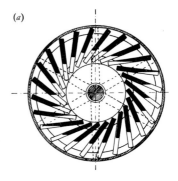

(*b*)
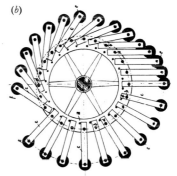

(*c*)
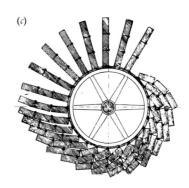

2.21 Three perpetual-motion machines described in a chapter on water-wheels written some time between the ninth and twelfth centuries AD.

(*a*) Machine with closed pipes partially filled with mercury and fixed round the rim of the wheel at an angle to the radial direction.

(*b*) Machine with mallets hinged to the rim of the wheel.

(*c*) Machine with multi-jointed arms hinged to the rim of the wheel.

3 *Civil engineering*

3.1 BUILDING TECHNOLOGY

The story of Muslim architecture – its derivation from classical, Hellenistic, and Iranian traditions and the assimilation of those traditions into a distinctively Islamic style – cannot be told here. Even a list of the largest, most architecturally successful of Islamic edifices would occupy more space than we have available. We can only mention, as examples, the Dome of the Rock (Fig. 3.1(a)), and the Aqsa mosque in Jerusalem, the Umayyad Mosque in Damascus, (Fig. 3.1(b)), the Alhambra Palace in Granada and the buildings of Ibn Tulun in Egypt (Fig. 3.2); many more examples could be given. Nor should we forget the many smaller but exquisite buildings that can still be found in all Islamic countries. We shall, however, confine ourselves here to the basic techniques of building, whether these were applied to architectural masterpieces or to humble dwellings.

The materials that Muslim builders had at their disposal depended on the area in which they were working. They included stone, rubble, baked bricks (*ajurr*), unbaked bricks (*tawb*), clay (*tin*) and timber; and in the Middle Ages, before the Lebanon had been deforested, cedar wood was plentiful for roofing. Syria (i.e. modern Syria, Lebanon, Palestine and Jordan) held to the tradition of building in dressed stone – also known as ashlar masonry – right through the Middle Ages and up to modern times. This is because Syrian limestone is a splendid building material; fairly easy to work, it is nevertheless resistant to weather and takes a beautiful amber tint on exposure. Ashlar masonry was also common in Egypt and in Tunisia, but it did not become widespread in the Maghrib until the sixth century AH (twelfth century AD) in Almohad buildings. Rubble or rough-hewn stone was used in Sassanid Iran and is still in common use in the Muslim world and elsewhere. It does not demand so much skill as ashlar work, but nevertheless it is a job for the craftsman. The stones must be placed together so that the interstices are neither too wide nor too narrow, and the surface of the wall must be even enough to

3.1 Two examples of early Islamic architecture.
Above The Dome of the Rock, Jerusalem, begun in the seventh century AD.
Below The Umayyad mosque, Damascus. Late seventh century AD onwards.

3.2 The courtyard and fountain of the mosque of Ibn Tulun, Cairo, with its spiral minaret in the background. Ninth century AD.

take a plaster finish. Mortar and plaster may be gypsum-based, or made from a mixture of chalk, sand, crushed fragments of tile and wood charcoal. The use of a strong mortar made from modern cement and sand is not satisfactory since it seems to cause cracking. Sometimes rubble walls are faced with ashlar or, as a cheaper alternative, only the joints and the outer five or six centimetres of the face are dressed, leaving a central boss of rough stone. This has a pleasing appearance once the stone has weathered.

Baked brick is used in all Islamic countries, but it is particularly characteristic of Iran. The bricks are of varying dimensions and may be cut at an angle or partly rounded off. They can be used alone or in combination with rubble in those parts of a building where accuracy of line is important. Brick functions as a horizontal bonding material alternating with courses of rubble, or as a vertical bond to maintain regularity of construction, especially at corners. Unbaked bricks, made by ramming earth and cut straw together in wooden moulds (Fig. 3.4), are still in common use in Sahara towns, and were employed very early on in arid regions such as Arabia and parts of Mesopotamia. They were used in addition to kiln-baked bricks in the building of the 'Abbasid capital of Samarra (third

century AH/ninth century AD), and at about the same time in Tunisia. Carefully moulded specimens have been uncovered in Tunisia; these measure 42 centimetres in length, half that in width and one quarter in thickness. Cobwork (*tabya*) is a form of concrete used for the construction of walls *in situ*; earth with which chalk and crushed baked earth or broken stones are often mixed is rammed between two boards kept apart by beams. The wall is plastered over, often in such a way as to simulate joints of heavy bond-work underneath. In the Muslim West cobwork became general in the fifth and sixth centuries AH (eleventh and twelfth centuries AD), especially in military building. Clay, the simplest of all building materials, was also used; it was excavated, moistened and placed in mould-boxes to dry in the sun.

When it was in plentiful supply, timber was adopted extensively in building work. The dome of the Dome of the Rock in Jerusalem consisted of a double skin of timber, doubtless Lebanese cedarwood, covered by lead sheets which were themselves covered by sheets of brass. Most of the houses in some towns and cities were built entirely of timber, for example at Bukhara in Transoxiana, and the houses in the port of Siraf in Fars were built of teak. More usually timber was used

3.3 Houses along the edge of the creek at Dubai, most of them with towers rising above them to catch the wind. The technique of producing an air current through buildings in hot climates by means of wind catchers probably goes back to ancient times. It became highly developed in the windier parts of Persia during the eleventh to the fifteenth centuries AD and later and from there spread to towns on the Gulf. The system was also used in North Africa. Air blows into the towers through vents facing the prevailing wind and passes down into the houses below, where it circulates through the rooms and provides a refreshing draft.

3.4. Making bricks in Egypt by pressing straw and mud into a wooden mould.

for the rafters, purlins and joists of roofs; in one type of construction, timber beams were built into the walls. Wherever possible, large timber baulks provided the foundation course for the walls of buildings.

The *muhtasib* (the Muslim censor of morals) exercised a close supervision over building construction. A number of wooden templates were kept in the mosque, each made to the standard size of a constructional member: one for the size of each wooden component, one for the baked bricks, one for the thickness of tiles, and so on. Using these templates the *muhtasib* made constant checks to ensure that the builders were adhering to the specifications. He also made regular checks of the mould-boxes used by builders for making baked bricks, raw bricks and tiles, in case these had become worn or distorted. Raw bricks were not to be used until they had whitened. Builders were required to keep stockpiles of special materials: bricks for lining wells, bricks for flooring, refractory bricks for lining ovens and furnaces, and special tiles for the roofs of

3.5 The building of the Red Fort at Agra, India depicted in a Mogul painting of the sixteenth century AD. On the right a clerk makes notes as the building materials are carried past him. Victoria and Albert Museum, London.

water-clocks. This supervisory function of the *muhtasib* was very similar to that of a modern clerk of works (see also the discussion of quality control in Chapter 10).

3.2 ROADS AND BRIDGES

In medieval times Muslim society was highly mobile. There were, of course, large sections of the population, farmers and urban labourers for example, who never travelled more than a few kilometres from their place of birth. But the exigencies of commerce, administration and warfare, together with the longing of all Muslims to make the pilgrimage to Mecca at least once in their lifetime, meant that the roads through the Muslim world were in constant use. Scholars also travelled widely in the pursuit of knowledge, and the great geographers wrote their books only after extensive travels in Islamic countries. Political frontiers were no barrier, although then as now customs formalities could be irritating for the weary traveller. Ibn Jubayr has left us an entertaining narrative of his encounter with Egyptian Customs officials at Alexandria in 578 AH/AD 1183. The works of geographers such as al-Muqaddasi and Ibn Hawqal are milestones in the study of geography, but they also served the purpose of providing information on routes and local conditions for merchants, government officials and postal couriers. All the great highways were described in detail: from Fustat to Upper Egypt and north to the Delta and to Syria, Iraq and Upper Mesopotamia; from Egypt along the North African coast to Tunisia and the Maghrib; from Iraq to Iran and then over the desert routes to Khurasan and Transoxiana; the Pilgrimage Routes to Mecca; and so on. The routes inside a given province were also described. Travellers were told the length of each stage, the kind of lodging, food and water available at each staging post, and any special hazards likely to be encountered on the journey. Wheeled traffic was rare. Camels, mules and donkeys were used for riding and as pack animals, although the Bactrian camel, the usual beast of burden in the Iranian highlands, was not suitable as a mount. The predominance of animal transport and the lack of rainfall made the metalling of roads and steppelands unnecessary, but in mountainous regions the roads had to be properly constructed and maintained. The institution of the state postal service (*barid* – see Chapter 4, section 7) ensured that the roads were mapped and that the towns and staging-posts en route were properly equipped for the reception of travellers. If there was no natural water supply at a staging-post, cisterns were built for the storage of rainwater. One instance of the efficiency of transport was the carriage of ice from Syria to Egypt during the summer months. This service was in operation in Fatimid, Ayyubid and Mamluk times (fourth to tenth centuries AH/tenth to sixteenth centuries AD). Five camel loads were sent every week; these were destined for the Sultan's palace and were paid for out of state funds. Streets in major cities such as Alexandria, Fez and Samarqand were paved with stone, while the *muhastib* ensured that the inhabitants of each quarter of the city met their obligations by keeping the streets clean, repairing potholes and providing drains. Every householder was responsible for the length of street which adjoined his property.

As far as river crossings were concerned, one of the commonest forms of river was the pontoon bridge. Fustat was connected to the island of Rawda by a bridge of 30 boats, and the island was connected to the other bank of the Nile by a bridge of 60 boats. At Hilla on the Euphrates there was a bridge of large boats, built for the pilgrims by order of the Caliph to replace a ferry. A steel cable was stretched across the river and secured to wooden anchorages on the banks; the boats were fixed to this cable. This kind of bridge is effective and relatively cheap to build, but it requires constant maintenance and is a barrier to shipping. Many of the rivers and canals were navigable, and often these were spanned by masonry arch bridges. There are few problems in constructing a single-span bridge with a semi-circular arch, where the load on the banks is mainly vertical, but difficulties arise with other types of design. With a multiple-arch bridge, the hardest problem is to ensure that the piers rest on firm foundations in the river bed (Fig. 3.6). This is not a great problem in canals and slowly-flowing

3.6 The multiple-arched Shahristan bridge, Isfahan, which dates from the twelfth century AD.

rivers, but it is a tricky business if the current is rapid. There is a record of a bridge near Marrakesh, built by engineers from Muslim Spain, being swept away when the river was in spate. Nevertheless, there are many examples of successful constructions of this kind. A more daring type of construction than the semi-circular arch is the single-span segmental arch, where the rise of the arch is less than half the span. This permits longer spans, but imposes a horizontal as well as a vertical load on the abutments. It is generally practicable only when the banks are of solid rock. Segmental arches did not appear in Western Europe until the end of the seventh century AH (thirteenth century AD), but were known in Islam long before this time. For example, we have the dimensions of a segmental arch bridge built over the River Tab in Iran at the beginning of the second century AH (eighth century AD). It had a span of 60 metres and a rise of about 10 metres.

3.3 IRRIGATION

When irrigation in Islam is considered, one naturally turns to the extensive canal systems in the valleys of the great rivers. And, indeed, large cities in arid areas, such as Baghdad and Cairo, could not have flourished in the absence of thriving agriculture based upon irrigation. The attitude to water as a precious source of life, however, extends into every Muslim community down to the smallest hamlet, because the nature of the water supply decides the size and prosperity of the community.

Wells, springs, streams, and underground sources are all used for growing crops and for domestic purposes. Thus we learn of a village community in the fourth century AH (tenth century AD) whose well was dry for most of the time; when it filled, at a certain time every year, it was used to irrigate the fields. Another community used wells to irrigate its fields by means of *saqiyas* (see Chapter 2, section 1) during periods when their river was dry. Wadi irrigation was also common. Dams were built across the wadis to impound the water that cascaded down them after a rainstorm. Irrigation was not used solely to sustain life, however; in areas with adequate rainfall it was commonly a means of increasing production or growing crops such as rice and sugar-cane, which could not be grown under ordinary rainfall conditions. For these reasons the Muslims introduced their methods of irrigation to the Iberian peninsula, together with a number of varieties of fruits and vegetables that were new to Europe. The impact of Muslim methods on the agronomy of Spain is reflected in modern Spanish, in which many of the words relating to agriculture and irrigation are of Arabic origin.

Bearing the foregoing in mind, we can now turn our attention to the major irrigation systems of the Muslim world, which provide much of technological and sociological interest. Civilisations based upon great rivers such as the Nile, the Tigris and the Euphrates had, of course, been in existence for millennia before the Arab conquests of the first century AH (seventh century AD). The basic techniques did not change with the advent of Islam, but the existing systems were extended and new canal works were constructed to meet the needs of the newly-founded cities. The techniques, being dictated by the regimes of the rivers, differ from one region to another. In Egypt the Nile floods begin predictably in the middle of August, reach a peak at the end of that month, and recede two months later, leaving a fresh fertilising sediment on the land. In ancient times man simply planted his crops in this fertile sediment, but as demand for food grew the system of basin irrigation was developed. Along the banks of the river, connected to each other and to the river by canals, large plots of land were provided, suitably levelled and at the correct elevation with respect to each other. Every season the flood water was allowed to run on to the plots by breaking the dykes; it was left to stand while the fertile silt settled. When the inundation receded, the water was drained back into the river, and there was no further irrigation until the following year. This system, which was the whole basis of Egyptian irrigation until the nineteenth century, was ideal for the Nile valley. The river is relatively steeply graded and the canal system was short; it was therefore kept silt-free by the flow of water, which also helped to flush out salts. No dams were built over the Nile, although longer canals were run to areas at some distance from the river, such as the Fayum depression. A disadvantage of the method was that it permitted only one harvest a year. Nevertheless a wide variety of crops was grown, planted on the fresh sediment at different times according to their growing season. Also, some cultivation was possible along the Nile even when its waters were low, since the water was raised to the level of the neighbouring fields by norias.

The rise of the Nile during the period of inundation was measured by the famous Nilometer (Fig. 3.7), completed in 247 AH/AD 861–2. This consisted of a tall graduated octagonal column, which served as a measuring gauge, standing in a stone-lined pit, roughly 6.2 metres square, with a staircase running down to the bottom. The last part of the pit was circular. The four sides of the upper pit were relieved by arched recesses in a style the Gothic architects called 'tiers-point', but they were three centuries earlier than any Gothic example. The pit was connected to the Nile by three tunnels at different levels. The measuring column was divided into 16 cubits and the 10 uppermost were subdivided into 24 divisions. The amount of land-tax due to the Sultan was assessed on the height to which the water ascended.

As in Egypt, the Muslims in Iraq inherited an irrigation system from their predecessors, in this case the Iranians (Sassanians). The Tigris and Euphrates are far more difficult to deal with than the Nile because the volume of water can vary enormously from one year to the next; this, combined with their sluggish rate of flow in the alluvial plain of lower Iraq, has

3.7 The interior of the Nilometer at Rawda Island, Cairo. Ninth century AD. The octagonal column on the right is calibrated in cubits to measure the height of the water of the Nile.

until recently caused frequent extensive flooding and changes
of course in both rivers. Several such changes have been
recorded in historical times. Fresh problems were posed in the
Islamic age by the rapid growth of newly-founded cities such as
Basra and Baghdad, which necessitated considerable extensions
of the existing network of canals. Since there is a slight
eastward slope from the Euphrates to the Tigris, large canals
were excavated between the two rivers below Baghdad. To the
east of the Tigris the Nahrwan canal, begun by the Sassanians,
was enlarged and equipped with a second inlet fed from a dam
across the Tigris below Samarra. The rivers Adheim and Dyala,
tributaries feeding the Tigris from the east, were also dammed,
and the canals led off from these dams formed the basis of
extensive irrigation systems (Fig. 3.8). Basra was founded in 17
AH/AD 638 as a military encampment to serve as a base for the

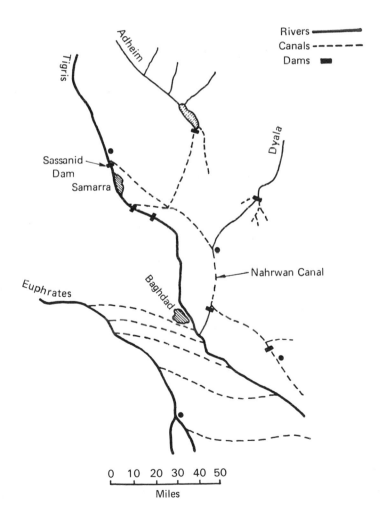

3.8 The canal network in the
Baghdad area as it was developed in
the Abbasid period using water
from the rivers Euphrates, Tigris,
Adheim and Dyala.

conquest of Iran; at the time the dwellings were simply temporary huts which were dismantled and stored when the troops were campaigning. About twenty years later the first permanent buildings were erected and Basra soon grew into a large city, which became a centre for commerce and overseas trade, for industry and finance, and for agriculture. It also became known for its active intellectual life, notably for the study of theology. The first main feeder canal to Basra from the Shatt al-'Arab was completed about 45 AH/AD 665, and during the following century a vast network of canals was constructed around the city to support the thriving agriculture.

A specialised irrigation technique was the utilisation of subterranean water by means of underground conduits called qanats. The qanat, one of the earliest examples of the difficult and hazardous operation of mining, is an almost-horizontal tunnel leading from an aquifer (a water-bearing stratum of rock, sand or gravel) to the point where the water is needed (Fig. 3.9(*a*)). A vertical shaft – the 'mother well' – is excavated at a location in the hills where there is known, or hoped to be, an aquifer. The route of the qanat is then set out on the surface from the mother well to the discharge point. Qanats may be quite short, but lengths of 8 to 16 kilometres are not uncommon, and some may be 30 kilometres or more. The depths of the mother wells also vary: some are less than 7 metres, though many are as much as 45 to 100 metres. The tunnel is excavated from the exit towards the mother well, the slope varying from 1 in 1000 in a short qanat to almost horizontal in a long one. At intervals of about 20 to 140 metres vertical shafts are sunk from the surface to the tunnel (Fig. 3.9(*b*)). These serve the dual purpose of supplying ventilation and providing a means for disposal of the spoil. A good aquifer

3.9(*a*) Cross-section of a *qanat* system for obtaining subterranean water.

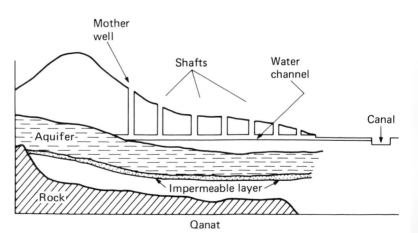

3.9(*b*) The course of a *qanat* in Iran marked at the surface by mounds of excavated material at the tops of the shafts

will yield a steady and dependable flow of water from year to year, while the passage of water along a tunnel aids cleanliness and the effects of evaporation are less than those encountered in lakes, cisterns, and open channels. In the Middle Ages qanats were widely used in Iran, North Africa and Spain; they are still in use in Iran today. In 1962 the distinguished French water engineer Henri Goblot estimated that about half the land under cultivation in Iran was irrigated by qanats.

The management of a large irrigation system was a major undertaking which was controlled by a department of state employing administrators, hydraulic engineers, inspectors, skilled workmen and labourers. The duties of the department included the construction of new canals and dams, the maintenance of existing canals and water-raising machines, and the allocation of water to farmers. When the excavation of a new canal was approved and funded, its exact line, gradient and cross-sectional profile were determined by the engineers and surveyors. The cubic content of the excavation was calculated and from this the number of workmen and supervisors required to complete the work in the allocated time could be estimated. The likely cost, derived from the total man-hours, could then be checked against the budget. Similar calculations were made for removing accumulated silt from existing canals, the work being done either directly by the department or by an outside contractor.

Water was allocated to farmers in two ways. The first was on a time basis. The channel leading from the canal into a farmer's fields was blocked by a small earthen dam. When he was due to receive his supply of water, the tiny dam was breached and the water allowed to flow into his property for a set period, after which the dam was closed again. In the alternative method the inlets to the fields were closed by wooden boards in which there were holes of a standard diameter. The supply was therefore continuous but varied with the rate of flow of the feeder canal. Some idea of the magnitude and importance of the administration of irrigation can be gained from a report made in the fourth century AH (tenth century AD) about the region of Marw in Khurasan. The superintendent of the irrigation systems based on the River Murghab had more authority than the prefect of Marw, and supervised 10 000 workers, each with a specified task.

3.4 DAMS

Dams were usually associated with irrigation works, being built over rivers to feed irrigation canals as part of integrated hydraulic systems which included sluices, regulators and flow dividers. Figure 3.8 shows the positioning of dams of the irrigation system in the Baghdad area, and there were similar layouts in Transoxiana and Syria. In the Iberian peninsula, Muslim engineers built river dams from the Ebro right round to the Guadalquivir in a conscious attempt to re-create the luxuriance of the Damascus Ghuta. These diversionary dams were usually of small size and made of earth with a core of rammed clay, but more imposing structures were also built to produce water-power as well as for irrigation. Al-Idrisi, writing in the middle of the sixth century AH (twelfth century AD), described one such dam on the Guadalquivir river at Cordoba. It was built of Egyptian stone in which marble pillars were incorporated to provide openings for three mills, each of which contained four water-wheels. Until recently the mills still functioned, though much changed from their original form. We have a description of a similar installation at the beginning of the seventh century AH (thirteenth century AD) near Tabriz. In this case there were two water-wheels. Yet three centuries earlier, about the year 370 AH/AD 960 the Buwayid Amir Adud al-Dawla created a massive hydraulic project on the River Kur in Iran (Fig. 3.10). In the words of al-Muqaddasi, 'Adud al-Dawla closed the river between Shiraz and Istakhr (Persepolis) by a great wall with lead foundations. And the water formed a lake and rose. Upon it on the two sides were ten norias as we mentioned for Khuzistan, and beneath each noria was a mill, and it is today one of the wonders of Fars. There he

3.10 Dam on the river Kur at Band-i Amir in Fars, Iran built about AD 960 to provide water for a large irrigation project.

built a city. The water flowed through the canals and irrigated 300 villages.'

A notable example of wadi irrigation, still to be seen about a kilometre from the north gate of Qayrawan in Tunisia, is provided by the two cisterns which impound the waters of the wadi Marj al-Lil (Fig. 3.11). The smaller cistern is a polygon with 17 straight sides averaging 6.25 metres in length, each corner being strengthened both internally and externally by a round buttress. Its internal diameter is 37.4 metres. This cistern is a decanting tank, where the mud settles. One of its sides is in contact with the sides of a much larger cistern, to which there is a circular channel of communication in the partition wall several metres above the bottom. The larger cistern has 48 sides with a round buttress at each corner; it has an internal diameter of 130 metres and a total depth of 8 metres. The installation was completed in the year 248 AH/AD 862–3.

3.5 SURVEYING

To determine the position – the longitude and latitude – of any place on the Earth's surface is valuable for various reasons, and vital to astronomers if they are to work out results of their observations of the positions of celestial bodies. One way of finding these co-ordinates for any place is by determining its meridian, i.e. the line passing due south of the place and continuing through the north celestial pole and through the zenith. The simplest method of determining the meridian is by measuring the altitude of a circumpolar star (i.e. a star close

3.11 view of part of the two
cisterns of the ninth-century AD
reservoir on the wadi Marj al-Lil
near Qayrawan in Tunisia.

enough to the celestial pole so that it always appears above the
horizon), while simultaneously measuring its horizontal angle
from some given point on the horizon. This is done when the
star is to the east of the observer, and then when it is to the
west. Bisecting the horizontal angle gives the meridian line.
After this it is fairly simple to fix the latitude by observing the
altitude of the Sun or star when it crosses the meridian. Several
other methods were also used by Muslim astronomers for
determining latitude.

Medieval methods for determining longitude were not, in
general, as accurate as those for finding the latitude because
complete precision requires the use of a reliable chronometer.
Such chronometers were not available until the middle of the
eighteenth century AD, so Muslim astronomers had to apply
other methods. They adopted two techniques. One was to
make observations of lunar eclipses from two different places,
noting the same event – the moment when the Moon moves
into the Earth's shadow, for instance – and then comparing the

results. The difference in time between the event at both places was a measure of their difference in longitude. The second method was to measure the east–west distance of one place from another of known (or assumed) longitude.

Once the latitude and longitude of two places are known it is possible to determine the direction of one place from the other and thus its azimuth, i.e. its bearing measured eastwards from the north point. One application of this calculation, determining the direction of Mecca from a given locality – its *qibla* – was of particular importance for medieval Muslim scientists. Solutions to the *qibla* problem proposed by leading astronomers between the third to the eighth centuries AH (ninth to fourteenth centuries AD) bear witness to the level of sophistication in trigonometry and computational techniques attained by these scholars. Since the azimuth of one place relative to another could be obtained, theoretically it would have been possible to have driven a road or a canal in a straight line between two towns. This was not practicable however, since routes were determined by terrain and by matters of land ownership, while canals had to be as close as possible to the areas of cultivation which they were to irrigate. Routes were therefore fixed bearing these practical considerations in mind.

Before excavating a canal it was necessary to establish not only its route but also to level the ground along that route from start to finish. The operation of levelling requires a horizontal sighting line which, in modern instruments, is provided by a telescope with crossed hair-lines inside the eyepiece and a spirit level to bring the base-plate of the instrument horizontal. Muslim surveyors used several instruments based on the same principle, though none of course had telescopes; they used open sights. One instrument made use of a metal triangle with metal hooks soldered to the two ends of one of its sides (Fig. 3.12). A plumb-line with a lead weight on its end was fixed to the centre of this side. Two levelling-staffs, graduated into divisions of about 12 centimetres which were themselves subdivided into divisions, were held vertically by assistants at a distance apart of about 7 metres. A wire was stretched tightly between the two staffs and the triangle was suspended by its two hooks at the centre of this wire. One end of the wire was moved up and down its staff until the plumb line passed through the lower corner of the triangle. A similar method was to take a piece of hardwood about 0.5 metres long and drill a longitudinal hole through it. A metal pendulum was fixed to a fulcrum at the centre of the hardwood to act as a plumb-line,

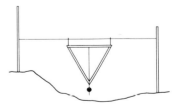

3.12 An Islamic surveyor's level, which used a metal triangle and plumb line.

and the wood then threaded on to a wire; levelling proceeded as before. A third method was to take a long straight reed and drill a hole through one of its walls into the central bore (Fig. 3.13). The reed was then held between the levelling-staffs and an assistant trickled water down a long woollen filament and into the hole. The reed was deemed to be horizontal when equal quantities of water issued from each end. Whichever method was used, the difference in level between the two points was recorded, the rear staff moved round to the next point on the route, and the procedure repeated. When the route had thus been surveyed, the total (i.e. the algebraic sum) of 'rises' and 'falls' from all the stations gave the difference in levels between start and finish. Similar methods were used to obtain the correct gradient when the canal was being excavated.

To obtain the height and bearing of distant objects, Muslim surveyors used the astrolabe. On the back of the instrument, in the lower semi-circle, there was a square, or sometimes two equal matching squares. The instrument shown earlier, Fig. 2.19, has only one square, and its vertical and horizontal sides are divided into 12 equal parts. Where there was a second square this might be divided into tenths or other fractions. (Choice of the number of divisions depended on the units of length in common use.) When the astrolabe was suspended freely, the alidade or sighting bar was adjusted so that a distant object whose height was required was viewed through the sights. Once this was done, the right-angled triangle formed by the alidade and the two sides of the square engraved on the astrolabe, allowed either the height of the object or its distance

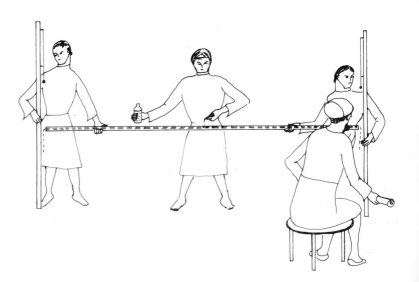

3.13 Checking the level by means of a hollow reed through which water is poured.

to be found from the graduated scales provided one of these two distances was known. However, if neither was known they could be determined by sightings with the astrolabe from different points on the same straight line. And if the astrolabe were supported horizontally, it was possible to view distant objects through the sights and record their bearings. Used in this way the astrolabe became a theodolite.

كانت رماحهم على كافهم فسوطهم لحث شديد فاذا وقع ذلك وفعلوا المخالف
على اصحاب الميسره فخرجوا محالفات وخرجوا الذين لهم مثلهم شرخرجوا المبتدئ
حرجه وبدوروا ناوردا واحدا ويقطع كل في ارضه

وهذا الميدان فهو حربي حدكله وفيه يتبين للفارس الماهرسرلانه لايفلت من
هذا الميدان حربشكان اوميدانا الاكل حاذق واذا فعت هذه الاسواط
دواحد من خلفه ورمحه من خلفه ورمحه على كتفه فليرديد به الى العنان ويقبض
بكلتاهما على عقب الرمح وحطه من كفه ويعطل من رمحته ومن مشارفي هذا الوجه

4 *Military technology*

4.1 ARABIC MILITARY TREATISES

Before the advent of the Ottoman Turks, the two greatest successes of Muslim arms in the Middle Ages were the Arab conquests of the first century AH and the victories of the Ayyubid and Mamluk armies in the sixth and seventh (seventh, and twelfth and thirteenth centuries AD). For the early period and indeed right up to the sixth century AH, there are no known military treatises as such, although the names of the earlier masters of the military arts have been preserved in some of the manuals of war. Anyone wishing to study military technology in the first five Islamic centuries and the vital role it played in external and internal affairs must therefore have recourse to the descriptions of battles and campaigns in the works of historians such as al-Waqidi, al-Baladhuri and al-Tabari. Not surprisingly, considering the time span and the widely differing techniques used by various Muslim peoples, there is as yet no general history of military affairs, though there are some valuable monographs, among which may be mentioned a treatise on weapons in pre-Islamic Arabia derived from a close study of poetry, and a work on military affairs under the Umayyads.

From the end of the sixth century AH (twelfth century AD) and onwards for about two hundred years, a considerable number of military treatises were composed. It has been suggested that the stimulus for these arose from the necessity of confronting the Crusaders. Certainly, the methods of warfare of both sides were influenced by this confrontation and the extent of this interdependence now needs to be investigated. Yet, at the same time, it must be remembered that the Muslims had been forced for centuries to oppose Western armies in Spain and Byzantine armies in Asia Minor, and had been under constant pressure from nomadic peoples on their north-eastern borders. It would seem then that the urge to write military treatises was probably inspired more by other factors, such as the warlike character of the Mamluk leadership and the menace of a possible Mongol invasion.

4.1 Horsemen taking part in a contest. Illustration from a Mamluk manual on horsemanship for cavalrymen. Fourteenth century AD. British Library, London.

93

Such treatises are usually categorised under three headings: first, *furusiyya*, i.e. horsemanship in its widest sense, then archery, and finally tactics, military organisation and weapons. (For treatises on gunpowder and firearms, however, see section 8 below.) Over fifty treatises covering these three categories are known to exist, and there can be no doubt that others lie undiscovered in the world's libraries. A few of them are of a literary nature, with little relevance to the realities of warfare, but most are practical manuals for the guidance of those responsible for training recruits.

The most important of the *furusiyya* treatises was composed by the great tournament master and lance-jouster Najm al-Din Ayyub al-Ahdab al-Rammah (d. 694 AH/AD 1294). Entitled *Kitab al-furusiyya bi rasm al-jihad* (*The Book of Horsemanship for the Holy War*), it exists in thirteen manuscript copies, many of them illustrated. It was the source book for all future work on the subject of cavalry exercise, tournaments and battle formations. There was also the exhaustive work *Nihayat al-su'l wa'l-umniyya fi ta'lim a'mal al-furusiyya* (*An end to questioning and desiring [further knowledge] concerning different exercises of horsemanship*) attributed to Muhammad b.'Isa al-Aqsara'i who was active about 800 AH/AD 1400. This treatise, of which nine manuscript copies are known, has been described as the most important of all the sources in Arabic on Muslim military organisation, training and theory (Fig. 4.1).

The archery treatises include descriptions of various types of bow, their manufacture and use, together with traditions relating to the exploits of celebrated archers. The earliest example we have is part of a manual of war written in Persian and having the title *Adab al-harb wa'l-shaja'a* (*Rules of conduct for war and bravery*). Its author was Fakhr-i Mudabbir, who dedicated it to the Delhi Sultan Shams al-Din Iltumish (reigned 608–33 AH/AD 1211–36), but of the sources in Arabic perhaps the most important of the treatises are those by Taybugha al-Baklamishi (d. 797 AH/AD 1394).

Works in the third category include such subjects as fortifications and siege warfare (including siege engines), camping and constructing pallisades, spying and stratagems, battle formations, types of commanders and their qualities, etc. In this last field we have two important treatises; the first of them, *Tabsirat arbab al-albab fi kayfiyyat al-najat fi al-hurub* (*Instructions of the masters of the skills of the methods of salvation in wars*), was written by Murda (or Mardi) b.'Ali al Tarsusi, and composed for Saladin about 583 AH/AD 1187. The second, *Al-tadhkirat al-harawiyya fi al-hiyal al-harbiyya* (*Things worth mentioning about warlike stratagems*), was by 'Ali b. Abi Bakr al-Harawi (d. 611 AH/AD 1214), and is a very thorough study in twenty four books of the Muslim army in the field and under siege. The unique Istanbul manuscript is dated 602 AH/AD 1205, and so was written within the author's lifetime.

4.2 CAVALRY

By the first century AH (seventh century AD) the cavalry had become the best armed and most numerous of the Byzantine troop formations. It seems also that the Iranians, with their horse-mounted knights, the *Asawira*, could put much larger cavalry forces into the field than the Arabs, for in the early days of Islam the number of horses in the army was small, particularly before the fall of Mecca. The type of open, level country best suited to cavalry had been well described by the author of a book on generalship, but it was precisely this type of country the Arabs avoided when they brought their enemies to battle. The decisive battles of the Yarmuk and Qadisiyya were won by infantry. Later, however, horses became more numerous and 'Umar I (ruled 31–41 AH/AD 634–44) had them collected for military use from all areas. As a result 4 000 became available at Kufa, a horse pasture for Muslim mounts was established in northern Syria, and gradually strategy changed, so that the force with which 'Amr b. al-'As conquered Egypt in 37–9 AH/AD 640–2 was composed mainly of horsemen.

The Islamic use of cavalry was helped in other ways, as for instance when the *Asawira* came over to Islam in a body during Abu Musa's conquest of Khuzistan from 17–21 AH/AS 638–42. However, this was only one of the more dramatic examples of the incorporation of non-Arab troops into the Muslim forces. The recruitment of the Khurasanis, Berbers and Turks is too well-documented to require elaboration here, yet all these peoples brought their own styles of combat and horsemanship with them. In consequence it would be inaccurate to speak of a single style of cavalry practice for the Muslim world as a whole. We can, however, briefly examine the warlike skills of the horsemen during the Mamluk period, for this was a critical time in Islamic history.

The arms of the Mamluk horseman (*faris*) included the sword, lance, bow, shield and mace. The mace, made of iron or steel with a cubical head, was secured under the stirrup leather, and the lance was held in one or both hands, not 'couched' or lowered for attack as it was in the West, at least for jousting (see section 3 below). Training took place in the *tibaq* (sing. *tabaqa*), the name given to the barracks of the Cairo Citadel which housed the military school. It began when the *mamluk* reached his majority, and was thorough and rigorous. Tuition in horsemanship lasted until he could handle a horse, both bareback and saddled, at a canter, a trot and a gallop, on the flat and over jumps. He had also to know how to care for his horse in case of sickness. In addition, training with the bow and lance was considered very important; the *faris* had to be able to strike a target from various angles and at different speeds of approach using both weapons. The *mamluk* was also fully trained to use his sword in a similar way (Fig. 4.2). The success of these methods is attested by Mamluk victories over the Crusaders and the Mongols.

4.3 EDGED WEAPONS

The sword (*sayf*) was the main weapon of Islamic warriors, both infantry and cavalry; it was used for personal defence, hand-to-hand fighting and single combat. Indeed, swords were the most highly esteemed of all weapons and were often given names; we have a record of many of these from the earliest days of Islam and throughout the medieval period. Yet it is not possible to identify a typical Islamic sword, because the construction,

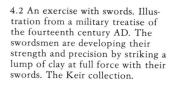
4.2 An exercise with swords. Illustration from a military treatise of the fourteenth century AD. The swordsmen are developing their strength and precision by striking a lump of clay at full force with their swords. The Keir collection.

length and shape varied from one area to another. In Arabia one of the distinguishing marks of a tribe was the length of the swords used by its members. The curved 'scimitar', often regarded as typical of Islamic weaponry, did not come into use until quite late – it may have appeared in the eighth century AH (fourteenth century AD), though the actual date of its appearance is still undecided. The commonest type of sword in use in the Islamic heartlands during the Middle Ages, and of which there are many examples in illustrations and as museum exhibits, was of the pattern shown in Fig. 4.3. The blade (*nasl*) had one cutting edge (*shafra*), which was curved for about one span (some 22 centimetres) towards the tip (*dhu'aba*). This curved section was called the *midrab* (chest), since this was the part with which one struck the target. The back (*matn*) was sometimes curved slightly over the length of the *midrab*. The hilt (*maqbid* or *nasab*) had a knob or pommel (*saylan*) and a cross-piece (*kulab*); hilts were made of steel, ivory, ebony or other hard material.

Swords were manufactured at a number of centres, though Indian swords were also in use in Arabia in pre-Islamic times and later. At the Battle of Yamama in 12 AH/AD 633 the Muslims' opponents were armed with Indian swords, and there are frequent references to them in the works of Islamic poets. It is possible, then, that Arab swords were superior to those from India. The poet al-Mutanabbi (d. 354 AH/AD 965) wrote: 'The swords of India are feared, and they are of iron: how then when they are Nizari, Arab?' Yemeni swords were famous, as were those from Damascus. (See Chapter 9 below for verification that Damascus swords were made in and near Damascus from steel produced from locally mined iron ore.) In Mamluk times the *faris* was trained to be able to judge the force of his blows exactly so that he could could kill or merely wound his antagonist according to circumstances.

The lance (*rumh*) was also very widely used in the Islamic world (Fig. 4.4). The sword was relatively expensive, whereas a simple lance could be made by fitting an iron spear-head to the branch of a tree. Longer lances of good quality wood and tipped with lance-heads of Damascus steel were, of course, considerably more costly and beyond the reach of the poorer members of the community. The shafts of such lances were sometimes made of bamboo; in this case the weapon was known as a *qanat*. The lengths of lances could vary greatly, the shortest being no more than about 2 metres while the largest were about 7 metres or even more. The main parts of the lance were the shaft (*matn*), the head (*sinan*) with a socket (*tha'laba*) for fitting over the shaft,

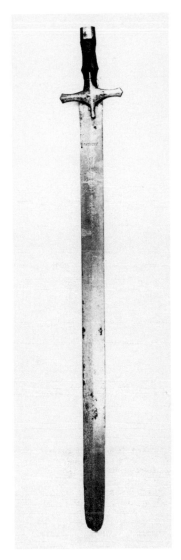

4.3 An Abbasid straight sword, the blade dating from the ninth century AD. Topkapi Sarayi Müzesi, Istanbul.

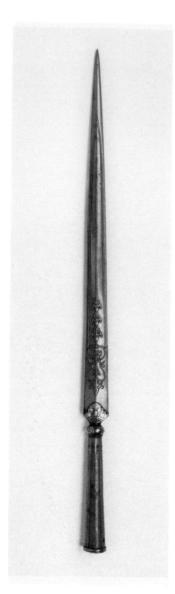

and a pointed ferrule (*zujj*) at the bottom of the shaft. Written instructions for the use of the lance were laid down by some of the *furusiyya* masters in Mamluk times, under the collective title *bunud* (sing. *band*). Najm al-Din summarised the rules for attack in 72 *bunud*, in each of which he explained in detail how the lance should be held and tilted when the opponent was attacked. The two-handed technique was widely used, as opposed to the 'couched' method prevalent in Europe. The assumption that the second method was superior to the first has recently been questioned and one historian has suggested that 'The survival of the two-handed lance technique suggests that there must have been more to recommend it than is generally supposed. Perhaps this is also indicated by the revival of the lighter weapon in later lance units in Europe, the Middle East, Central Asia and India'.

There were, of course, other weapons in the armoury of Muslim warriors, but we can do no more than list them here. The javelin (*harba* or *'anaza*) was a throwing spear, although short lances were also used as missiles. Knives (*khanjar*) were worn at the waist or under the clothing, and there were two distinct types of shield, the *daraqa* made of hide and the wooden or metal *turs*. The mace (*dabbus*) has already been mentioned.

4.4 THE BOW AND THE CROSSBOW

A distinctive feature of archery in the Muslim world, compared with the West, was the high esteem in which archers were held. In the West knights did not deign to use the bow, which was an infantry weapon. In Islam, on the other hand, many notables were skilled archers and distinguished themselves in battle using the bow. The craftsmen who made the bows, arrows and ancillary equipment were also highly regarded. A second feature that distinguished an Islamic archer from his Western counterpart was the use of the composite bow. The wooden bows used in the West were known in Islam, particularly Arabia, but the composite bow was the standard type in Muslim armies from the early conquests to Renaissance times and beyond.

Composite bows have a long history, having been known in ancient Egypt. It seems probable, however, that they entered the Muslim armoury during the conquest of Sassanid Iran, where this type of bow was widely used. Over the centuries the construction of the bow changed in certain details and there were always variations from one region to another, but the type of bow illustrated in Fig. 4.5 represents the normal pattern,

4.4 Persian chiselled-steel lance-head. Eighteenth century AD. Victoria and Albert Museum, London.

which was standard equipment in the Ayyubid and Mamluk armies. This, the most effective weapon developed before the invention of firearms, required great skill in manufacture. Unfortunately it is impossible here to describe the very interesting methods of construction of what was a very complex design except to say that it consisted of an inner core of wood, with a reinforcement of horn on the side facing the archer and an outer layer of sinew. The bow was 'reflex', i.e. its curvature before it is tautened is in the opposite direction to that afterwards. When it was strung it was naturally pre-stressed by tension in the sinew and compression in the horn. This added considerably to the power of the weapon. Bow-strings were often made from silk.

The fletcher was also a skilled craftsman. Arrows were made from reeds or wood – the former was the preferred material – and arrow heads fabricated in a number of shapes and sizes depending on the use for which they were intended. The flights, usually quite small to minimise drag, were made from the feathers of birds of prey. Ancillary equipment included the quiver (*ja'aba* or *kinana*) and the thumb-ring (the Muslim archer drew with the thumb, not with the fingers as in Europe). A long period of training was needed for the archer to reach the necessary level of skill but, as a result, Muslim cavalry armed with the bow were formidable opponents. The weapon had a range of 500 metres or more, and could penetrate mail body armour ('chain-mail') at 150 metres if fitted with an arrowhead of triangular cross-section.

The use of the crossbow was not widespread in Islam before the middle of the sixth century AH (twelfth century AD), and even after this time it was regarded as more suitable for sieges and to be shot from ships than for field warfare – it took too long to draw and was too cumbersome for use on horseback. In the later Middle Ages, though, it was preferred to any other kind of bow in Muslim Spain. It was called *qaws al-rijl* (lit. 'foot-bow') in Arabic and *zanburak* in Arabic, Persian and Turkish. One type had a stirrup at the end of the stock; the foot was placed in this stirrup (*rikab*) and the string was drawn back by a hook on the end of a rope. Another type was drawn by using a windlass (see next section).

4.5 SIEGE ENGINES

Medieval artillery consisted of many beam-operated machines, quite different from the catapults of classical times that depended on the resilience of wood or twisted fibres to provide

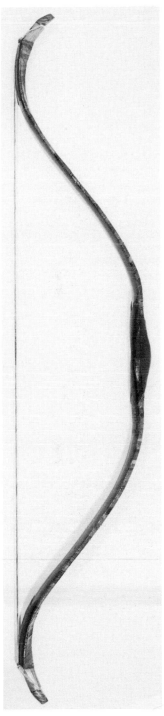

4.5 A Syrian Mamluk composite bow. Reconstruction by Edward McEwen from a description in a manuscript of the fourteenth century AD. Lieutenant-Commander W. F. Paterson.

the impetus for missiles. Such a missile thrower, the powerful traction trebuchet (Fig.4.6), entered Islam from China by way of Central Asia towards the close of the first century AH (seventh century AD). It consisted of a wooden spar provided with an axle which was supported on bearings at the top of two wooden towers. At the end of the short arm was a special attachment to which a number of ropes was fixed. In some types this attachment consisted of a single piece of hardwood (cf. Fig. 4.9, below) but in the version shown here it was made of iron and divided into two legs, each of which terminated in a

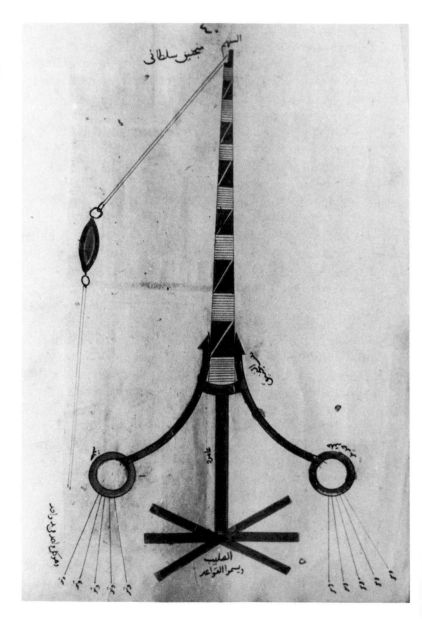

4.6 A traction trebuchet for throwing missiles. It is shown without its supports in this drawing, which comes from a manuscript of the fourteenth century AD. Topkapi Sarayi Müzesi, Istanbul.

ring. At the other end was a sling with a pouch for the missile. One end of this sling was attached to the underside of the spar and the other, which was made into a loop, was slipped over a projection at the end of the spar. A team of men was stationed on the ropes, while the artilleryman held the missile in its pouch. When he gave the signal the men pulled on the ropes and he released the pouch at the critical moment. When the spar reached a certain point in its upward swing, the loop slid off the projection and the missile was released. Missiles could weigh up to 50 kilograms and ranges were of the order of 50 metres.

The more powerful counterweight trebuchet (Fig.4.7) came into use in Islam during the second half of the sixth century AH (twelfth century AD). Its place of origin is still undecided, but the balance of evidence is in favour of a Muslim origin. Superficially similar to the traction trebuchet, it had a heavier

4.7 A counterweight trebuchet for hurling heavy missiles. Fourteenth century AD. Topkapi Sarayi Müzesi, Istanbul.

beam, its towers were more robust, and the sling was longer. At the end of the short arm, instead of an attachment for the ropes there was suspended a box filled with lead or stones. The machine was drawn back by a winch (indicated by a circle at the bottom-left of the figure) whose rope was attached to the long arm of the beam. To set the machine in motion the artilleryman pulled on a rope attached to a special hook. The missiles could be as heavy as 230 kilograms but were usually somewhat lighter, and ranges up to 300 metres were attainable. The counterweight trebuchet was in widespread use in Islam during the seventh century AH (thirteenth century AD), and featured at Kubilai's siege of Fan-cheng in AD 1272; in China the machine appears to have acquired the name of the 'Muslim phao [throwing machine]'. Yet as early as Abbasid times (second to seventh centuries AH [eighth to thirteenth centuries AD]) military engineers had been put in charge of catapults, trebuchets and battering rams.

The pedestal crossbow (*qaws al-ziyar*) was first known in Islam in the sixth century AH (twelfth century AD) (Fig. 4.8). This was drawn using a windlass that operated a rack-and-pinion gear. A multiple shot crossbow (*charkh kaman*) came into use about the same time. After it had been drawn, it could be operated by one man in the keep of a fortress and so could deceive the enemy into believing that a number of crossbow-men were present. As Fig. 4.9 indicates, siege engines were used by the besieged as well as by the besiegers. In addition to hurling solid missiles, all these engines could be used to throw incendiary and explosive projectiles.

4.6 FORTIFICATIONS

There was no tradition of constructing fortifications in pre-Islamic Arabia, where the only town provided with substantial walls was Ta'if in the Hejaz. It was therefore inevitable that the Arabs adopted the methods of fortification already in use in the countries which they conquered. In later centuries, as military architecture developed, there was much cross-fertilisation between Byzantium, Islam and the West, ideas passing from one area to another as improvements in siege techniques compelled military architects to seek constantly for matching improvements in defences.

Most Islamic towns and cities were provided with a wall and quite often with a ditch or moat outside it. The moat was particularly useful in hindering the operation of sapping or undermining the foundations of the walls. As an additional

4.8 A pedestal crossbow. The windlass wheels are shown at either end of an axle through the stock. The pinion wheel is shown faintly at the lower right-hand corner of the illustration. Fourteenth century AD. Topkapi Sarayi Müzesi, Istanbul.

protection, the larger cities usually had an outer wall as a first line of defence. A common feature in most cities was the citadel (*hisn, qal'a, quhandiz*), the final place of resistance for the garrison when the other defences were overrun. It might be a simple tower (*burj*) or a massive castle with thick walls of ashlar masonry with a heavily-fortified double gate at the top of a steep ramp as its only means of access. Such an edifice, with its own water supply and food stores, could hold out for months against a besieger. The citadel at Aleppo was a particularly fine example of this type of building (Fig. 4.10). A specifically Muslim type of fortification was the *ribat*, a castle garrisoned by dedicated warriors. They were erected along frontiers and sea coasts, and on important highways.

4.9 Siege engines on a tower. On the right a traction trebuchet, in the centre a counterweight trebuchet and on the left a missile-throwing machine powered by the torsion of twisted hair or sinew. Fourteenth century AD. Topkapi Sarayi Müzesi, Istanbul.

4.7 MILITARY COMMUNICATIONS

During the early Arab conquests communications between the Caliph in Medina and his commanders in the field was by means of camel-mounted couriers. In Umayyad times (first to second centuries AH/seventh to eighth centuries AD) a regular postal service (*barid*) was established, based on similar systems already in use in Byzantium and Sassanid Iran. The *barid*, which was used for the transmission of all kinds of information, civil and military, reached a high stage of efficiency during the Abbasid

Caliphate in Baghdad (second to seventh centuries AH/eighth to thirteenth centuries AD), where a government department was responsible for the service. Postal stages (*markaz*) were erected along all the main routes of which there were no less than 930 in the Empire. The messengers rode mules in Iran and horses or camels elsewhere. In the third century AH (tenth century AD) the Buwayhids also employed 'runners', perhaps to ensure greater secrecy. For urgent messages pigeons were used.

Military communications were particularly efficient in Mamluk times (seventh to thirteenth centuries AH/thirteenth to sixteenth centuries AD). There were staging posts all the way from Cairo to Alexandria, Damietta and Upper Egypt, while other routes led from the capital to Damascus, Aleppo and the Euphrates. When, early on, the Mamluks were engaged in hostilities with the Mongols on the northern frontier, there was a chain of signal beacons that ran from the Euphrates through Palmyra, Damascus, Baysan and Nablus to Gaza. When danger threatened, fires were lit in succession on these high points. The pigeon post was also widely used by the Mamluks and there were pigeon towers (*burj*) in many places in Egypt and in Syria.

4.10 The citadel of Aleppo. View of the lower gatehouse, fortified access ramp and upper gatehouse with part of the main circumference walls beyond. The citadel mostly dates from the thirteenth century AD, when it was rebuilt; it was partly rebuilt again later.

4.8 INCENDIARY WEAPONS, GUNPOWDER AND CANNON

The subject of incendiary weapons or 'military fires', gunpowder and cannon is one of the major issues in the history of technology. In fact, so many conflicting papers and books have been written on the subject during the last two hundred years that it is easy to become confused in the maze of contradictory conclusions. In particular, the subject of gunpowder and the use of cannon arouses nationalistic feelings, and personal prejudices become very apparent.

It is not hard, of course, to understand the reasons. For here we are dealing with one of the most important inventions of all time, a turning point in history that has affected its course to a greater degree, perhaps, than nuclear weapons in our own time. But unlike the nuclear bomb, which appeared forcefully and suddenly, gunpowder moved very slowly from China to Muslim lands and thence to Europe; its effective development and utilisation took several centuries.

4.8.1 Incendiary weapons

From the start of Islamic history, incendiary weapons were used on various occasions, both in local conflicts and against the Byzantines. The Muslim armies of the Abbasids (second to seventh centuries AH/eighth to thirteenth centuries AD) formed special incendiary troops (*naffatun*) who wore fireproof clothing and threw incendiary materials (Fig. 4.11). Military fires had been used in the Near East from ancient times, due it seems to the existence of natural seepages of *naft* (petroleum). In Arabic, however, the word *naft* was also used to denote military incendiary materials, whether of petroleum origin or not. The incendiary materials used in warfare in pre-Islamic times included: (*a*) liquid petroleum, which was available in Iraq, Iran and from the shores of the Caspian Sea; (*b*) liquid pitch; (*c*) mixtures of pitch, resin and sulphur; (*d*) mixtures of quicklime and sulphur, which ignited on contact with water; and (*e*) mixtures of quicklime and sulphur with other flammable materials such as bitumen, resin, *naft*, etc. that also ignited on contact with water. All these materials continued in use with the advent of Islam, but after the second century AH (eighth century AD) important developments took place.

About the year 54 AH/AD 673 a Syrian architect from Baalbek called Callinicus defected to Byzantium; this was less than forty years after the establishment of the Arab government in Syria

4.11 Illustration from a military treatise depicting incendiary troops, above, wearing special fire-proof clothing covered with lighted fire crackers and, below, with rockets. Fourteenth century AD. The Keir Collection.

and just before Constantinople (Istanbul) was besieged by the Muslims that same year. It seems that Callinicus had brought with him the secret of a new fire which helped the Byzantine Empire defend its capital for centuries against Muslim attacks, as well as those of the West Europeans and the Slavs; not until 857 AH/AD 1453 was the city conquered by the Muslim Ottomans. This new fire was called 'Greek fire' by the Crusaders, though it was never called 'Greek' by the Byzantines.

The mastery by the Muslims of the art of distillation (see Chapter 6), together with their inheritance of the technical skills of pre-Islamic civilisations and their control of the sources of petroleum, led them to develop more powerful incendiary techniques and keep them under continuous development. An important element in the decisive battles of the Crusades from the days of Saladin (Salah al-Din) in the sixth century AH (twelfth century AD) to the fall of Acre some 120 years later, was the use of incendiary weapons.

Many historians have tried to discover the precise composition of these incendiary materials. They agree that, in addition to the flammable substances just mentioned, the mixtures contained a secret ingredient which made them particularly effective. From analysing the historical and archaeological evidence, most have come to believe that this ingredient was saltpetre. However, a smaller group has suggested that the secret lay in the use of distilled fractions of petroleum. From an analysis of Arabic sources it appears that both opinions are correct. Distilled *naft* was an important ingredient in the mixture, but saltpetre came to be used also as another major ingredient. We now know that distillation became an established process in the early days of Islamic science, though the story of the early use of saltpetre is still not quite as clearly defined, as we shall see in a moment.

Various methods were used to hurl incendiary substances. One was by means of what was known as a 'siphon' (*zarraqa, mizraq, naffata*), a bronze piston pump from whose nozzle a jet of burning liquid was projected (Fig. 4.12). A brass box full of *naft* was attached to the pump by pipes and so made a compact unit. An igniting element or *warda* (lit. rose) was fixed at the tip of the nozzle and lit when the device was to be used: 'A jet of fire (*shihab*) one lance long issues which will burn the enemy who is opposite in combat.' But the more common method of incendiary warfare was to fill containers of various sizes with *naft* or other inflammable mixtures and then fix them to arrows or pour them into grenades or pots that could be hurled by hand, by machines or shot as rockets.

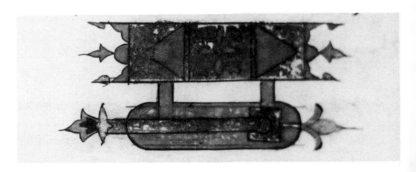

4.12 A *zarraqa*, or siphon, for emitting a jet of burning liquid. Fourteenth century AD. Topkapi Sarayi Müzesi, Istanbul.

4.8.2 Grenades and fire pots

The size of incendiary containers ranged from very small pots to large ones, and many military terms were applied to them. One common size was the grenade (*karaz, karraz*) which was of glass or, more usually, of clay. Many of those which have been found in Egypt, Palestine and Syria date from the Crusades and have an aerodynamic shape (Figs. 4.13(*a*) and (*b*)). A close examination of them shows traces of saltpetre. The larger size of fire-pot was the *qidr* (Fig. 4.14), which was hurled by trebuchets (Fig 4.15). Military treatises of the sixth to eighth centuries AH (twelfth to fourteenth centuries AD) are full of descriptions of the various sizes of container, typical among them being *Kitab al-furusiyya wa'l-manasib al-harbiyya* (*The Book of horsemanship and the engagements of war*) by al-Hasan al-Rammah (d. 694 AH/AD 1294) who lived and flourished in Syria and was an *ustadh* (master) of military science.

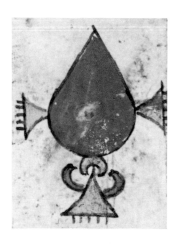

4.13(*a*) Illustration of a grenade, from a manuscript of al-Rammah. Thirteenth century AD. Bibliothèque Nationale, Paris.

4.8.3 Saltpetre

In English the word 'saltpetre' refers to potassium nitrate, the salt used in gunpowder after AD 1500, though the substance itself was known in England at least two centuries earlier. The same applies to the word *barud* in Arabic, and we should not attach much importance to it; its origin is still uncertain and largely remains a study for philologists. Certainly Ibn al-Bitar defined *barud* in 638 AH/AD 1240, and many historians have given this date an undue importance. Yet saltpetre was known

4.13(*b*) Three Islamic grenades made of earthenware. Musée National du Louvre, Paris.

4.14 A *qidr*, or larger-sized incendiary missile, from a manuscript of al-Rammah. Thirteenth century AD. Bibliothèque Nationale, Paris.

much earlier and its mention as *barud* by Ibn al-Bitar does not mean that it was previously unknown. Indeed it was already familiar though under other names. As a noted historian of technology has remarked 'the only certain fact in this perplexing subject is that it is useless to base our ideas on exact identifications of the names of "salts" given by medieval authors with the substances clearly distinguished by modern chemists. The old authors made a thorough confusion of the nitrates and carbonates of sodium and potassium'.

Evidence of this is to be found in a number of instances. For example, Jabir ibn Hayyan describing the preparation of what we now call nitric acid used the term 'flowers of nitre', which may well refer to a crystalline form of saltpetre, while in a later Arabic manuscript written in Syriac characters and probably composed in the fourth or fifth centuries AH (tenth or eleventh centuries AD) saltpetre is listed among the 'seven salts'. Its descriptions cover *buraq al-sagha* (borax – the hydrated sodium borate used by jewellers) which, it says, is white and resembles *al-shiha* (i.e. saltpetre), and lists it immediately afterwards, describing it as 'the salt that is found at the feet of walls'. Saltpetre was also known under other names: flower of assius (*shawraj*); wall salt (*milh al-ha'it*); snow of China (*thalj al-Sin*); salt of China (*milh al-Sin*); *al-shiha*; *ashush*; tanner's salt; *barud*; and sometimes as a kind of borax, alum, and so on. In the Islamic East the earliest mention so far known of the word *barud* to denote saltpetre is the manuscript with Syriac characters mentioned above. In his *Kashf al-asrar* (*Uncovering of secrets*) of 622 AH/AD 1225, al-Jawbari mentioned the name *al-barud al-thalji* (snowy or snow-like saltpetre), while according to Ibn

4.15 A trebuchet for flinging incendiary missiles. Illustration from a manuscript of al-Rammah. Thirteenth century AD. Bibliothèque Nationale, Paris.

al-Bitar who wrote about 638 AH/AD 1240, the word *barud* was in current use in the Maghrib not only by physicians but even among ordinary people. The fact that it had filtered down to the general public indicates that it must have been known for a considerable time.

4.8.4 Gunpowder in military pyrotechnics

The important question of the first use of gunpowder in Islamic countries and in the West is one of the main issues in the history of military technology. Shawar, the Wazir (Vizier) of the last Fatimid Caliph al-'Adid allied himself with King Amalric of Jerusalem so that he could remain in power, but this alliance with the Franks was to cost Egypt a great deal. In addition to a high tribute, the Franks demanded that one of their garrisons be stationed in Egypt and that a High Commissioner be appointed to Cairo. This caused widespread unrest and public discontent, with the result that a quarrel broke out between Shawar and his allies over the humiliating terms. But this was not all; Shawar was soon besieged in Fustat (now Old Cairo) by the Franks, and in his despair he decided to burn the city. According to al-Maqrizi 20 000 pots of *naft* were used and the fire, which occurred in 564 AH/AD 1168, continued burning for no less than 54 days. Subsequent excavations at Fustat have revealed many of the fire-pots still in good condition, and tests and analyses have shown that they were Syrian grenades (*karraz shami*) which even now contain traces of gunpowder.

With the rise of Saladin in 533 AH/AD 1139 a new era of military pyrotechnics began. The Muslims used incendiary weapons in every battle, and the story of the technician from Damascus who prepared *naft* pots which destroyed the siege towers of the Crusaders is well known. According to many historians incendiaries containing gunpowder were the deciding factor at the Battle of al-Mansura in 647 AH/AD 1249 when King Louis IX of France was taken prisoner. Both sides relied heavily on the skills of their engineers, but the mastery of the Muslims in the use of incendiary weapons gave them a decided superiority. Indeed it has been said that these weapons 'were real artillery and the bombardment had a terrifying effect on the Crusaders'. The famous chronicler Jean, Sire de Joinville (AD 1224–1319), who was one of the fighting officers at the battle, recorded that when the French commander saw the 'Saracens' preparing to discharge the fire 'he announced in panic that they were irretrievably lost'. The fire was discharged, it is said, from a large ballista (giant crossbow) in 'pots of Iraq' (*qidr'Iraqi*). These were a well-known type of incendiary, as we shall see in a moment. De Joinville wrote 'It was like a big cask and had a tail the length of a large spear: the noise it made resembled thunder and it appeared like a great fiery dragon flying through the air, giving such a light that we could see in our camp as clearly as in broad daylight'. When it fell it burst and liquid was ejected, spreading a trail of flame. James Partington, the celebrated historian of chemistry, remarked that 'the Crusaders believed that anyone struck by it was lost ... and it seems to have been regarded as a kind of old-fashioned atomic bomb'. Though incendiary weapons had been used since the time of the first Crusade some hundred and fifty years before, the effects had never been so terrifying; the cause was the secret ingredient, gunpowder.

From the time gunpowder was introduced, military engineers began to play an increasing role. Corps of engineers were formed, and artisans such as smiths, carpenters, bronze founders, *naft* craftsmen and others came under the command of military engineers who were responsible direct to an army Amir. With their siege machinery and gunpowder, they were the effective elements when in 690 AH/AD 1291 Acre was besieged and fell, putting a final end to the Crusades. During this siege, it was said that the Sultan's trebuchets and catapults flung their 'pottery containers filled with an *explosive mixture* at the walls of the city or over them into the town', and that the Sultan had 'a thousand engineers against each tower'. These engineers were busy sapping the crucial defences so that when the walls were undermined and 'began to crumble' the Mamluks could readily force their way into the ruins. Yet the book of al-Hasan al-Rammah, which was compiled around 679 AH/AD 1280, had already recorded what had by then become an established experience and tradition, as can immediately be realised from its use of many technical terms relating to gunpowder technology. From this text we can readily appreciate that twenty years earlier de Joinville was only describing a bombardment by the very same pots (*qudur*) as had appeared in al-Rammah's book.

4.8.5. Early cannon

Ibn Khaldun, who wrote his history about 779 AH/AD 1377, described what are clearly cannons in his account of the siege of Sijilmasa in the Maghrib by Sultan Abu Yusuf a century earlier. He claims that the Sultan installed siege engines ... and gunpowder engines (*hindam al-naft*), which project small balls (*hasa*) of iron. These balls are ejected from a chamber (*khazna*) placed in front of a kindling fire of gunpowder; this happens by a strange property which attributes all actions to the power of the Creator.

But cannon did not appear suddenly in the Maghrib. As we have seen, *barud* was already a familiar product there, and gunpowder had been used in fire-pots during the Crusades. In fact in the Maghrib and in Spain there are historical reports which seem to have been overlooked but which deserve to be investigated now. José Conde, the Spanish historian, claimed that in 601 AH/AD 1204 cannon were used by the Almohad Caliph al-Nasir in his siege of al-Mahdiyya in North Africa, and Peter, Bishop of Leon, reported the use of cannon in Seville in 646 AH/AD 1248. In addition, cannon appeared in the Islamic East in the second half of the seventh century AH (thirteenth century AD), as we shall see. Indeed, we would advance the view that in the Maghrib, where petroleum was not available, cannon may have developed into a siege engine somewhat earlier than in the Islamic East, and that the appearance of cannon at Sijilmasa as described by Ibn Khaldun was a natural development the veracity of which need not be doubted.

In the Mamluk kingdom cannon of a lighter type appeared in battles against the Mongols, who suffered several setbacks after their destruction of Baghdad in 656 AH/AD 1258. The first defeat of the Mongol Hülagü's army by a Mamluk force, led in this instance by Sultan Qutuz, took place in 658 AH/AD 1260 at 'Ayn Jalut in Galilee and was one of the decisive battles of history. The last battle occurred at Marj al-Suffar, south of Damascus, in 702 AH/AD 1303 when the Mamluks defeated the Mongol army of Ghazan in another decisive battle that brought the menace of the Mongols to an end. The new cannons were not yet truly effective weapons for they were still in an early stage of development. Nevertheless there are several military manuscripts in Leningrad, Paris, Istanbul and Cairo which not only report the use of light cannon in battles with the Mongols but also say that the 'Egyptians' had a cavalry force specially equipped with such cannon (*midfa'*) (see Fig. 4.19 below) and with crackers (*sawarikh*) which used to frighten the enemy and cause confusion in their ranks. In some of the manuscripts reference is made to 'the defeat of Halawun at Jalud', and one also speaks of their use against Ghazan. We have then two further dates for battles in which early cannon were used by the Mamluks, one in 658 AH/AD 1260 and the other in 702 AH/AD 1303. But since the cannon had developed into a siege engine in the Maghrib by 672 AH/AD 1274, it seems reasonable to assume that it was invented before the battle of 'Ayn Jalut in 658 AH/AD 1260.

There is an account in the writings of Lisan al-Din b. al-Khatib (d. 776 AH/AD 1374) of the later use of cannon in the siege of Huescar, north-east of Granada, in 724 AH/AD 1324. Ibn al-Khatib was not only a minister in the Nasrid kingdom but also its literary historian, and the siege took place during his lifetime. He reported that when the Sultan of Granada besieged Huescar 'He bombarded the upper part of the strong tower with a heated ball using the great engine which functions by means of *naft*. This bombardment caused ruin like thunder and the besieged surrendered unconditionally'. Next he quotes a poem written by the scientist and poet Abu Zakariyya Yahya b. Hudhayl in tribute to the Sultan, in which the thunder, lightning and destruction caused by this miraculous weapon were described.

It was during this period that cannons as siege engines became common in the Mamluk kingdom. Shihab al-Din b. Fadl al-Allah al-'Umari (700–749 AH/AD 1301–1349), historian, encyclopaedist, high government official, and an expert in state affairs, wrote a number of books, among them *al-Ta'rif bi'l mustalah al-sharif* (*The noble [book] of definitions of established custom*), which was a guide for senior government officers (741 AH/AD 1340). Al-'Umari devotes a chapter to siege engines in action during the reign of Sultan al-Nasir, which ran from 709–741 AH/AD 1309–1340. Six kinds were in common use: the *manjaniq* (trebuchet), the *ziyarat* (mechanical crossbow), the *sata'ir* (protective coverings), *khita'i* (arrows), the *makahil al-barud* (gunpowder cannon) and *qawarir al-naft* (pots of *naft*). The last three were gunpowder weapons and al-'Umari gives a literary description of each. His remarks about cannon refer to gunpowder and to the destructive power of red-hot balls which break arches and damage structures.

In a series of sieges and battles in Spain between 1340 and 1343 AD both Western and Arabic sources state that cannon took part. In 741 AH/AD 1340 cannon were used by the Muslims at the battle of Tarif, and also in 743 AH/AD 1342 at the Siege of Aljazira. The iron balls were fired from cannon charged with gunpowder and it is reported that the Earls of Derby and Salisbury, who were both at the battle, were the persons responsible for bringing back a knowledge of firearms to England. It is also believed by some Western historians that the Spaniards derived their knowledge of artillery from the Arabs of Granada, who had early on become acquainted with the use of gunpowder. Thus as with other things, the transfer to Europe of knowledge about gunpowder and cannon took place by way of Spain.

In the year of the Aljazira siege, the Syrian and Egyptian Amirs decided to overthrow the newly appointed Sultan al-Nasir Ahmad because they found him unfit for his high office. They therefore sent a force to al-Karak and besieged him there, but it is reported that he 'installed on top of the citadel five *manjaniqs* (trebuchets) and many *madafi'* (cannon)' and so defended himself.

The first battle in the West in which cannon are reported to have been used was in 1346 at Crécy. English cannon were also deployed to block the entrance to Calais harbour during the same campaign.

We have given the chronology of the early use of cannon because of its importance. After 743 AH/AD 1342 the development of the weapon was continued by the Mamluks who used them extensively in siege operations, though gradually their manufacture spread to other Islamic countries, and the Ottomans soon adopted them on a large scale (Fig. 4.16). The most spectacular operation involving cannon was the capture of Constantinople (Istanbul) by the Ottomans in 857 AH/AD 1453. One bronze gun in the siege had a bore of over 88 centimetres and the ball it fired weighed over 270 kilograms. A ball which struck a Venetian ship cut it in two and another report claims that in this case the ball weighed no less than 400 kilograms and was fired from a distance of 2.4 kilometres. Each pair of such large guns required, it is said, 70 oxen and up to 1000 men to move them.

4.8.6 The early technology of gunpowder and firearms

Purification and crystallisation of saltpetre
In al-Hasan al-Rammah's book mentioned above (section 4.8.2, p. 109), we find a description for the purification and crystallisation of saltpetre. This is the first account of such a process and it is important because effective gunpowder cannot be made without pure saltpetre. There are, however, similar accounts of the purification process in later Arabic manuscripts.

Gunpowder recipes
There are more than 70 recipes for gunpowder in al-Rammah's book, but in the Arabic chemical work written in Syriac

4.16 Cannon being used by the Ottoman army in the siege of a Hungarian fortress. Sixteenth century AD. Topkapi Sarayi Müzesi, Istanbul.

characters which the French nineteenth-century chemist and historian of science Marcellin Berthelot dated as from the fourth or fifth centuries AH (tenth or eleventh centuries AD), there are seven recipes. In the military treatises which followed al-Rammah's we find scores of recipes, and the total number in all manuscripts must amount to several hundred. All the same, such recipes can be classified into particular types with, of course, a great many items of each type, and specialised

4.17 Cannon with adjustable mounting. Fifteenth century AD. Topkapi Sarayi Müzesi, Istanbul.

technical names abound. The gunpowder compositions (mainly saltpetre, sulphur and charcoal) are given in special chapters, though sometimes a whole manuscript is devoted purely to a collection of recipes. On reading these, however, it soon becomes evident that one recipe can serve for several purposes, but in some manuscripts we learn what a certain type of recipe will do. For instance, the group of recipes called *saymudaj* was used for making fuses, incendiary arrows and wheels, crackers and flying rockets. Others were suitable for fire-pots or for cannon, and some just for amusement and for fireworks.

Fuses

Al-Rammah used two kinds of fuse, the *ikrikh* and the *warda* (lit. rose). The *ikrikh* was a cotton cord impregnated with sulphur and then coated with a layer of wax and other tinder material. Such fuses were also called *dhakhira*. Apart from sulphur, gunpowder was also used, and instructions for preparing fuses of all kinds are to be found in the military treatises.

Rockets

Rockets for carrying incendiary material were a frequently used weapon (Figs. 4.18 (*a*) and (*b*)). One type was an arrow (*sahm*) which was provided with a gunpowder charge for taking off and driving it to its target; it also carried an incendiary grenade. Both the gunpowder fuse and the grenade's fuse were ignited before launch. Instructions were given for the weight of gunpowder and the type of paper to be used for the cartridge,

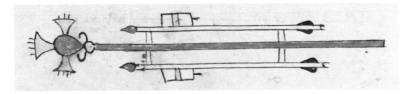

4.18(*a*) Illustration of a rocket, from a manuscript of al-Rammah, Thirteenth century AD. Bibliothèque Nationale, Paris.

together with the ratio of the rocket's diameter to its length. It was claimed that one design, an arrow with guiding vanes on both sides and called *sahm tuli* (long arrow) or *sahm sa'i* (going arrow), made with 70 *dirhams* (218 grams) of paper and 90 *dirhams* (280 grams) of gunpowder (*dawa*) would carry one *ratl* load of any kind, i.e. about 0.5 kilograms. It was said, too, that it could be made to reach the target, discharge its incendiary material, and then returen to the point from which it started.

Another type of rocket was the *tayyar* (the flying one). In one size, the *tayyar tuli* (long [distance] flyer), 150 *dirhams* (468 grams) of paper and 150 *dirhams* of gunpowder were used; it was also known as *al-majnun* (the mad one). A third type was the *fattash* (explorer), the wings of which could be made of paper or leather. Flown like a kite, it was equipped with incendiary material for dropping on citadels and ships.

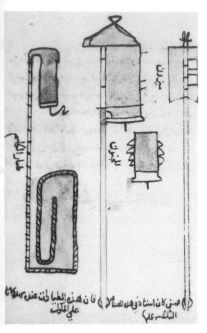

4.18(*b*) Two kinds of rocket (centre and right) and a fuse (left). Fourteenth century AD. Süleymaniye Kütüphanesi, Istanbul.

Torpedoes

Al-Rammah's manuscript contains a description of a torpedo designed to travel on the water's surface (Fig. 4.19). It was a pear-shaped vessel made from sheet-iron and filled with gunpowder and incendiary materials. Two or three rockets were used for propelling it towards its target by burning jets at the rear while the projectile itself was burning at the front. The long rods of the rockets helped to steer the torpedo because they acted like a rudder.

The qidr (*pot*)

According to al-Umari this was one of the main siege weapons. Al-Rammah and other military writers mentioned several types – the Iraqi, the Maghribi and the Ajami. One description of a *qidr* (cf. Fig. 4.14 above) which was thrown by a *manjaniq* (trebuchet, see Fig. 4.15 above) runs as follows:

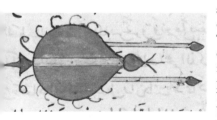

4.19 Illustration of a torpedo designed to travel on the surface of water. From a manuscript of al-Rammah. Bibliothèque Nationale, Paris.

take three *ratls* [1.5 kilograms] of black rosin and melt, while in the same *qidr* sprinkle one *ratl* [0.5 kilogram] of [a substance] of the quality called *daw* [light]. Leave the contents to cool, then put in one hundred 'Dirkawiyya' *fattash* [crackers] . . . with a felt bag impregnated with oil on the top of each. Put in also four smaller glass pots full of seeds and incendinary mixtures and then throw into the pot cut pieces of *tuz* [a particular kind of tree root] and cottonseed and make a paste of these by means of a mineral *naft*. Put in a net of copper wire. Inside there will be one *ratl* [0.5 kilogram] of *dawa'hadd* [a strong chemical] and a ring of black *ikrikh* [fuse]. If you wish to throw the *qidr*, coat the pan and the legs of the *manjaniq* [trebuchet] with *kathira* [tragacanth] and alum. Then give fire to the rose [the fuse] and throw. The *qidr* should be the same weight as the stone of the *manjaniq* [trebuchet].

Early cannon used against the Mongols

As mentioned earlier, several military treatises reported the use of light, portable cannon to frighten Mongol cavalry and cause disorder in their ranks. The battles in which this occurred took place between 658 and 702 AH/AD 1260 and 1303. The method was to choose a squadron of cavalry and fit the knight's lance with gunpowder crackers, while the knight himself wore a fireproof helmet and fireproof clothing, both being covered with crackers (see Fig. 4.11, above p.107). His horse, likewise clad in a fireproof covering, also carried crackers. Infantry accompanied the knight, some with clubs and fire-sprinklers, others with light cannon (*midfa*), as in Fig. 4.20. The whole

4.20 Two illustrations from a military treatise of the fifteenth century AD depicting light cannon (*midfa*). *Above* A horseman and two infantrymen with burning fire-crackers and a *midfa*. *Below* Two men with various incendiary weapons. One of the men is preparing a *midfa* for firing. Oriental Institute, Leningrad.

squadron marched in front of the army and started the explosions when they encountered the enemy, though several other tactics could be adopted to provide an element of surprise before the actual attack. In an Istanbul manuscript instructions are given for loading the cannon used in these operations; they run as follows:

description of the *dawa'* [strong chemical] which you put into the cannon: *barud* [saltpetre] ten *dirhams* [30 grams], charcoal two *dirhams* [6 grams], sulphur one *dirham* [3 grams]. Grind them finely and fill one third of the cannon, not more. Tamp in securely with the plug after you have rammed the charge. Put in the ball or the arrow and give fire by means of the fuse. Measure the *midfa'* under the hole. If it is deeper than the hole then it is defective and will strike the gunner.

5 Ships and navigation

5.1 SHIPBUILDING

Shipbuilding was a major industry in Islam, both for the construction of merchant vessels and for building and fitting out warships. Apart from the main shipyards, there were private yards on the banks of the great rivers and the shores of the Gulf and the Red Sea. These were engaged in building the many varieties of small craft which can still be seen in those waters today. It is not possible here to enter into a detailed discussion of the various types of vessel in use during the medieval period of Islam, though it should be mentioned that they ranged from small oared skiffs to merchantmen of over 1000 tonnes capacity and warships capable of carrying 1500 men. Writing in the fourth century AH (tenth century AD), al-Muqaddasi lists the names of several dozen kinds of vessel, and still more types came into use during the ensuing centuries.

All Muslim shipping displayed certain characteristics. Merchant ships were usually sailing vessels, with a wide beam relative to their length to provide maximum storage for cargo. Warships were leaner and were either oared or fitted with sails, depending on the functions they were to fulfil. All ships and boats were carvel-built, i.e. their planks were laid edge to edge (Fig. 5.2), not overlapped as they were in the clinker-built vessels common in northern Europe. In the eastern part of the Muslim world, the planks were sewn together with ropes, but in the Mediterranean iron nails were used; in both cases the timbers were caulked with pitch or tar. Ropes for the rigging and anchors were made of hemp or papyrus, while a distinctive feature of the rig of Muslim ships was the lateen sail attached to a heavy spar suspended at an angle to the mast. In the Mediterranean the lateen sail was three sided but in the Red Sea and further east it had a fourth, very short, forward side. This too can be called a lateen sail but, more correctly, a settee sail. In this eastern area the mast slanted forward, which was less usual in the Mediterranean. The first positive evidence for the use of the lateen sail in the Mediterranean comes from the third century AH (ninth century AD) but it was probably adopted

5.1 Boatbuilding in Bahrain, still using simple tools and traditional techniques.

123

5.2 Thirteenth-century AD illustration of an eastern Muslim boat. It is carvel built and the planks are stitched together. Bibliothèque Nationale, Paris.

there before this time. The lateen is not easy to handle, but once mastered its use enables a ship to sail considerably closer to the wind than the usual square rig, and so take a less indirect route.

Apart from some shipborne expeditions to Sind during the first Islamic century, little of their shipping in the Indian Ocean was warlike; most was concerned with trade. The situation was very different in the Mediterranean, where no Islamic state could have survived for long without adequate naval forces. As a result, there were many naval dockyards in the Muslim world and they became so familiar to Western seamen that the Arabic expression for a dockyard *dar al-sina'a* has entered European languages as, for example, in the English word 'arsenal'. In the east there were shipyards at Ubulla and Basra on the Shatt al-'Arab, at Siraf on the Iranian side of the Gulf, and at Suhar in 'Uman. At first the Muslims had used existing Byzantine

5.3 A *gaiassa*, an Egyptian lateen-rigged river boat.

dockyards but these soon became insufficient for their needs, and in 54 AH/AD 673 the first dockyard to be built in Islam was installed on the island of Rawda in the Nile at the site of modern Cairo. Shortly after shipbuilding facilities were constructed at Acre and at Tyre. There were other yards at Alexandria, Damietta and Fustat. The Abbasid Caliph al-Mutawakkil (d. 247 AH/AD 861) paid particular attention to the Egyptian shipyards, as did the governor Ibn Tulun (d. 270 AH/AD 884), who built 100 warships at Rawda, together with many smaller vessels. In the west there were naval dockyards at Tripoli and Tunis in North Africa, and at Seville, Almeria, Pechina and Valencia in Spain. In addition, warships were also built by the Muslims at Messina and Palermo which between them employed thousands of men.

Before embarking on their conquest of Egypt, the Fatimids consolidated their naval power in North Africa by extending

5.4 A Bahrain pearling boat. It has the settee sail and forward-raking mast typical of Islamic boats of the Gulf and Indian Ocean.

the facilities for constructing warships at the arsenal at Tunis; they even excavated a hillside to make an anchorage where 200 ships could be accommodated. They also built a completely new port and dockyard at Mahdiyya on the Tunisian coast, which was completed in 305 AH/AD 912. Its dock was cut out of a rock face and could accommodate 30 large ships. Their policy was continued by the Ayyubids and the Mamluks. For example, in 566 AH/AD 1170 Saladin had ships made in sections in the Egyptian dockyards, then transported these on camel-back to the Syrian coast where they were assembled. His assembly yard continued in operation for supplying ships for the battles against the Crusaders.

The provision of the necessary materials for shipbuilding was a constant concern of Muslim rulers. The most important material, of course, was high-quality timber, but there were also the ropes required for rigging and as anchor cables, iron for nails, anchors and the shackles, and thimbles for the cables.

In addition, stout cloth was needed for the sails. In the west there was no problem, since timber was abundant in Spain, Sicily and the Maghrib, and there were also iron mines in all these regions. In Egypt, however, although forests for the production of wood known as *sant* (*Acacia nilotica*) were cultivated, there was insufficient timber to meet the needs, and the deficiency had to be made up by imports from the Maghrib and from Sicily. Iron was also imported from the same sources. There was, however, abundant locally-grown hemp for rope-making, and sails were provided by textile factories in the Fayum.

5.2 NAVIGATION

Muslim ships sailed to every part of the known world. Besides the Mediterranean area and the North African coast, Spain, Egypt, and Syria were all part of Islam, as was Sicily in the third and fourth centuries AH (ninth and tenth centuries AD), and large numbers of ships traded within this vast empire. There was also constant traffic along the east–west routes and there were, in fact, seldom any barriers to commerce. For example, in the sixth century AH (twelfth century AD) Ibn Jubayr could start his return journey from Acre, which was then in Crusader hands, and interrupt it for some weeks in Norman Sicily. Again there was direct trade between Byzantium and the North African ports, and on the Caspian Muslim merchants on the southern shores had commercial links with the Khazars in the north.

In the south-eastern Mediterranean, Qulzum was the port for shipping Egyptian and Syrian goods to Jidda and thence to the holy cities of Mecca and Medina – the same route as that taken on the annual pilgrimage – while the port of Aden was the commercial centre for trade to Abyssinia and to the east African coast as far as Zanzibar and Madagascar. It was from Iraq and the Gulf ports, however, that mariners set sail on the voyages which captured public imagination. Indeed, shorn of their magical elements, the tales of Sinbad in the *Thousand and One Nights* reflect the realities of commercial life during the Abbasid Caliphate at the height of its prosperity, for the ports of Siraf in Iran and Suhar in Uman were important centres for eastern trade, with Basra, of course, the greatest of them all. Ships did, however, also sail direct to Baghdad, where the banks of the Tigris and the main canals were lined with wharves. Muslim ships went as well to India and Sri Lanka, to Malaya, the Philippines, Indonesia and China, not as voyages of explo-

5.5 The decorated stern of an 'Umani *ghanjah*. The *ghanjah* was an ocean-going trading ship which on occasion was armed.

ration but as regular sailings of convoys of merchant ships; indeed, there were communities of Muslim merchants in important foreign ports, including Canton.

In the days of sailing ships and before the perfection of astronomical and other means for the exact determination of one's position at sea, the business of navigating a ship to its destination meant that master mariners needed an array of skills at their command. It was common for a tradition of seafaring to persist in certain families, with the result that a body of acquired knowledge was passed from one generation to the next. In earlier days this tradition was oral, but by Abbasid times it had become codified in writing. In the fourth century AH (tenth century AD) al-Muqaddasi made a point of conversing with the sea-going fraternity at the Gulf ports and found their information for sailing to India and beyond relied on maps, books and files. These, he discovered, contained charts of coastlines and maps of sea areas divided into squares of longitude and latitude, as well as directions of prevailing winds and data about tidal conditions. Hazards such as rocks and shoals and the likelihood of turbulent winds were familiar to all experienced sailors, while the approaches to Basra, the entry into the Red Sea and the Straits of Messina were all known to be dangerous areas. And as far as determining one's position was concerned, this could be ascertained by various signs – the colour of the sea, the nature of the sea-bed, the sighting of different kinds of birds and, of course, familiar landmarks, for mariners did not venture too far from the shore

5.6 A passenger-carrying
Mesopotamian river boat,
rowed by a crew of three.
Thirteenth century AD.
Bibliothèque Nationale, Paris.

if they could help it. Scientific aids were not, however
completely lacking and their variety and accuracy increased
during the Middle Ages.

The usual method of determining latitude was by measuring
the altitude of the Pole Star, for which the Muslims used the
unit of one finger (*isba'*), approximately equal to 1.5 degrees,
and the *zam* which was one eighth of this. The observations
themselves were done with an instrument known as the *kamal*;
this consisted of a plate to the centre of which was attached a
string divided into fingers by knots. The observer held the
string to his nose and, when it was taut, moved the plate until
the Pole Star was on its upper edge and the lower edge
coincided with the horizon (Fig. 5.7). The length of the string
gave the altitude in fingers and *zam*. Knowing the latitude of his
destination, a sea captain would sail to that latitude and then
follow it until he reached the end of his journey. The
introduction of the mariner's compass to Islam about the
beginning of the seventh century AH (thirteenth century AD)
marked a significant step in the progress of navigation. The
phenomenon of magnetism and the discovery of the magnetic
needle had been made in China centuries before this, but there
is some doubt about who introduced the pivoted-needle
compass for use in ships. Given that the navigational methods
of Muslims and Chinese were remarkably similar, it would seem
that it could have been invented by either nation.

The summit of Islamic achievement in navigation is represented in the writings of Ibn Majid, who lived in the second

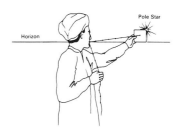

5.7 Use of a *kamal* to measure
the altitude of the Pole star,
from which the latitude could
be calculated.

half of the ninth century AH (fifteenth century AD). His sources of knowledge came from the skills of his forefathers, enriched by his own exprience of forty years at sea and combined with extensive reading of the works of Arab geographers, astronomers and navigators. Ibn Majid gave the Portuguese navigator Vasco da Gama accurate instructions for sailing from East Africa to India, and was unsurprised by the instruments da Gama showed him, saying they had long been in use in Arab ships.

5.3 NAVIES

The Arabs were very quick to appreciate the necessity for naval power to maintain and consolidate their dominions. Within a decade from their conquest of Egypt they were challenging the Byzantines for command of the eastern Mediterranean: Cyprus was occupied in 30 AH/AD 649, Rhodes in 52 AH/AD 672. With the conquest of North Africa and Spain some forty years later, Muslim naval supremacy over the whole of the Mediterranean was established and remained unchallenged for the next two centuries. Expeditionary forces from North Africa occupied Sicily in 211 AH/AD 827 and frequent raids were then made on the coasts of Italy and southern France.

In the early days ships were built in Egypt and Syria by indigenous shipwrights, and were of similar construction to those made for the Byzantine navy. Seamen were also recruited from the local population, although the fighting men on the ships were Arabs. With the passage of time, however, these distinctions disappeared and shipbuilding and naval warfare became wholly Muslim enterprises. Indeed the Muslims became highly skilled in both branches of nautics, and made significant advances. Their developments in ship design included big warships like the *shini*, a large galley powered by 143 oars. In 326 AH/AD 972 the Fatimid Caliph Mu'izz li Din Allah supervised the construction of 600 of these vessels in the dockyard at Maqs in Egypt. Another type of large warship was the *buttasa*, a sailing ship that could hoist as many as 40 sails, and there is a record of one having a complement of 1500 including crew and men-at-arms. Others were the *ghurab* (lit. crow), probably named from the shape of its prow, and the *shallandi*, a large decked ship used for carrying cargo. These last two names have passed into European languages as 'corvette' and the lesser known 'challand'. There was also the *qurqura* (Latin *cercurus*), a large Cypriot vessel for carrying supplies for the fleet, while there were also a number of smaller vessels designed for specific purposes such as supply, ship-to-shore communications, reconnaissance, pursuit and interception. Most of them were oared, but the *shubbak* (a Mediterranean fishing boat) had sails in addition to banks of oars.

The larger vessels carried missile throwers and machines for discharging incendiary material (Fig. 5.9), besides complements of skilled archers. Sea battles were fought, at least in the early phases, at a distance, but all ships carried grappling irons for making fast to the gunwales of enemy vessels and many battles were decided by hand-to-hand fighting between the crews and the marines of opposing fleets.

5.8 Illustration from a thirteenth-century AD manuscript of a ship on the Euphrates, its mast broken in a storm, and propelled by oars alone without the aid of sails. Oriental Institute, Leningrad

5.9 A ship carrying grenades, from a manuscript of al-Rammah. Thirteenth century AD. Bibliothèque Nationale, Paris.

6.1 Rock-crystal ewer from
Egypt. Late tenth century AD.
Victoria and Albert Museum,
London.

6 *Chemical technology*

6.1 ALCHEMY, CHEMISTRY AND CHEMICAL TECHNOLOGY

When we look at industrial chemistry in Islam we find that there is not much to be gained by attempting to differentiate between 'alchemy' and 'chemistry'. The Arabic world *al-Kimya* was used to denote both in their technological aspect, thus covering those processes concerned with metallurgy and those involved with the distillation of petroleum, or perfumes and of other materials, as well as the manufacture of dyes, inks, sugar, glass, and a host of other products.

In addition to its concern with technology, in some cases alchemy became associated with more metaphysical and philosophical aspects, such as matters concerned with the cosmos and the spirit. Reactions to this side of alchemy varied; some distinguished scientists such as Jabir and al-Razi, believed in the transmutation of metals while others equally distinguished, such as Ibn Sina and al-Kindi, did not. But both sides dealt with technological subjects; the works of Jabir, al-Razi, al-Kindi and others are all full of technological knowledge to which modern industrial chemistry and chemical engineering owe a great deal. Indeed, Jabir and al-Razi (known to the West as Geber and Rhazes respectively) were the most distinguished scientists in the history of chemistry and chemical technology in Islam, and their works exerted a dominating influence on later generations of Muslims and Europeans.

6.2 ALCHEMICAL EQUIPMENT

Arabic alchemical works describing processes and equipment used in *al-Kimya* are numerous. Indeed, it has been said that by about 280 AH/AD 900 'such a degree of exact knowledge of chemical substances and apparatus was displayed that historians may henceforward be justified in pre-dating the birth of scientific chemistry by, in all probability, at least 900 years'.

Al-Razi (d. 313 AH/AD 925) gave a full account of alchemical

133

equipment in his *Kitab al-Asrar* (*The Book of Secrets*), dividing it into two categories: (*i*) that used for smelting and other heating processes, and (*ii*) equipment for processing chemical substances (*tadbir*). Table I gives his list, which includes items inherited or developed by the fourth century AH (tenth century AD). Additions and modifications were, of course, made in later times.

Table 1. *Chemical equipment in al-Rhazi's* The Book of Secrets

(1) Equipment for melting and heating

1	Blacksmith's hearth (*Kur*).
2	Bellows (*Minfakh* or *Ziqq*).
3	Crucible (*Butaqah*).
4	Descensory (*But-bar-but*; lit. a 'crucible on a crucible', the upper one having its bottom perforated with holes).
5	Ladle (Persian: *Mashu*; Arabic: *Mighrafah* or *Mil'aqah*).
6	Tongs (Persian: *Ambur*; Arabic: *Masik* or *Kalbatan* – the last named being large blacksmith's pincers).
7	Shears (*Muqatti'* or *Miqta'*, plural *Maqati'*).
8	Hammer or pestle (*Mukassir*).
9	File (*Mibrad*).
10	Semi-cylindrical iron mould (*Rat* or *Misbakah*).

*(ii) Instruments and apparatus used in alchemical processes (*Tadabir*)*

1	Curcurbit or retort for distillation (*Qar'*) and the alembic or the head of a still (*Ambiq*) having a delivery tube.
2	Receiving flask (for distillate) (*Qabilah*).
3	Cucurbit and 'blind alembic' (i.e and *ambiq* without a delivery tube).
4	Aludel or closed vessel in which reactions can occur (*Uthal*) (Fig. 6.4).
5	Beakers (*Aqdah*, singular *Qadah*; *Jam*, plural *jamat*). A similar though perhaps larger vessel was the *Batiyah*).
5a	Glass cups (*Kizan*, singular *Kuz*).
6	Bottles or flasks (*Qannani*, singular *Qinninah*).
7	Phials (*Qawarir*, singular *Qarurah*).
7a	Rose-water phials (*Ma'wardiyah*).
8	Earthenware jars with lids in which substances were heated (*Barani*, singular *Barniyah*).
9	Cauldron in which substances were dissolved (*Mirjal* or *Tinjir*).
10	Earthenware pots (*Qudur*) glazed inside with corresponding covers (*mikabbat*).
11	Sand bath on which a vessel could be heated by a fire underneath. Apparently this had no special names beyond that of earthen pot (*Qidr*).
12–16	Various forms of furnace or stove
12	Large baker's oven (*Tannur*).
13	Small cylindrical stove used for heating the aludel (*Mustauqad* or *Mauqid*).
14	Small model of potter's or lime-maker's kiln (*Atun*).
15	Brazier or chafing dish similar to that used by food-hawkers, the glowing charcoal being contained in a tray on the top of an oven (*Tabashdan* or *Kanun*).
16	A stove with perforated sides, half filled with charcoal, and mounted on three legs, and in which a receptacle containing substances to be calcined (roasted) or brought into combination, was placed. It appears to have been something like a navvy's fire-bucket, but the top was closed with a cover. (*Nafikhu nafsih*).

6.2 Islamic glass vessel used in sublimation and distillation. Tenth to twelfth century AD. Science Museum, London.

17	Mortar (*Mihras*) and its pestle (*nisab*). The mortar was sometimes made of glass.
18	(*a*) Flat stone mortar (*Salayah*); (*b*) stone roller for use with the *salayah* (*Fihr*).
19	Clay box in which layers of substances to be calcined or treated were placed. After the box had been closed by a luted cover, fire was kindled over it to heat the contents (*Durj*).
20	Round mould (*Kurah*) in which filings mixed with suitable reagents were placed in order to subject the mixture to the action of fire.
21	A covered iron pan (*miqlat* – usual meaning 'frying pan') used for calcining hair in the preparation of sal-ammoniac (chloride of ammonia).
22	Hair cloth, in which substances were tied and left in a moist warm atmosphere so that they slowly deliquesced and could be removed in the form of a strong solution.
23	Glass funnel (*Qim'*) in which the drippings from the hair cloth were caught. The funnel was inserted into the mouth of a glass bottle.
24	Sieve (*Minkhal*) made of hair or silk.
24a	Filter (*Rawuq*) made of linen (*khaish*).
24b	Filter made of a cup (*kuz*) with a perforated bottom, the holes being covered with a layer of pieces of hair or fibre.
25	Dish or platter (*Sukurrujah*).
26	Basket (*Sallah*) or felt covered cage (*qafas*) used in the process of 'burial' under a covering of dung. Either was inverted over a bottle in the mouth of which was a funnel containing the substances to be dissolved, and the whole was buried in dung.
27	Lamps (*Qanadil*, singular *Qindil*) for imparting a gentle heat.

6.3 ALCHEMICAL PROCESSES

Al-Razi's scheme of work can be divided into the following processes. In them he often used well-known alchemical terms, some of which were later adopted in scientific chemistry.

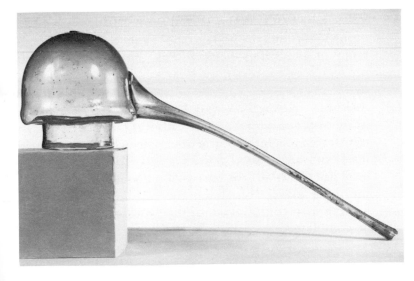

6.3 Glass alembic from Egypt. Sixth to eighth century AD. Victoria and Albert Museum, London.

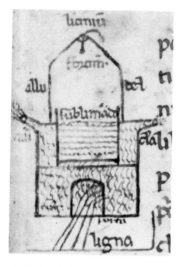

6.4(*a*) An aludel, the closed vessel with an annular shelf and close-fitting cover used in sublimation, illustrated in a thirteenth-century AD manuscript of a work written by al-Kathi in the eleventh century AD. It is shown in position over a furnace.

6.4(*b*) An aludel being heated by the circulation of hot gasses rising from a wood furnace below it. Illustration in a Latin manuscript of a treatise by Geber. Thirteenth century AD. Bibliothèque Nationale, Paris.

(*a*)   *Distillation* (*Taqtir*). This involved using the cucurbit and alembic and catching the distillate in a receiver (*qabila*).

(*b*)   *Sublimation* [i.e. vaporisation without the intermediate formation of a liquid state] (*Tas'id*), conducted by means of an aludel (*uthal*). (The word *tas'id* is used almost synonymously with *taqtir* [distillation]). The aludel is illustrated in Figs. 6.4 (*a*) and (*b*), Fig. 6.4(*a*) being from a manuscript by al-Kathi written in 426 AH/AD 1034 and available in Arabic, while Figs. 6.4(*b*) and 6.4(*c*) come from a Latin manuscript of Geber (Jabir) dating from the late thirteenth century AD.

Sublimation was widely employed as a method of purifying such substances as sulphur. In these figures we see the pot (*uthal*) which contains the substance to be sublimed; this was usually made of clay and glazed on the inside, though it was sometimes fabricated in glass, iron or stone. It had an annular shelf or gutter into which the sublimate could collect. The pot was mounted on a furnace or athanor (*al-tannur*). On top of the pot was a conical or bowl-shaped cover.

There was a simpler form of sublimation in which flasks (*qannani*) were used; this was termed 'constriction', 'strangulation' (*takhniq*) or 'incubation' (*tarkhim*). The substance, either by itself or mixed with oil if its 'essence' was required, was placed in the flask. It was then heated gently to remove any moisture or oiliness and, finally, after the mouth of the vessel had been sealed, was heated strongly until the substance sublimed into the neck of the flask.

(*c*)   *Purification* in a descensory vessel (*Istinzal*). The substance was placed in the upper of the two crucibles (the one with holes in its base). When heated the substance fused and dropped through the holes to the lower crucible, leaving a scum of impurities behind. This was a metallurgical process (see Chapter 9), and a variation of it was known as *tajsid*.

(*d*)   *Assation* or roasting (*Tashwiya*). In this process the substance was moistened with water in a mortar (*salayah*) and then transferred to a luted bottle or cup, which was then hung inside another vessel that was placed on the fire. After the head had driven off the excess of moisture, the mouth of the inner vessel containing the substance was closed; heating then continued until the process was thought to be complete.

This process is interesting for its recognition of the use of an air-bath to obtain a moderate degree of heat.

(e)   *Cocotion* or digestion (*Tabkh*). This was another form of roasting (*tashwiya*), generally conducted in the presence of excess moisture.

(f)   *Amalgamation* (*Talghim* or *Ilgham*), or mixing substances with mercury. It was often employed as a preliminary step to sublimation and calcination.

(g)   *Lavation* or washing (*Ghasl*). Apparently this was another preliminary to sublimation.

(h)   (i)   *Calcination* (*Taklis*). This was a similar process to roasting (*tashwiya*), but the luted vessels were placed directly in contact with the fire, and heating continued until the substance was reduced to an almost impalpable powder.

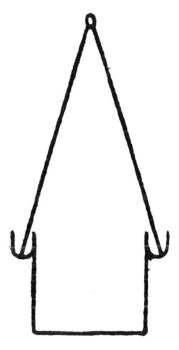

6.4(c) Another drawing of an aludel from the same manuscript as 6.4(b).

(ii) *Ceration* (*tashmi'*) or reducing to a wax-like consistency. This took place after a substance had been freed from an excess of impurities by one or more of the processes just described. It resulted in a product which, when dropped on to a heated metal plate, melted readily without the appearance of flames.

(iii) *Solution* (*hall* or *tahlil*), meaing a 'loosening' or a 'disintegration' of the particles of a substance. It indicated a further physical change beyond that which had already occurred during the process of ceration. In his *Kitab al-Asrar* (*Book of Secrets*), al-Razi describes eight methods of subjecting substances to this process of solution, among them the use of acids or 'sharp waters' (*al-miyah al haddah*). This last brings to mind the fact that al-Razi is credited with the discovery of mineral acids.

(iv) *Combination* (*tamzij*). Al-Razi gives three methods of bringing this about:
(1) Trituration or pulverisation, followed by assation (roasting);
(2) Trituration followed by ceration;
(3) Combination of solutions.

(v) *Fixation* (*'aqd*) or coagulation. This was usually the last part of the whole process and was performed either by assation or in the 'flask and pot' by burying in dung (*dafn*), or by heating in the 'blind' alembic.

(a)

(b)

6.5 Two types of still for making
rose-water and other substances,
illustrated in a manuscript of
al-Kindi. Ninth century AD.
Süleymaniye Kütüphanesi, Istanbul.

6.6 Distillation using a glass
retort. From a sixteenth century AD manuscript in Syriac
and Arabic. British Library,
London.

6.4 DISTILLATION

Distillation was a most important process in Islamic chemical
technology. It was utilised on large scale in making pharmaceutical preparations and in industrial production in both
peace and war. The Muslims became masters of this art and
their knowledge and experience was transmitted to the West;
indeed, the very terms for distillation equipment in European
languages are derived from the Arabic.

All kinds of distillation equipment were used, but we shall
illustrate only two main types. Figures 6.5 (*a*) and (*b*) shows the
distillation equipment used by al-Kindi, who worked in the
middle of the third century AH (ninth century AD) and is
described in his *Kitab Kimya' al-'Itr wa al-Tas'idat* (*Book of Perfume
Chemistry and Distillation*). In Fig. 6.5(*a*) the still is of the retort
type, with no annular rim but set on a water-bath above the
stove. In Fig. 6.5(*b*) the still is provided with an annular ring and
is set in a stove gently heated by charcoal or coal.

The Muslims are credited with the development of the
distillation apparatus classically known in chemistry as the
retort, but also called the 'pelican' or 'cucurbit' because of its
bird-like or gourd-like shape. In this case the still-head ceased
to be a separate entity and better cooling resulting in the
collection of an increased amount of distillate came about of
itself if the side-tube were made long enough. Figure 6.6 is a
drawing of a retort in a Syriac and Arabic manuscript. The
Arabic inscription *al-ᶜawjā* means 'the apparatus which is
curved or bent'.

At these early times, Arabic manuscripts do not show any
water-cooling sleeve round the side-tube. Nevertheless it
seems to have been appreciated that cooling the tube would
improve condensation of the vapours, and sponges, cloths or
rags periodically moistened with cold water were placed round
the top of the still. On present evidence it is usually suggested
that the use of cooling water was a later development that
occurred in the West. All the same, a word of caution is needed
because though the distillation of alcohol requires external
cooling of the retort or of the side-tube, our present knowledge
of Arabic technical and chemical manuscripts is still in its
preliminary stages, and it is too early to come to definite
conclusions about water-cooling in Muslim alchemy. However,
it is significant that the cooling-bath that embraced the whole
upper part of the still was always known as the 'Moor's head'.
Moreover, it did not appear in illustrations in the West until
about AD 1485, (though a picture of a water-jacket for cooling

the side-tube did appear in 1420), while specific descriptions of it in Western alchemical literature came only in about 1570. In his monumental history of early Chinese science and civilisation, Joseph Needham has been sensitive to the curious paradox by using the name 'Moor's head' for this, the most effective cooling device in Renaissance Europe. He comments: 'No explanation of the origin of this term seems to have been attempted by historians of chemistry, but it is hard to believe it was purely pejorative and does not betray to us some influence from the world of Islam'. Needham has also observed that the Moor's head was used in 'Moorish lands' and we may note that it has also been seen in use there in more recent times. Figure 6.7 illustrates a Moor's head for a steam distillation apparatus from Algeria; stills of this kind were also seen by Western travellers in Syria in the early eighteenth century AD. Thus it seems more likely that the Moor's head was of Moorish origin, though further research is needed to substantiate Islamic influence.

6.5 ALCOHOL

The most important of the great chemical discoveries in the Middle Ages were alcohol and the mineral acids. The key to finding them was distillation and, as masters of the art of distillation, the Arabs obtained both at an early date. This seems, however, to be at variance with the claims of some historians of science and technology who have advanced the idea that the earliest account of the distillation of wine occurred in the twelfth century AD in the *Mappae Clavicula*, a treatise on the preparation of pigments which is attributed to Adelard of Bath, who translated it from writings of the important physicians at Salerno in southern Italy that also date from the same century. The account appeared also in the next century in the *Liber Ignium*, a book on 'Greek fire' and gunpowder, possibly written by Marcus Graecus.

Adelard was a notable translator of Arabic into Latin and it seems clear that the *Mappae Clavicula* was written under Arabic influence. Similarly transmission from Spain could have led to the development of alchemy at Salerno, since it is known that the translation of Arabic alchemical treatises into Latin only began in the twelfth century and that it was these which gave rise to Western alchemy. The same can be said about the *Liber Ignium* and the present view is that, as we now have it, this text is of the late thirteenth century and also owes much to Arabic influence. As some historians have pointed out, there is an additional factor which underlines the importance of Arabic

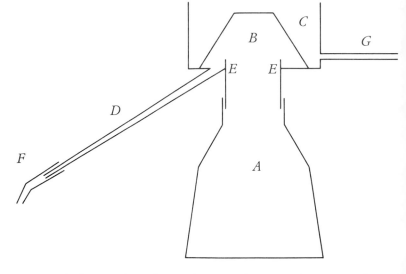

6.7 An Algerian 'Moor's head' apparatus for distilling herbs and flowers for use in medicines. The herbs are placed in the vessel *A* with water and heated. The steam emitted rises to the condenser *B* where it is cooled by water in the trough *C*. The fluid formed runs down the sloping sides of *B* to the gutter *E* and thence down the tube *D* and through its nozzle *F* into a collecting bottle. As the water in *C* heats up it can be drawn off through the tube *G* and cold water added at the top to replace it.

texts, and this is that the earliest author cited as describing distillation of alcohol is Michael Scot, yet another of the great translators of Arabic manuscripts into Latin. Scot was in Toledo in 1217 before moving to Bologna three years later.

Returning now to the works of the great Muslim chemists, we find that several of them clearly described the distillation of wine using specialised distillation equipment. Thus after describing the apparatus (Fig. 6.5), al-Kindi in his *Book of Perfume Chemistry and Distillation* says: 'In the same way one can distill wine using a water-bath, and it comes out the same colour as rose-water'. The addition of sulphur to the distilled wine is found in a work of al-Farabi (fourth century AH/tenth century AD), while Abu al-Qasim al-Zahrawi (who died about 404 AH/AD 1013 and was known in the West as Abulcasis) described the distillation of vinegar in an apparatus similar to that used for rose-water, adding that wine could be distilled in the same way. Again, Ibn Badis (d. 453 AH/AD 1061) in his *Kitab 'Umdat al-Kuttab* (*Book of the Supports of the Scribes*) described how silver filings pulverised with distilled wine could provide a means of writing in silver.

The properties of alcohol were also noticed by Jabir. Thus he says: 'And fire which burns on the mouths of bottles [due to] .... boiled wine and salt, and similar things with nice characteristics which are thought to be of little use, these are of great significance in these sciences'. This flammable property was utilised extensively from Jabir's time onwards and we find various applications of the recipe in Arabic military and chemical treatises of the sixth and seventh centuries AH (twelfth and thirteenth centuries AD), such as those by Hasan Mohammad al-Iskandari and Hasan al-Rammah. It is, incidentally, worth mentioning that it is in such manuscripts that we meet with the first designs for a portable gas lighter.

It is important to note that the various Arabic chemical recipes not only found their way into the twelfth and thirteenth century books attributed to Adelard of Bath, the Salernian doctors, Marcus Graecus, and Michael Scot, but also those of Roger Bacon, Albertus Magnus and others of the same period. Thus the assumption that alcohol was first discovered in the West is incorrect; it is based on the *Mappae Clavicula* yet this is similar to the passage from Jabir just quoted, and which appeared in various forms in other Arabic manuscripts. Indeed, none of the recipes in the *Mappae Clavicula* differ from Jabir, though they do not speak about the distillation apparatus of al-Kindi, al-Farabi and al-Zahrawi which were also specifically mentioned, nor do they refer to any method of cooling the still-head.

6.6 PERFUMES, ROSE-WATER AND ESSENTIAL OILS

In Islamic lands the distillation of rose-water as well as other perfumes and the scented oils in plants and flowers – the 'essential oils' – grew to become a true industry. We do not come across this industry in the older civilisations, nor in contemporary ones, and this has led historians to believe that it was a genuine Muslim industry that originated during the Islamic era.

An important centre for the manufacture was Damascus, though there were other important distilleries at Jur and Sabur in Persia, and Kufa in Iraq. It flourished too in Muslim Spain. The industry's products were exported, being sent for instance from Damascus and Jur to other Muslim countries and even as far east as India and China.

How significant this perfume industry was thought to be is exemplified by the fact that a number of technical books were prepared for the use of manufacturers. Al-Kindi's treatise, which contained 107 methods and recipes, has already been mentioned but unfortunately it is the only one to have survived out of nine Arabic titles on the subject mentioned by Ibn al-Ishbili. However, some later books are still in existence such as al-Jawbari's *Kitab al-mukhtar fi kashf al-Asrar* (*Book of disclosure of the Secrets*) from the seventh century AH (thirteenth century AD), which described the preparation of rose-water, and one of 664 AH/AD 1266 by the historian 'Umar b. al-'Adim. In the next century, the rose-water industry in Damascus was described by al-Dimashqi (d. 727 AH/AD 1327) in his *Kitab Nukhbat al-Dahr* (*Book of the Flower of the Age*). Figure 6.8 illustrates the technique he described and, comparing it with al-Kindi's method for wine and other substances as well as rose-water and shown in Fig. 6.5 (see above, p.138), we can see that it marked a step forward from the retort illustrated there. Of course, in the descriptions of industrial installations we often find the use of mass-ovens; back in the sixth century AH (twelfth century AD) Ibn al-Ishbili said that these contained anything between 16 and 25 cucurbits. In Fig. 6.8 we see such a steam oven being used; its fire was regulated by openings in the furnace itself and the cucurbits, which stood on mats, were placed in circles over the pan of water which produced the steam. Such circles of cucurbits, fitting on top of one another, might reach one and a half times the height of a man. The necks and mouths of the cucurbits emerge from the steam oven to the outside where there are alembics, which thus have their necessary cooling sufaces in the open air; receivers or 'suckers' (*radda'at*) were attached to receive the distillates. Fig 6.9 shows another industrial installation for rose-water, but using a hot-air oven instead of a steam one.

There was, however, another source of books on the subject other than those obviously concerned with it. This arose because distillation was also of importance in the agricultural industry, with the result that we sometimes find mention of the preparation of rose-water, for instance, in books on agriculture. Thus in the sixth century AH (twelfth century AD) al-

6.8 Steam oven for the distillation of flowers to make rose-water. Illustration from a manuscript of *Kitab nukhbat al dahr* by al-Dimashqi. Fourteenth century AD. Bibliothèque Nationale, Paris.

Ishbili gave a technically-important account in his *Kitab al-Filaha* (*Book of Agriculture*) where, incidentally, he also cited the methods of distillation used by the famous physician and surgeon al-Zahrawi (Albucasis to the West) who worked two centuries earlier.

As well as rose-water and the essential oils produced by distillation, the industry included the manufacture of such preparations as musk, ambergris, 'abir (a perfume), *mahlab* (an essence from the *Prunus mahaleb*), *ban* (another from the horse-radish tree *Moringa oleifera*), *ghalia* (a perfume from musk and ambergris), and several others. Clearly, the perfume and cosmetics industry was a flourishing one, reflecting a better quality of life. Indeed, in the second to third centuries AH (eighth to ninth centuries AD) a famous singer and musician of

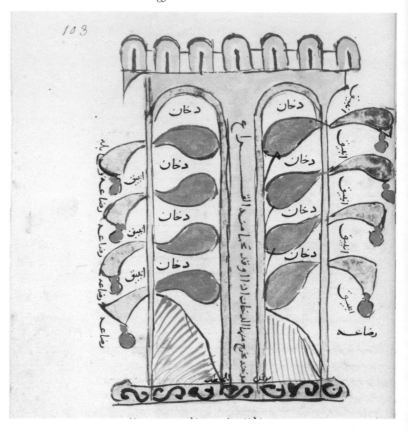

6.9 Hot air method of distillation of flowers from *Kitab nukhbat al-dahr* by al-Dimashqi. Fourteenth century AD. Bibliothèque Nationale, Paris.

Muslim Spain known as Ziryab ('Blackbird') opened 'a genuine beauty institute where the arts of applying cosmetics, removing superfluous hair, using dentifrices, and dressing the hair were taught'.

6.7 PETROLEUM AND PETROLEUM REFINING

Today petroleum is the most important product of Muslim lands and probably the most significant material, affecting the lives of many nations and the international policies of the major powers. It is not generally realised, however, that petroleum was also significant in Islamic history. Crude petroleum (*naft*) was produced and distilled extensively; it had a strategic importance in war and was used also in every-day life.

The word *naft*, which can mean either crude oil or the light distillates, was defined more specifically by Muslim scientists. Usually they called crude oil 'black *naft*' and the distillates 'white *naft*', even though some crude oils are white in their natural state. As to the distillation process, we have excellent descriptions in Arabic literature, such as that in al-Razi's *Kitab Sirr al-Asrar* (*Book of the Secret of Secrets*), probably of the late second century AH (ninth century AD). From this we learn that black *naft* was first mixed with white clay or sal ammoniac into a 'dough like a thick soup' and then distilled. Such light distillates or white *naft* were used by him to 'soften or loosen' some solid substances, such as certain gems and minerals. Moreover in his chemical and medical work al-Razi made use of oil lamps (*naffata*) for gently heating chemicals; the fuel for these was either vegetable oils or petroleum.

The oilfields of Baku were developed on a commercial scale by the Muslims at an early date, and it is reported that in 272 AH/AD 885 the Caliph al-Mu'tamid granted the revenues of the *naft* springs to the inhabitants of Darband. There are several accounts of Baku oil and al-Mas'udi, after visiting them about 302 AH/AD 915, wrote that 'vessels carrying trade sail to Baka [Baku] which is the oilfield [mine] for white *naft* and other [kinds]; and there is not in the world – and God knows better – white *naft* except in this spot'. In the seventh century AH (thirteenth century AD) wells were dug in Baku to get down to the source of the *naft*, and it was at this time that Marco Polo reported 'a hundred shiploads might be taken from it at one time'.

Other Arabic sources record crude oil production in Iraq, where there were oil seepages on the eastern bank of the Tigris along the road to Mosul. Arab travellers reported that it was produced on a large scale and was exported, Dawud al-Antaki (David of Antioch) writing that the crude oil was black and that 'it is distilled, and the first fraction (*daf'a*) of the distillate is white, the next black. If the black fraction is distilled again it joins the first [fraction]'. Other Arabic reports give information on crude oil production at Sinai in Egypt and Khuzistan in Persia.

Besides its extensive military applications (see Chapter 4), petroleum was used as a fuel and a medicine. Marco Polo wrote of Baku oil: 'This oil is not good to use with food, but it is good to burn, and is also used to anoint camels that have the mange. People come from vast distances to fetch it, for in all the countries round about they have no other oil'.

The properties of the light fractions of distillation were noted. Any such fraction had 'a power of attracting fire so that it may burn suddenly without fire but by a motion', and strict instructions were given for its distillation, storage and use. Petroleum spirit was also prepared, confirming what has been said earlier about the distillation of alcohol, which is similarly volatile. It had various uses and in his *al-Najum al-Shariqat* (*The Radiant Stars*) Abi al-Khayr al-Hasani (tenth century AH/ sixteenth century AD) described how to mix it with the resin sandarac to prepare a waterproof varnish. He called the petroleum spirit 'pure *naft* oil' and described how it could be tested:

drop one drop of it on a sheet of white paper, place it against the Sun and look. If you see a trace of oil similar to that of other oils then it is mixed and bad, and it will spoil all you do. If there is no trace of oil on the paper then it is good and pure, so put in it glass-ware and guard it.

Besides crude petroleum and its distillates, asphalts were also abundant. Particularly in Iraq *Qir* or *Qar* (pitch) and the *Zift* (pitch or asphalt) were produced and exported, having been known and used in this region by earlier civilisations, though their use was extended in Muslim times. They became familiar in building construction, especially for baths, and in ship-building, while they were also adopted as ingredients in the recipes for many incendiary weapons. They were also distilled to give lighter fractions. Again, oil shale was known to produce *naft*, as al-Dimashqi reported:

Among the oily organic (*nabatiyya*) stones are the stones of Musa's grave east of Jerusalem from which petroleum is produced if [they are] broken and placed in the cucurbit as is the case with rose-water. If lighted these stones burn like wood.

6.8 DISTILLATION AND EXTRACTION OF INDUSTRIAL OILS AND FATS

6.10 Apparatus for distilling oils and fats from a military treatise by al-Rammah. Thirteenth century AD. Bibliothèque Nationale, Paris.

Another industry that was important in both peace and war was the extraction and distillation of those vegetable and animal substances from which oils, fats and waxes could be prepared. Al-Kindi's compendious *Book of Perfume Chemistry and Distillation* described how to extract oils from cotton-seed, from mustard and from other seeds, and the military writer Hasan al-Rammah (d. 694 AH/ AD 1294) wrote about the distillation of *qitran* (tar), pine wood, pine resin, apricot seeds, frogs, and other materials. Figure 6.10 shows one of his distillation installations. In another military manuscript of the same period there is a long chapter on the distillation of similar substances, and in both we find evidence of advances in the techniques and equipment used. Both manuscripts also give instructions for separating water and oil in a distillation process, while there are several other manuscripts which are likewise rich in information.

6.9 ACIDS

The discovery of mineral or inorganic acids is of immense importance in the history of chemistry and chemical technology. They are the products of the distillation of alum, sal ammoniac (chloride of ammonia), saltpetre (potassium nitrate) and common salt in various proportions, as well as of vitriol. (Vitriol, it should be remembered, was a term used in early times for hydrated sulphate crystals, and sometimes for the mineral copperas (iron sulphide); in later times it became synonymous with sulphuric acid.)

Muslim alchemists were immensely curious; every substance known to them was subjected to a range of chemical reactions. Being masters of distillation this was one of the processes they were bound to use, so that it is not perhaps astonishing that they should have produced mineral acids at some stage or another. The surprise of some historians over this achievement is probably due largely to a widespread neglect of those alchemical treatises devoted to the transmutation of metals and the processes involved in the hunt for an elixir of eternal life. Yet it was during their extensive experiments with elixirs that Muslim scientists discovered much of the basis of modern chemistry of which the mineral acids are part.

In the space here we cannot elaborate on this viewpoint and any remaining controversy about the Muslim contribution will have to be settled by the study and publication of relevant Arabic texts, most of which are still unexplored. The delay in this work, as Sarton rightly said, constitutes a serious gap in our knowledge of the history of chemistry. Nevertheless, some comments can be made.

6.9.1 Nitric acid

The historian of chemisty E.J. Holmyard cites a description of making nitric acid from the Arabic manuscript *Sanduq al-Hikma* (*Chest of Wisdom*) by Jabir. It runs as follows:

Take five parts of pure flowers of nitre, three parts of Cyprus vitriol and two parts of Yemen alum. Powder them well, separately, until they are like dust and then place them in a flask. Plug the latter with a palm fibre and attach a glass receiver to it. Then invert the apparatus and heat the upper portion (i.e. the flask containing the mixture) with a gentle fire. There will flow down, by reason of the heat, an oil like cow's butter.

Analogous instructions appear in the Latin work *Summa Perfectionis* by 'Geber' and is thus a translation of a Jabir manuscript, possibly his *Kitab al-Istitmam* (*Book of the Completing* [*of Knowledge?*]).

6.9.2 Aqua regia

Aqua regia was a mixture of nitric and hydrochloric acids, and was obtained by adding salt or sal-ammoniac to nitrate and vitriol and then distilling, as is reported in the Latin texts of works by Jabir. Yet such combinations were given in other Arabic manuscripts and this is perhaps not surprising since these materials were very familiar to Muslim alchemists. Indeed, in an Arabic manuscript written in Syriac script but with additions made probably in the seventh century AH (thirteenth century AD) a variety of early Arabic chemical materials are given; we even find sal-ammoniac, saltpetre and vitriol together in one recipe. In another, though later, manuscript describing the manufacture of artificial diamonds and gems, there is also frequent mention of the spirit of vitriol, spirit of alum, spirit of saltpetre and spirits of salts (hydrochloric acid), all occurring in combination. Incidentally, it is worth noting here that while nitric acid alone will dissolve silver and is therefore used for separating small quantities of gold from silver, it is aqua regia that will separate silver from gold.

6.9.3 Sulphuric acid

This important acid was produced by Muslim alchemists starting with Jabir. It can be made by distilling vitriol or alum or by the combustion of sulphur. In one of his recipes al-Razi called it 'water of distilled alum' and he used it as one of the reagents which he prepared beforehand and kept for use in his alchemical work. He also described the way to obtain this 'water' by distilling vitriol. And in the fourth century AH (tenth century AD) even al-Mas'udi, who was not a chemist but a geographer and historian, described a few chemical reactions, among them the reaction of *al-kali* water with the *zaj* or vitriol water (sulphuric acid). He noted, too, the red colour that resulted and commented on the dangers that could come from 'subliming vapours and vitriolic fumes and other mineral exhalations'.

In the Arabic manuscript in Syriac mentioned when discussing aqua regia, the preparation of sulphuric acid is also described. It says: 'take three parts of vitriol (*zaj*) and three parts of sulphur, pulverise them well and distil them on dry fire. A yellow water distils.' Similar distillation recipes for sulphuric acid are given more than once and it is clear that this acid was often prepared and stored for further use, as al-Razi did. The author of the Syriac text calls the acid 'water of vitriol and sulphur', and in this and other Arabic manuscripts it is also sometimes called *ruh al zaj* (spirit of *zaj*).

6.9.4 Hydrochloric acid

This was known as *ruh al-milh* (spirit of salt). Al-Razi gave the following recipe:

Take equal parts of sweet salt, bitter salt, Tabarzad salt, Indian salt, salt of *al-qili* and salt of urine. After adding an equal weight of good crystallised sal-ammoniac, dissolve by moisture, and distil [the mixture]. These will distil over [to give] a strong water which will cleave stone instantly.

In other Arabic manuscripts there are other recipes in which sal-ammoniac and vitriol are distilled together.

6.9.5 Organic acids

Besides the mineral acids some organic acids such as vinegar were produced in large quantities, while vinegar itself was also distilled to give acetic acid. Silicic acid (a compound of silicon, oxygen and hydrogen) which can be used to make substances that are insoluble in water was another familiar product; it was obtained from bamboo.

6.10 ALKALIS

Soda and potash were in great demand for making glass, glazes and soap. Natron and plant ash were the sources.

6.10.1 Natron

This is crude sodium carbonate; it was found in its natural state in Egypt in the Western Desert and was exported widely. It was from the Arabic *natrun* that the European variant 'natron' was derived and thus the symbol 'Na' for sodium.

6.10.2 Al-Qali

This was obtained from the fused ashes of a low, woody shrub found in Syria and variously called ashnan, ushnan and shinan. It is of the family Chenopodiaceae and has the botanical name

Salsola soda while chemically it is about 80 per cent potassium carbonate with some 20 per cent sodium carbonate.

The ashes of wood, especially oak, were also utilised. Al-Razi described the concentration and purification of *al-Qali* and of oak ashes to give pure potassium carbonate and sodium carbonates. Abu Mansur Muwaffak (fourth century AH/tenth century AD) was, however, the first to make a clear distinction between sodium carbonate (soda) and potassium carbonate (potash), which are similar in so many respects.

6.10.3 Caustic soda

Caustic soda or sodium hydroxide was never produced on a commercial scale but it is of historical importance to note that al-Razi knew how to prepare it. His recipe ran as follows:

Take one *mann* [about 1 kg] of white *al-Qali* and an equal quantity of lime and pour over it [i.e. the mixture] seven times its amount of water, and boil it until it is reduced to one half. Purify it [by filtration or decantation] ten times. Then place it in thin evaporating cups (*kizan*), and then hang in [heated] beakers (*jamat*). Return what separates out [to the cup], raise it [the cup] gradually, and protect from dust whatever drops from the cups into the beakers, and coagulate it into a salt.

6.10.4 Lime

Lime (*kils*) was quite abundant. Used in soap-making, as a building material, and for military purposes (see Chapter 4), it was produced by burning stones or marble. When slaked with water it was known as *nura*.

6.11 SOAP

Hard soap was first produced by the Arabs, only later spreading to Europe. Soap manufacture became an important industry in many Islamic lands, especially in Syria. Coloured perfumed toilet soap as well as some medicinal soaps were made and exported, and Syrian towns like Nablus, Damascus, Aleppo and Sarmin were famous for their products. The basic process used olive oil and *al-Qali*, though sometimes *natrun* was added. One method of manufacture was given by Dawud al-Antaki and ran as follows:

Take one part of *al-Qali*, and half a part of lime. Grind them well and place them in a tank. Pour five times water and stir for two hours. The tank is provided with a plug hole. When the stirring is stopped and the liquid becomes clear, the hole is opened. When the water is emptied plug the hole again and pour water and stir, then empty, and so on until no taste is left in the water. This being done while keeping each water separate from the other.

Then take from the pure oil ten times the quantity of the first water and place on a fire. When it boils feed it with the last water little by little. Then the water before the last until at last you feed it with the first water. Then it becomes like dough. Here it is ladled out [and spread] on mats until it is partially dry. Then it is cut and placed on *nura* [slaked lime]. This is the finished product and there is no need to cool it or wash it with cold water while cooking. Some add salt to the *al-Qali* and lime in half the quantity of lime. Others add some starch just before cooking is over. The oil can be replaced by other oils and fats such as the oil of carthamus.

The alchemical treatises such as those of al-Razi sometimes also give recipes for soap. It is worth noting too that al-Razí also gave a description of a process for producing glycerine from olive oil.

6.12 GLASS

Glass-making is an ancient industry which began with the civilisations in Egypt, Mesopotamia and Syria. Even the later advances that occurred during Roman times were confined to Syria and Mesopotamia, whose basic technology has scarcely been improved upon in Europe and elsewhere down to modern times.

With the rise of Islamic civilisation the early glass industry underwent a renaissance. Not only the traditional centres took part in this revival; new centres developed as well. The resulting Muslim glass treasures, which are now distributed among museums throughout the world, bear witness to the unique characteristics of the glass made in each centre.

The glass of the third century AH (ninth century AD) made at Samarra is considered peerless in its quality, but Samarra was not Iraq's only glass-making centre. Others included Mosul, Najaf and places in the Baghdad region. In Syria glass from Damascus was renowned throughout Islamic history, though there were other manufacturing centres at Aleppo, Raqqa, Armanaz, Tyre, Sidon, Acre, Hebron and Rasafa. There were manufactures in Egypt at Alexandria and Cairo as well, while glass was also made in Persia, Spain, in the Maghrib, and in other Muslim lands. But Syria remained the major glass-making country for many centuries until, in fact, the rise of the Venetian glass industry in the thirteenth century AD.

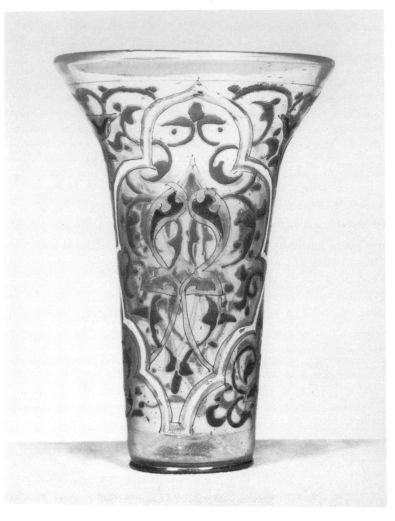

6.11 Syrian glass beaker with enammelled and gilt decoration, probably made in Aleppo. Thirteenth century AD. Victoria and Albert Museum, London.

There were various factors that led to the transfer of glass-making technology from Islam to the West. The first phase came, it is believed, as early as the fifth century AH (eleventh century AD) when Egyptian craftsmen founded two glass factories at Corinth in Greece. Here they introduced contemporary techniques of glass manufacture, but the factories were destroyed during the Norman conquest of Corinth in AD 1147 and the workers carried off westwards, to contribute to the renaissance of Western glass-making in medieval times. Then, in the thirteenth century AD, Mongol conquests drove large numbers of glass-workers from Damascus and Aleppo to glass-making centres in the West. In addition to all this, there seems to have been some transmission of glass technology from Islam to the West due to contacts made during and after the Crusades.

Finally, as mentioned previously (Chapter 1), a treaty for the transfer of technology was drawn up in June AD 1277 between Bohemond VII, the titular prince of Antioch, and the Doge of Venice. It was through this treaty that the secrets of Syrian glass-making were brought to Venice, everything necessary being imported directly from Syria – raw materials as well as the expertise of the Syrian-Arab craftsmen. Once it had learnt them, Venice guarded the secrets of the technology with great care, monopolising European glass manufacture until the techniques became known in seventeenth-century France.

6.12.1 Materials

Islamic glass was made by fusing together two main ingredients, woody ashes (*al-Qali*) and sand or flint (silica). Lime came with the sand in the form of sea shells. It was therefore of the soda–lime–silica type, and a typical analysis would give 65 per cent silicon oxide, 15 per cent sodium oxide and 9 per cent calcium oxide, plus other oxides like that of magnesium. Of course, *al-Qali* was a major Syrian product, made in such quantity that it was exported; in the early sixteenth century the Italian writer on technology, Vannoccio Biringuccio, could say in his compendious *Pirotechnia* that in glass-making 'one takes ashes made from the herb saltwort that comes from Syria'. Ordinarily the *al-Qali* was used in the concentrated form of the salt *milh al-Qali* described by al-Razi, though it was also sometimes used in its non-concentrated form.

In addition to the main ingredients, manganese dioxide was added in order to produce 'colourless transparent clear glass'. This was possible because, although most sands contain sufficient iron oxide to give a greenish or brownish glass, manganese dioxide oxidises the iron and neutralises the resulting yellowish colour by its own purplish tint. This property was not known in ancient times, but was observed by Jabir and frequently mentioned in Arabic literature. Thus 'magnesia' became an essential ingredient with the sand and *al-Qali*. Colours, when required, were produced by adding small amounts of metallic oxides, and in an Arabic manuscript on alchemy we find recipes for colouring glass black, blue and sapphire blue, brick red, yellow, and pistachio green.

6.12.2 Furnaces and tools

Furnace installations in glass-works were big enough for commercial production and employed several workers. Such factory-scale equipment could produce large objects and is described in an Arabic manuscript. The furnace was provided with six chambers, three of them on top of one another, making in effect a three-storey building which was dome-shaped and formed the major part of the factory. The lowest chamber was occupied by the fire, the middle one by the crucibles in which the glass was melted, and the uppermost for annealing the glass products once they have been fashioned. This description fits the remains of a furnace at Corinth, and also those described by Biringuccio.

Figure 6.12 illustrates a furnace shown in an Arabic manuscript

6.12 Furnace for making artificial rubies and sapphires, illustrated in a manuscript of about the sixteenth century AD. Forschungsbibliothek Gotha.

probably from the tenth century AH (sixteenth century AD). It was used for making artificial rubies and sapphires like the *'ain al-hir* (eye of the cat). Figure 6.13 shows a small glass furnace at Armanaz near Aleppo, which is still in operation. As for the tools used in glass-making, these have shown little change over the centuries, and Figs. 6.14 (*a*) and (*b*) illustrate those now in use at Armanaz. They are the same as those used in Europe in the nineteenth century, and in Islamic and European countries during the Middle Ages.

The main items were the iron blow-pipe and an iron rod called a *bolin* (pontil), which is applied hot to the bottom of a partially formed glass article for ease of manipulation until the glass-maker has finished. Other tools are shears, pliers and similar items.

6.12.3 The manufacturing process

The raw materials – the sand, *al-Qali* and magnesium, if any – were first subjected to heating and melting in a pot (*qidr*) to purify them. This is the 'fritting' process that eliminates some of the gaseous products. Next the 'frit' is crushed, mixed with waste broken glass, loaded into crucibles and placed in a high temperature (i.e. in the middle chamber of the three-tier furnace) where it melts into glass. Using the blow-pipe, the glass-maker extracts a piece of viscous glass from a crucible through one of the holes in the walls of the furnace and then blows with the mouth or uses a mould.

Blowing was the last major revolutionary technique in glass-making to be invented. A Syrian development of the first century AD, basically it has not undergone any significant

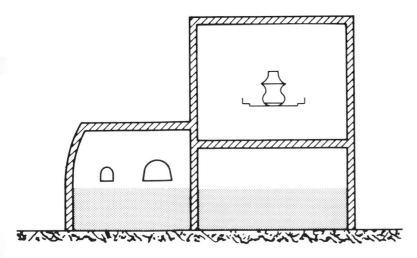

6.13 Cross-section of a small glass furnace at Armanaz, near Aleppo.

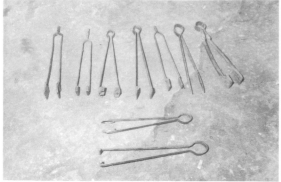

6.14 Glass making tools used at Armanaz, near Aleppo.

modification for nineteen centuries. It is still a fundamental method both of the traditional glass-maker and of the modern glass factory; the only modern change has been the introduction of elaborate machinery for mass production.

The blower's art was maintained at a high pitch in Syria and other Islamic countries and still exists at Damascus, Aleppo and Armanaz. And, as we have seen, it was from Syrian craftsmen that at a later date the Venetians learned the skill.

6.12.4 Decoration techniques

Decoration was performed either during the manufacturing process, to give mosaic glass and moulded patterns, or after objects were shaped but while they were still warm, giving 'trails' and 'blobs', indentations, ribbing and nipples. Decoration could also be carried out after the glass had cooled by cutting, enamelling and gilding. We shall discuss each of these in turn.

Mosaic glass

Glass with mosaics of various patterns and colours was made in ancient times but then manufacture ceased. The art was revived early in Islamic history, but it was a costly process and its use was always restricted to those rich enough to afford it.

Moulded patterns

These were made by means of blowing into a mould (Fig. 6.15), though there were variations in Persia and Samarra over the way this was done. One variation was to blow first into a patterned mould and then into a plain one; this caused the pattern (usually ribbing) to appear raised on both the inside as

6.15 Glass bottle blown in a two-piece mould. Persian, tenth or eleventh century AD. Victoria and Albert Museum, London.

well as the outside walls of the vessel and was known as 'optic' blowing.

Trailings and blobs

This form of decoration was used extensively on early Islamic glass (Fig. 6.16). Trailings presented some difficulty because it

6.16 Blown glass bottle with applied decoration of trailings and blobs. Probably Syrian. Sixth to eighth century AD. The Toledo Museum of Art, Ohio.

was hard to obtain a regular pattern by manipulating long, slender threads of viscous glass while the object was rotated at the end of a blow-pipe. Blobs were not such a problem; they were added by letting glass droplets fall on to the vessel and then fusing them into its walls.

Indents, ribs and nipples

These were made while the object was still hot, the glass-maker using tools such as the pincers to make the decorations.

Cut glass

Cut glass and cut crystal became an important method of decoration (Figs. 6.1, 6.17). In the third and following centuries AH (ninth century AD onwards) a renaissance of fine or colourless crystal-type glass occurred in some Muslim countries. Hollow and relief carving was done by a wheel fed with water and emery, while engraving was carried out using diamond, flint or other similar tools. Glass-cutting techniques were not introduced into the West until the later Middle Ages.

The engraved Islamic goblets and bottles of Samarra resembled rock crystal in their thickness and precious stones in their dark colouration. The imitation of precious stones was, indeed, a common feature in Islamic art, and such imitations became accepted in the West as works of exceptional beauty.

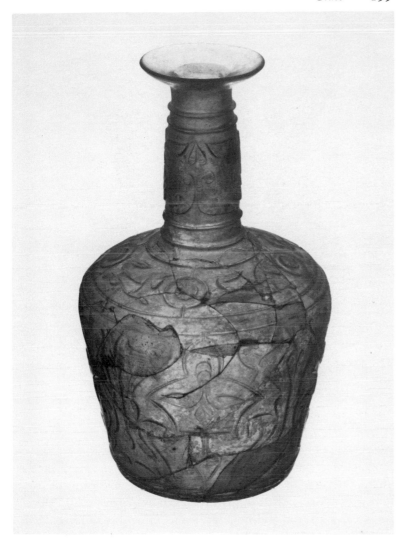

6.17 Persian cut-glass bottle. Ninth to tenth century AD. Victoria and Albert Museum, London.

Lustre and enamelling

These were other high achievements in Islamic glass-making. Like glass-cutting, the art was developed in Muslim countries during the Middle Ages. Lustred glass, made in imitation of lustred pottery, was prepared in Egypt, Syria and other Islamic lands from the second to fourth centuries AH (eighth to the tenth centuries AD).

But the most important achievement in decorating glass-ware was the art of enamelling of colourless and coloured glasses, such as those used for drinking glasses, in lamps for mosques, and other items (Fig. 6.18). Such enamelled glass was made largely if not entirely in Syria at the glass-works in Raqqa, Damascus and other cities between the sixth and eighth

6.18 Enamelled and gilt glass mosque lamp. Syrian, fourteenth century AD. Victoria and Albert Museum, London.

centuries AH (twelfth and fourteenth centuries AD). Decoration was with true enamel, applied as a powder and fired *in situ* and not with enamel paint as was Roman glass, so that Islamic enamelled glass-ware is characterised by its glossy sheen in contrast to the matt appearance of the Roman.

6.13 CERAMICS

Innovation in ceramics reached a high level in the Muslim civilisation. Yet surprisingly, though ceramics form one of the glories of Islamic art and technology, achievements in this field are known only to historians or art; their relation to science and technology has not been explored.

Pottery is, of course, one of the oldest arts and crafts, being developed first by the ancient civilisations of Egypt, Mesopotamia and the Near East in general. This same area, including Persia, was also the birthplace of Islamic ceramics.

6.13.1 Shaping pottery

Three main techniques were used by Muslim potters: hand fabrication, throwing on a potter's wheel, and casting or forming in a mould. We shall deal with each in turn, but first a word about the material used. This was clay, prepared by slaking with water and then screening through a sieve. In addition, its composition was adjusted by adding finely-ground quartz pebbles or flint to the slaked clay. Once prepared, the purified and pliable clay was kneaded with the feet (Fig. 6.19), and again before shaping, though this time the smaller pieces were kneaded by hand.

Hand fabrication

In this method, pots were formed either from one lump of clay or from coils. In using coils the potter shaped the pieces into circles and placed them on top of each other to form a cylinder. As the shaping progressed, the cylinder was smoothed and the coiling continued until the final shape was reached. Later a combination of coil-forming and throwing was sometimes adopted. However, the hand fabrication technique is still used

6.19 Kneading clay with the feet at a pottery in Fez, Morocco.

in Muslim lands because it is considered convenient for some products, such as large vessels and in ceramic hardware for building.

Throwing on a potter's wheel

This was the technique adopted by most potters and utilised a 'kick-wheel' which was a heavy treadle-disc turned by the potter with his feet (Fig. 6.20). Much Islamic pottery shows evidence of having been formed on such a wheel which, of course, pre-dates the advent of Islam even though it is still in use today.

A kick-wheel of an early Aleppo potter was typical, consisting of two horizontal discs made of wood (though other materials were sometimes used), the upper one being the wheel on which

6.20 A potter working at a foot-operated wheel, Bursa, Turkey.

the clay was worked. It was about 30 centimetres in diameter and projected 10 centimetres above a table or platform. The lower disc was the actual kick-wheel; it was some 70–80 centimetres in diameter and fixed 30 centimetres above the ground. Connection between the two discs was by a vertical shaft of wood or steel, which extended below the lower disc and rested on a pedestal standing on the ground. Later, a ball-bearing was fitted where the shaft passed through the platform just below the upper disc. The potter was seated in front of the upper disc or 'working-wheel'.

To throw a pot, a lump of kneaded clay was placed on the working-wheel, centred, and a hole formed in it; then, by manual dexterity, the potter 'threw' the pot into the desired shape. Using hands and fingers he would form the body of the pot first, followed by the neck (Fig. 6.21). The base could be formed using a modelling tool. Immediately after shaping the pot, it could be decorated with grooves by applying a toothed modelling tool to the soft surface while the wheel was still rotating.

After being shaped the pot was taken off the wheel using a knife or string to cut it away and carried to the drying room, where it was left until it was leather-hard. Then the pot was replaced on the wheel, re-centred, and turned with templates and other tools to remove surplus clay and give the final shape. After removing the marks caused by turning, handles were attached as needed, the handles themselves being made from strips or rods of clay.

6.21 A potter throwing a pot on the wheel, Bursa, Turkey.

Forming in a mould

This technique was carried out using various methods. In later times there was *casting*, where a porous mould was filled with a clay mush and then emptied after a time (Fig. 6.22). Due to the mould's porosity, water escaped from the mush where it was in contact with the walls of the mould. At those points the mush would stiffen and when the mould was emptied, cling to its interior. With further drying the layer formed shrunk and separated from the walls of the mould.

Another moulding technique was to take clay of a similar consistency to that used for throwing, put it in a mould and

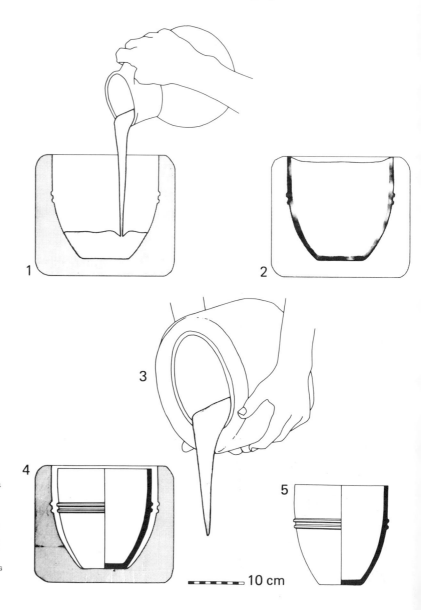

6.22 Method of casting pottery in a mould using a clay mush. 1. the mould is filled with clay mush. 2. The porous mould absorbs water from the mush adjacent to it and the outer layer of clay stiffens. 3. The rest of the mush is emptied out of the mould. 4. The stiffened clay dries and shrinks. 5. The pot is removed from the mould.

10 cm

then press it to the walls with the fingers; alternatively, it could be placed in the mould while throwing. A decorated mould could be used if desired. Moulding is still used by Muslim tilemakers.

6.13.2 Firing pottery

Pottery kilns in Islamic countries were the outcome of a long process of development that occurred in Egypt, Mesopotamia and Persia. Yet if we study existing kilns of the present time and those of ancient civilisations, we shall see that the basic designs are the same.

The simple vertical kiln still in use in modern Iran, Syria or England is not much different from the kiln of Mesopotamia built in the fourth millennium BC. It is a simple up-draught kiln which has been used all over the world (Fig. 6.23). The usual design had an under-flow fire-chamber, the fire itself burning in an adjacent side hearth so that the hot gases were made to pass to the fire-chamber and thence upwards through holes into the upper baking-chamber where the pottery was stacked. Flue gases then passed out through a chimney on the top or through smaller holes in the dome.

6.23 Pottery kiln in Fez.

Kilns differed widely in size depending on how large the pottery might be that they were expected to fire, and temperatures also varied. Moreover, the up-draught kiln was not the only design. Another was the down-draught type, which was developed from it (Fig. 6.24). Here, instead of rising through the dome, the hot gases descended between the stacks of pottery until they reached ground level, where they then escaped through openings connected to a chimney at the side.

Al-Biruni remarked that a pottery kiln was used for preparing the frit (the first melting of raw materials for glass-making) which was to be used in glazing (see below). Figure 6.25 is taken from an Arabic manuscript and illustrates a kiln for glazing (*mina*) artificial jewellry. It displays the general features of the vertical kiln, with a dome, a lower fire-chamber, a chamber above this for the wares that were to be glazed, and a multiple upper flue outlet for the spent gases. A door allows access to the upper chamber so that wares can be inserted and retrieved.

6.13.3 Glazes

Most glazes were a kind of glass and were applied both to the inside and outside of pottery, either to render it impervious to water or for decoration. Two main kinds were used, an alkaline glaze and a lead glaze. Both had their origins in ancient Egypt and Mesopotamia.

The *alkaline glaze* was made from quartz and soda, potash and, sometimes, ordinary salt. Such glazes are extremely transparent, but they tend to become iridescent and the range of colours which can be used with the glaze is very limited.

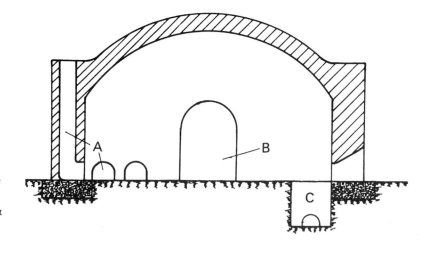

6.24 Cross-section of a down-draught kiln in Persia. Hot gasses from the fire pit C on the right rise up through the stacked pottery B to the ceiling and are then drawn down to the chimney openings A at ground level on the opposite side.

6.45 A kiln for glazing artificial jewellery. Illustration from a manuscript of the sixteenth century AD. Forschungsbibliothek Gotha.

Moreover, not all clays will take an alkaline glaze satisfactorily; an admixture of sand in the body of the pot is necessary for adhesion.

Lead glaze contained red lead (*isrinj* – Pb_3O_4). In Arabic countries such glazes were composed of flint (silica) and *isrinj*, the lead being used as a flux for the flint as it lowered the firing temperature. Lead glazes permitted a much greater range of colouring than did the alkaline type, but were apt to smudge and run. Nevertheless, they are still the potter's most important glaze.

Normally glazes are transparent and colourless but can be

given colour by the addition of *metal oxides*. Copper was a main colouring agent in Islam; as copper oxide it produced a turquoise blue in an alkaline glaze and a green in a lead glaze. If rust (ferric oxide – Fe_2O_3) was dispersed through a lead glaze it provided a yellow or orange colour, and under reducing conditions (i.e. when some oxygen was removed) it became ferrous oxide (Fe_2O), which gave a pale green tint.

Combinations of copper, iron and other minerals were also used. Mixing copper with varying amounts of ferric oxide gave olive greens, and whereas opaque ferric oxide produced red, mixed with antimony it provided a yellow. Cobalt gave a deep blue and manganese a purple, while other combinations gave a variety of other attractive colours.

Glazes with or without metal oxides could be applied either to unfired leather-hard pottery or to already fired vessels, though it was more usual to use the latter.

For lead glazing the potter mixed the ingredients (which could be flint, sand and red lead) and ground them, adding water until he had a homogeneous liquid. Any metal oxide required was then added. The liquid was then applied to fired pottery either by dipping or in some other way, and then the coated ware were re-fired in the kiln.

It was, however, possible for the potter to buy glazes already prepared by specialist craftsmen; in such cases a frit in the form of an alkaline glass was prepared. To make this, the raw materials (flint, quartz and *al-Qali*) were finely ground, mixed, and then placed in a ladle which was heated in a special kiln for several hours until the mass had melted into a clear glass. The ladle was then extracted and the molten glass poured into a pit filled with water. The quenching broke the frit into granules, which were ground and stored for later use.

When he received this frit, the potter mixed it with metal oxides of his choice and added some other ingredients, such as white clay, potash and vinegar. He then added water to the mixture, which was then carefully ground until it became a homogeneous liquid. This was applied to previously fired pottery by dipping or pouring, and then glazed.

Practices such as these, though sometimes with modifications, were adopted during different Islamic periods, and are still used today.

6.13.4 Innovations in Islamic ceramics

Having now briefly mentioned the main techniques for making pottery and glazing it, a few remarks about some Islamic achievements in the art of ceramics will not be out of place.

Some historians divide Islamic ceramics into three periods: and early period (up to the beginning of the fifth century AH/ eleventh century AD and including Umayyad and early 'Abbasid times); a middle period (fourth to ninth centuries AH/ tenth to fifteenth centuries AD); and a late period (after about the ninth century AH/fifteenth century AD). We shall begin with the early period.

Early 'Abbasid wares discovered at Samarra as well as at many other sites can readily be divided into six types:

(i) Common unglazed pottery;
(ii) Monochrome alkaline-glazed ware;
(iii) Lead-glazed ware decorated in relief;
(iv) Lead-glazed ware decorated with splashes and streaks, or mottled, together with Sgraffiato ('scratched') ware;
(v) Tin-glazed ware, including lustre painting;
(vi) Under-glaze painted ware;

One of the main Islamic achievements of this period was the invention of tin glazing. It is said that this was known in ancient Mesopotamia, forgotten and then rediscovered in the third century AH (ninth century AD). When added to a lead-silicate glaze a tin-oxide glaze produced a successful imitation of Tang creamy-coloured porcelain from China. Another advantage of tin oxide was not only that it became possible to paint on its unfired matt surface, but also that the paints did not run when the pottery was fired, as happened when they were applied direct to a pottery surface under a lead glaze. This brought about some of the finest achievements in Islamic painted ornamentation, and was the origin of the majolica and delft painted ware of Europe that appeared from the fourteenth century AD onwards.

Another Islamic innovation of this period was lustre-painted ware (Fig. 6.26). Here metallic pigments were painted over opaque-white tin glaze and fixed into that glaze by a second firing. The result was that the lustre-painted surfaces gave an iridescent and glittering reflection. Some of the main types of decoration of this kind were gold lustre on a white background, ruby lustre either on a white background or with other colours, and a polychrome lustre with a copper or silver-metallic shine.

During the middle Islamic period the most important achievement was the invention of white-body pottery. This was attained by using a new composite material made from powdered quartz, white clay and potash, and came about by the desire of Muslim potters to equal Chinese porcelain. When fired, the new material produced a very hard semi-transparent body which, after the eighteenth century AD, became known in Europe as soft-paste porcelain.

This new white pottery was accompanied by a re-emergence of alkali glazes using powdered pebbles and potash. When such glazes were used on it they fused excellently and slip or white glazing was no longer necessary. This use of alkali glazing was helped by the discovery of borax as a flux. We have already seen that pre-made alkaline glazes or frits were known, but it is worth noting that al-Biruni, in giving a recipe for a frit made from ground quartz and potash, also mentioned the use of borax or, in Arabic, *tinkar* (a cruder form of borax) as a flux.

White ware and alkaline glazing led to the invention of several new glazing techniques. Space precludes our mentioning all of them, though reference must be made to one, *mina'i* (enamel), which was a form of overlgaze painting. Here, using a crucible, the potter melted an alkaline pigment with the appropriate pigments. After cooling he powdered the melt to provide his enamel, which could be made in a range of seven colours; it was applied over an opaque white. Such over-glaze colours were fixed to the ware by a low-temperature second firing.

This was the golden age of Islamic ceramics, both for pottery and for tiles. Kashan in Iran was the most prominent centre. Here in 700 AH/AD 1301 Abu al-Qasim al-Kashani, a member of a local family of potters, wrote an important book giving details of Islamic ceramic techniques. Figures 6.26, 6.27 and 6.28 illustrate selected items from the three periods.

6.14 INKS AND PIGMENTS

In a civilisation where learning and the arts played an important role, great care was taken in the manufacture of writing and painting materials, and there are several Arabic technological manuscripts which are rich in details connected with the production of inks, pigments, and glues, as well as with paper-making, bookbinding and other related subjects. One such is *Umdat al Kuttab . . .* (*The Handbook of Scribes and the Tool of the Wise*) by al-Mu'izz Ibn Badis (*c.* 416 AH/AD 1025), though there are several others which dealt with similar subjects.

6.26 White glazed earthenware
dish from Mesopotamia painted
in yellow and brown lustre.
Ninth century AD. Victoria and
Albert Museum, London.

6.27 Earthenware bowl from Raqqa,
painted with coloured glazes.
Thirteenth century AD. National
Museum, Damascus.

6.28 Painted earthenware dish from Isnik, Turkey. About AD 1500. Victoria and Albert Museum, London.

6.14.1 Black inks

Two main types of black ink were used. One was permanent, with its blackness due to minute particles of carbon; the other was an ink in which the colour was due to tannate of iron. Carbon for the permanent ink was obtained from the soot of various oils and fats such as linseed oil and petroleum, or ground charcoal derived from different types of seeds.

A typical method of producing lamp-soot or lamp-black was to have a four-wick lamp burning linseed oil. On top of the lamp there was a dome-shaped cover with a hole in it, and above this were six other similar covers, forming a chimney. The wicks were lit and the oil burned until it was exhausted, then the soot that had gathered inside the chimney was collected using a feather. Next, the soot was sieved and subjected to further treatment until a fine powder was obtained.

For permanent ink, gum arabic (obtained from a species of acacia) was commonly used as a binder, though glair (made from whipped white of egg) was an alternative. However, other inks were also described in Arabic manuscripts, among them a blue-black ink derived from crushed gall-nuts and ferrous sulphate which is still in use today.

6.14.2 Pigments

Pigments impart colour without penetrating far below the surface and are normally applied either as inks or washes suspended in water or as oil paints. In the *Handbook of Scribes and the Tool of the Wise* Ibn Badis gives details not only of coloured inks but also of oil paints and lacquers. Such pigments were applied by pen or brush, and were used for writing and for painting miniatures on paper, leather, wood and other surfaces.

For *black pigment* the normal colouring substance was carbon obtained from lamp-black or special charcoals as already described.

A *white pigment* came mainly from white lead (*isfidaj*), though bone white was also mixed with it sometimes.

Red pigments were available in a variety of shades. The main constituents were cinnabar (*zanjfar*) – the red or crystalline form of mercuric sulphide – and red lead (*isrinj*), though sometimes a clayey ironstone containing red veins among the clay was used. Lac, a dark red resinous incrustation deposited on certain trees by the lac insect (*Laccifer lacca*), was also processed for its pigment and detailed instructions for its preparation were published.

Yellow pigments were derived mainly from orpiment (*zarnikh asfar*) – arsenic trisulphide – though yellow ochres (forms of clayey iron ores) were also used. In addition massicot (monoxide of lead) was mentioned in Arabic texts, as also saffron, which was employed together with other pigments.

Blue pigments came from the mineral lapis lazuli, though azurite (a form of copper carbonate) was also used, as was indigo.

Green pigments were mainly derived from the basic copper carbonate verdigris (*zinjar*) and from mineral malachite. In addition different greens, including those with plant-like hues, were manufactured by mixing other varieties of pigment.

If they were water-based, all these pigments required a *binding medium*, which was usually mixed with the pigment. Gum arabic was the most common binder, though glues (especially fish glue) and glair were employed. *Oil paints* were mainly used for miniatures in books and for coating such surfaces as wood. From a manuscript of the tenth century AH (sixteenth century AD) we have detailed information on the preparation of such paints and the techniques of applying them. In making them a solution of the gum resin sandarac mixed with linseed oil was prepared, then the colouring pigment was added, together with a distillate of naphtha, and the whole vigorously mixed.

6.14.3 Varnishes

Paintings were protected with a varnish; a typical recipe of the tenth century AH(sixteenth century AD) was to add a naphtha solvent to a thick mixture of sandarac and linseed oil. The resulting solution was applied two or three times to the surface being protected.

6.15 DYES

Dyeing was an important and specialised industry, closely related to the manufacture of textiles (Fig. 6.29). Until the advent of modern synthetic dyes, only vegetable and animal substances were available for dyeing. Yet it must be remembered that classical and later literature does not reveal the whole range of dyes actually used because these involved craft secrets which were never committed to writing but only handed down from father to son. Even so sufficient research into those dyeing techniques that are mentioned in Arabic sources has not so far been undertaken.

Red dyes were the most important because they provided a lively and luxurious colour. One significant source was the lac insect itself and others of the Coccidae family, the bodies of the females giving colours ranging from a brilliant red to scarlet. In Arabic literature they were referred to as *Qirmiz*, hence our words 'crimson' and 'carmine', and dyes of this kind were reported in several texts. There were other insect-based dyes, however. One known as 'cochineal' and derived from another insect of the same family (*Coccus cacti*) came from Armenia and was distributed to Muslim countries, while there was also the type called 'Qirmis proper' (*Kermococcus vermilio*) that came from Mediterranean lands and from Persia. There are descriptions of how to extract dye from both.

Another valuable source of red was the madder plant (*fuwwa*) (*Rubica tinctorum*), which was grown in most Muslim lands and in Persia. The dye was obtained from its roots. It became such an important product that Ibn al-Bassal, for example, went so far as to give a description of its cultivation.

A third source of red dye was the privet henna (*Lawsonia inermis*) that was grown in Syria and Egypt. However, Ibn al-Ukhuwwa advised the *muhtasib* authorities against dyeing with henna rather than *fuwwa*, because the latter was more stable. A red dye could also be extracted from *baqqam* (*Caesalpinia sappan*, known now as brazil wood), but again textbooks written for the *muhtasib* warned against its unstable colour.

Incidentally, it was previously mentioned that the lac insect was used both as a source of dye and of shellac. It must be made clear, however, that its use was not an Arabic invention, for it was known first in India and China.

The main source of *blue dyes*, was an indigo plant (*nil* or *nila*) (*Indigofera tinctoria*). A major product, it was grown in most Islamic lands and especially Palestine, as well as being imported from India. Indigotin, the chemical compound responsible for the blue colour, was obtained from the leaves of the plant by a

6.29 Dyeing cloth. Illustration from a manuscript of the sixteenth century AD. British Library, London.

process that was described in Arabic literature, while at the end of the sixth or beginning of the seventh centuries AH (twelfth or thirteenth centuries AD) its cultivation was also detailed by Ibn al-'Awwam.

A variety of materials were available for *yellow dyes*, important among them safflower (*'usfur* or *qurtum*) (*Carthamus tinctorius*); colouring matter was obtained from its petals and florets. Three other major sources were saffron (*za'faran*) (*Crocus sativus*), turmeric *(kurkum)* (*Curcuma longa*) and *wars* (*Memecylon tinctorium*). In addition, pomegranate rinds and sumach leaves were used both as dyes and as tanning agents.

Green dyes were obtained by dyeing with blue and yellow, though some green vegetable dyes came from the Thymelaeacae family, which includes such plants as Daphne (*Daphnae cnidum*), known in Arabic as *mathnan* or *mithnan*.

Tyre and Sidon were famous from ancient times for their *purple dyes*. They used the secretion of the tiny shellfish *murex*, which was boiled, and cloth dyed in the resulting liquor. Not much information is available on the process even though murex or purple dyeing was carried on in Syria until a century or so ago.

Black dyes were made primarily from galls with added iron sulphate (*zaj* or green vitriol). Sometimes this was superimposed on deep indigo.

Mordants or fixatives were required to make most dyes adhere to the cloth fibres, and aluminium sulphate or alum, known as 'alum of the Yemen' (*shabb Yamani*), was used. Pure alum was, therefore, always an important ingredient in the dyeing process.

7.1 Persian decorated-leather book-
binding. Sixteenth century AD.
Victoria and Albert Museum,
London.

7 Textiles, paper and leather

7.1 THE TEXTILE INDUSTRY

Textile manufacture was the leading Islamic industry. This is
perhaps not surprising, since it supplied society with that most
necessary commodity, clothing, which is second only to food as
a basic need. The standard of Muslim textiles was high.
Research into Islamic improvements of the different steps in
manufacture has not been undertaken yet, but the notable rise
in quality could only have been attained by technological
development at every stage of the process. The industry was
extensive, the volume of production high, and the number of
workers engaged in it prodigious. It was partly regulated by the
State, which had its own workshops and factories for producing
the special garments (*tiraz*) for caliphs, rulers, high-ranking
officials, army officers, and as official presents. Consequently
some textile workers received a daily wage, while others sold
their products privately either to the State or direct to
merchants.

That the Islamic industry had an appreciable effect on the
West is evident from a study of Arabic and Islamic words for
textiles which have found their way into European languages.
Thus for example in English we have such words as damask,
muslin and mohair.

7.1.1 Fibres

Wool was the oldest fibre used in Muslim textiles. Fine woollen
cloths were produced in Egypt and other Islamic lands, and
different qualities of sheep's wool were recognised; some were
considered suitable for weaving into cloth, others for carpets.
The inner hair coat of the Angora goat known as mohair (from
the Arabic *mukhayyar*), was used for fine shawls and for the
smooth cloth of coats, while camel hair was to be found in some
other fabrics.

Sheep were shorn with a pair of shears (see Fig. 7.2) and
before the raw wool was spun it was sorted according to quality,
then cleaned, degreased, and combed.

179

7.2 Sheep shearing in Turkey.

From ancient times Egypt was famous for its *linen*, but under Islam its manufacture spread to Iran and other countries. Flax from Egypt was also exported to various Muslim countries as well as to Europe, where it predominated until about 700 AH/AD 1300. Certain industrial cities such as Tinnis and Damietta became famous for their linen textiles. The industrial organisation of their factories was highly developed and a considerable degree of care was taken in the various stages of manufacture. Indeed, the technology used was the most advanced available in the Middle Ages and was adopted by contemporary European linen manufacturers.

Flax was specifically processed to extract the fibres, the plant stalks being placed on wooden or stone blocks and beaten with mallets. The broken stalks were then combed, first to remove any woody tissue, and next to split up and separate the bundles of fibres.

Cotton was known in India and ancient Egypt but it became an important textile only after the advent of Islam. Indeed, one of the results of the Muslim agricultural revolution (see Chapter 8) was that cotton plantations spread throughout all Islamic lands, in the east as well as the west. Fine cotton was manufactured and exported to various countries, including China and the Far East.

It was the Arabs, too, who introduced the cotton textile industry into Spain in the second century AH (eighth century AD). Here it flourished before spreading to France in the sixth century AH (twelfth century AD), Flanders a hundred years later, Germany in the eighth century AH (fourteenth century AD), and England a century after that. It was to become a major factor in the industrial revolution three centuries later.

During the Middle Ages, Europe also imported cotton from Muslim lands, the best coming from the Syrian cities of Hama and Aleppo. Syria, in fact, remained the main source for cotton until later times, when Egyptian cotton became so highly esteemed.

In manufacture, the cotton pods or 'bolls' were processed before spinning. Ginning was the main method for separating the fibre from the seeds; it included grading the cotton and cleaning it from impurities. Instructions on assessing the quality of ginned cotton and its freedom from seeds and husks were given in the manuals (*alhisba*) prepared for the guidance of the *muhtasib*.

Silk is the product of the silk-worm (the caterpillar or larva of moths of the *Bombyx* family), which feeds on white mulberry leaves and then envelops itself in a cocoon composed of one continuous silk filament. The technique of obtaining this silk was either to expose the cocoons to the sun so that the larvae would die in them, or the caterpillars were destroyed by plunging the cocoons into boiling water. In either case the silk filaments were then wound on reels, except in those cases where the cocoon covering was tangled, when it had to be spun like wool or cotton.

The silk industry was transmitted from China to the Near East in the sixth century AD, before the arrival of Islam. However, it was under the Muslims that its manufacture became important, with the result that in due course Islamic silk replaced Byzantine in the European markets, dominating them until the seventh century AH (thirteenth century AD).

7.3 A Turkish woman beating
cotton to remove impurities
before spinning.

Indeed, silk remained the most important Islamic export to the
West until the nineteenth century.

The Islamic state established the silk industry in all Muslim
lands, from India and Turkestan in the east to Sicily and Spain
in the west. State factories produced silk bearing the name of
the ruler, place of manufacture, name of the factory manager,
and the year when made. Such material found its way
westwards, to be used in churches as covers for the tombs of the
saints. Even now there are still silk covers in some churches
bearing the Arabic holy passage *La Ilaha illa Allah* ('There is no
god but God'), and until recently Islamic silk textiles remained
a highly valued commodity in the West. Figures 7.5 and 7.6
show some examples. Moreover, the artistic use of colour and

7.4 Preparing cotton fibres for spinning by *left* carding and *right* combing. Sixteenth century AD. British Library, London.

7.5 Persian woven-silk fabric with a Kufic inscription and a design of animals. Formerly in the church of Saint Josse, Paris. Tenth century AD. Musée National du Louvre, Paris.

pattern in Muslim silk textiles became an inspiration to European designers (Fig. 7.7). The influence first appeared in Spain and Italy, and then spread throughout Europe. It can also be seen in the decorative designs of the garments worn by subjects in Italian, Spanish, French, German, and Dutch paintings (Fig. 7.7).

7.6 Silk fabric made in Spain during the Muslim period, woven with a design of peacocks and stylised Arabic lettering. Eleventh to twelfth century AD. Musée de Cluny, Paris.

7.1.2 Textile machinery

Spinning is the process of drawing out and then twisting or winding textile fibres into a continuous thread. Various forms of spindle for doing this were developed among ancient civilisations. The more common type, which was used mostly by women, was a short tapering stick notched at one end and weighted by a whorl or disc of stone, clay, metal or wood, at the other. The disc acted as a primitive flywheel; the spindle was twirled to twist the thread, which was then wound on it. Spindle specifications are to be found in manuals for the *muhtasib*. Figure 7.8 shows such a spindle being used.

7.7 Carved panels on wooden doors in the Cathedral of Notre Dame, Le Puy, France. The border pattern down the sides is derived from an Arabic inscription and was probably inspired by designs on Islamic textiles imported into France. Twelfth century AD.

As well as the hand-spindle, the spinning wheel came into use. The history of the spinning wheel has been a subject of great significance to historians of technology, for not only did it represent a step forward in textile manufacture but it was also important in the development of mechanical engineering. This is because it incorporates the early application of an endless belt or rope drive and probably demonstrates the first use of a flywheel in a machine. At one time controversy arose about the invention of the spinning wheel: claims were made for its origin in China, India and even in Europe. However, the spinning wheel appeared in Europe only at the end of the seventh century AH (thirteenth century AD), whereas an illustration of such a device in China has been found dating from two hundred years earlier. It is also clear that the spinning wheel was one of the many benefits introduced by the Arabs during their period in Sicily and Spain, where they took it along with knowledge of silk culture and the way to use a machine for twisting the threads of several cocoons into one strong thread.

Ibn Miskawayh, who died at a very great age in 421 AH/AD 1030, was an historian, physician and philosopher; in his main work *Kitab Tajarib al-Umam* (*Experiences of Nations*) he wrote about a machine for spinning silk:

7.8 A woman holding a spindle is included (on the right) in this detail from a village scene illustrating a manuscript of the *Maqamat* of al-Hariri. Thirteenth century AD. Bibliotheque Nationale, Paris.

Have you ever seen the silk spinner [*ibrism*] winding it [silk?] on a number of distaffs [*mighzal*] attached to hooks on polo-sticks [*sawladjan*] [as it were] or glass? I said I had. He went on: Do you not know that all the trouble of the worker consists in setting up and arranging the machine; after that he has only to watch the tails of the distaffs and keep on twisting them? Now we have arranged the machines the distaffs are revolving, the silk is taut, and the winding is proceeding; but if we leave the place, the force of rotation will weaken, there being no motive power to renew it; it will begin to slacken, the velocity of revolution of the distaffs will be reduced, and they will begin to unwind, rotating in the opposite direction. No one will be there to attend to them so that, one by one, they will fall off, and finally none will remain.

This description, which comes only as a metaphor during a dialogue, was not intended to be a full technical description; nevertheless, it is still quite useful. It makes clear that, after reeling, the threads of silk were wound on spools, two or three being wound together for strength, while the twisting or throwing of the silk threads is a process similar to spinning. Ibn Miskawayh was referring either to silk-thread multi-spindle throwing, or to a twisting machine that was used in the third century AH (tenth century AD) in the Eastern Caliphate of Islam. This was the machine the Arabs later introduced to Sicily and which appeared in Italy at the end of the seventh century AH (thirteenth century AD).

Unfortunately, Muslim engineers did not describe or illustrate the machines used widely in everyday life; they took them for granted. As a result we do not find pictures of textile machinery, though a rare illustration was found in a manuscript of Muqamat by al-Hariri, dated 636 AH/AD 1237 and showing a girl operating a wheel (Fig. 7.9). The machine depicted could have been either a spinning wheel or a spool-winding wheel. However, the date of this manuscript is much later than the early use of these wheels, as Ibn Miskawayh's text indicates.

After spinning, a series of preparatory operations were undertaken before weaving took place. These included reeling (removing yarn from the spindle), winding (filling the weft spools), and warping (preparing the warp for attachment to the loom).

Weaving is, of course, the major operation in manufacturing textiles and is carried out on the loom. The basic principle is to interlace one set of filaments or threads (known as the warp), with another series (known as the weft), the loom holding taut the length-wise warp while the cross-wise weft is woven in. The loom is certainly one of the greatest single achievements in the history of civilisation, though it is not a single invention but the result of a series of contributions and improvements. Historians of technology are still discussing its origin, trying to decide whether it was in Syria and the Near East or in China. Whatever the final outcome may be, it is undeniable that significant original developments took place in Syria and Egypt before the advent of Islam, and various types of looms, including drawlooms, were in use there. Under Islam these looms continued to develop, as we can see from the striking advances in the quality and the wide variety of Muslim textiles.

Foot treadles to lift and lower alternate warp threads were added, and looms with these became so common that in Spain the poet al-Rusafi (d. 573 AH/AD 1177) mentioned them in one of his poems. In the horizontal loom, when one treadle is depressed the shuttle is thrown from one hand to the other through the gap or 'shed' so formed between the warp threads and the fabric is then beaten with a 'reed' (a device rather like a comb that spaces the threads evenly). Then the other treadle is depressed to open the 'counter shed', the shuttle again passed through, and the weft beaten home. With two treadles and two 'heddles' (sets of parallel cords for guiding the warp threads), only plain or 'tabby' (striped) cloth can be woven. With more of both, however, simple patterns can be produced.

In the Near East textile designs of patterns and decorations went beyond the production of mere geometrical shapes. They developed into figures representing animals, mythical birds, humans and even hunting scenes. However, such complicated

7.9 Another illustration from the *Maqamat* of al-Hariri, showing a girl working at either a spinning wheel or a spool-winding wheel (the same machine was often used for both purposes). Baghdad, Thirteenth century AD. Bibliothèque Nationale, Paris.

designs required the capacity to lift individual warp threads at will; the device invented for doing this was the draw harness (Fig. 7.10). Such drawlooms were developed further by Muslim weavers until they had a highly sophisticated machine in their Tiraz factories.

An interesting description of drawlooms in a silk textile factory in Alexandria was reported by al-Nuwairi. Al-Sultan al-Ashraf Sha'ban (d. 778 AH/AD 1376) visited the works and the report runs as follows:

He [the Sultan] was conducted to *Dar at-Tiraz* [the textile factory] by his minister. He dismounted, entered and went up the staircase to the place where there were looms and stores. He observed every weaver at his loom weaving decorated textiles and [also saw] complete cloths [*badlat*] of different colours, already folded for the use of the harem.

He went round the looms, observing them and putting his head below them to see their lower parts, and enjoyed himself by looking at the weavers while they were working and throwing their shuttles to and fro. He raised his head to see the tops of the looms where the 'draw boys' raised up and [then] lowered the top threads; he observed how the motifs of birds, geometric designs [*dalat* and *shaderwanat*] and other patterns were produced by these threads that went up and came down until each of the bird and other motifs were completed.

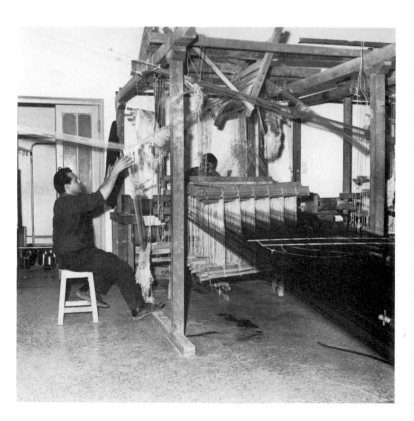

7.10 A draw loom for weaving brocade in Fez, Morocco.

He continued to go round looking at every kind [of thing] until he passed by an old weaver working at his loom, throwing his shuttle once to the right and once to the left and producing in this way a beautiful fabric like spring flowers.

The Sultan then saw what was [stored] in the *Dar at-Tiraz* of Alexandria, namely, brocade [*zarakish*], striped cloth [*raqm*] and golden silk robes [that were] completely finished. He chose some of these to be sent with him and left the rest until they should be completed.

Specifications were issued in the manuals for the *muhtasib* about the widths and lengths of woven silk cloth, the number of divisions in the weaver's comb and minimum possible weights. Regulations similar to those of al-Saqati occur in the municipal ordinances of Christian Seville and Toledo, clearly indicating the continuity in silk-weaving procedures. The diffusions of complex textile designs from Muslim Spain and Sicily to Italy and the rest of Europe also imply the concomitant diffusion of the drawloom.

Finishing. After weaving, fabric was subjected to a certain number of *finishing operations* before it was considered ready for sale. First, the woven cloth was inspected and all extraneous matter was picked out. Then woollen cloth was fulled (pressed) in order to felt it and thicken it; it also often underwent subsequent washing or 'scouring'. Linen was beaten too, so that its surface was improved, and then washed. The *daqqaq* or beater was the craftsman who carried out the fulling and beating; his was a separate craft from weaving, the beaters being subject to control by the *muhtasib*.

After fulling and scouring, the cloth was stretched in the open air for drying. Then followed the bleaching of wool, cotton and linen by the *qassar* (bleacher) and, finally, pressing.

7.1.3 Trades and crafts in the textile industry

It is possible to gain an idea of the importance of the Islamic textile industry by looking at a classification of trades and crafts in Damascus as given in *Kitab al-hisba* (*Book of Complaints* [*for the muhtasib*]) of Ibn al-Mubarrid (tenth century AH/ sixteenth century AD). He started his classification with weavers, claiming there were 100 types (*sinf*). He then gave a list of ten kinds of cotton weavers, more than twenty types of linen weavers, more than forty for silk (where drawboys were also employed to help the master weavers on the drawlooms), more than ten for rugs and carpets, and more than five for canvas and sacks.

7.11 Traditional carpet weaving in Persia.

Other trades and crafts related to the textile industry included merchants who sold new cloth, and those who traded in used cloth and rags. There were also merchants of silk and threads, bleachers, beaters, dyers, spinners, and various other craftsmen. All were organised into their own guilds and were subject to quality control by the *muhtasib* and to trade regulations issued by the government.

In the state textile factory at Alexandria there was a director general for the factory (*nazir*), while an inspector (*musharif*) assisted him and stored the finished products. The *'amel* made up the accounts and kept an eye on everything in the factory, while the *shahid* dealt with financial administration. In other Islamic cities these officers were not always the same.

7.2 PAPER

The introduction and spread of the paper-making industry in the Near East and Western Mediterranean was one of the main technological achievements of Islamic civilisation. It was a milestone in the history of mankind.

The early history of paper is now becoming clear. While it is possible that during the third century BC some types of paper were made in Asia, a more reliable date is that of AD 105, when paper was being produced in China from mulberry bark. It has, however, also been claimed that the Chinese of that time eliminated all non-Chinese centres for paper-making in Asia and so monopolised its manufacture. Whatever the truth of this, Arabic sources report that their paper industry started at Samarqand in the middle of the second century AH (eighth century AD) when some Chinese prisoners of war were taken there after the Battle of the Talas River in 133 AH/AD 751. Al-Qazwini, quoting another source, said 'Prisoners of war were brought from China. Among these was someone who knew [about] the manufacture of paper and so he practised it. Then it spread until it became a main product for the people of Samarqand, from whence it was exported to all countries'.

With the introduction of paper-making to the Muslim world and its spread during the second to fourth centuries AH (eighth to ninth centuries AD) a revolution took place in the industry. Writing material was freed from monopoly and paper became a very inexpensive product.

The oldest extant Egyptian paper bearing Arabic script dates from the period 178–97 AH/AD 796–815, though the earliest-dated paper only goes back to 256 AH/AD 874. However, we also know that factories for paper-making were established in Baghdad at the end of the second century AH (eighth century AD), and according to the historian of science Robert Forbes, there were floating paper mills on the Tigris by the fourth century AH (tenth century AD). Paper mills then spread to Syria and were established at Damascus, Tiberias, Tripoli, and other places. Egypt followed, with a mill at Cairo, and then North Africa, where Fez became a noted paper-making centre. Finally the manufacture of paper reached Muslim Sicily and Spain, Jativa in the Valencia region becoming famous for its products. Only later did paper-making spread to Europe and then rather slowly, the first paper mill being established at Fabriano in Italy in 1276 AD; it took another century and more before a mill was established at Nüremberg in Germany in 1390.

The manufacture of paper created a cultural revolution. It facilitated the production of books on an unprecedented scale, and in less than a century hundreds of thousands of manuscripts spread throughout the Islamic countries. Books became available everywhere and the profession of bookseller (*warraq*) flourished; in Baghdad alone at the end of the third century AH (ninth century AD) there were more than a hundred premises at which books were made. Private libraries abounded, while public libraries were established everywhere, Baghdad containing no less than thirty six at the time of the Mongol devastation in AD 1258. Science, literature, philosophy and all fields of knowledge became, for the first time in the history of the Near East, available to all literate persons in every Muslim country.

The historian George Sarton expressed his astonishment that our word for paper should not have been derived from the Arabic in acknowledgement of the Arabs' great service in bringing it to the West. The probable reason he gave was that paper was mistakenly taken to resemble papyrus, and since no single word was used in Arabic for it, the word 'paper' came to be adopted. Yet there is a word in the paper-making industry that reminds us of the role of the Arabs in bringing the invention to Europe: this is the word 'ream' in English, 'resma' in Spanish, 'risma' in Italian, with similar words in other European languages. These all derive from the Arabic word *rismah*, meaning a bale or bundle of paper, though the word now refers to a specific quantity, either 480 sheets or, frequently, 500 or 516.

7.2.1 Technology of paper-making

We have already mentioned *Kitab 'Umdat al Kuttab* (*Book of the Supports of the Scribes*) by Ibn Badis. The eleventh chapter of the book describes the method of making paper from flax, and it runs as follows:

Description of the manufacture of *Talkhi* paper. Take good white flax and purify it from its reed. Soak it in water and shred it with a comb until it is soft. Then soak it in the water of quicklime for one daylight and one night until the morning. Then knead it by hand and spread it out in the sun all daylight until it is dry [see Fig. 7.12(*a*)]. Return it to the water of quicklime, not the first water, and keep it for the whole of the second night till the morning. Knead it again by hand as before and spread it out in the sun. This is repeated during three, five or seven days. If you change the water of quicklime twice daily, it would be quicker. When it becomes extremely white, cut it by the shears into small pieces, then soak it in sweet water for seven days also and change the water every day. When it is free from quicklime, grind it in a mortar while it is wet. When it is soft and no knots are left, bring it into solution with water in a clean vessel until it is like silk. Then provide a mould of whatever size you choose. The mould is made like a basket [from] samna reeds. It has open walls. Put an empty vessel under the mould. Agitate the flax with your hand and throw it in the mould [see Fig. 7.12(*b*)]. Adjust it by hand so that it is not thick in one place and thin in another. When it is even, and is freed from its water while in the mould, and when you have achieved the desired result, [drop] it on a

7.12 Three photographs of
papermaking in Kashmir in 1917.
Above Pulp drying and bleaching in
the sun.
Centre The pulp placed in the
mould.
Below Sheets of paper drying on a
wall.

plate, and then take it and stick it on a flat wall [see Fig. 7.12(*c*)]. Adjust it by your hand and leave it until it dries and drops. Then take fine wheat flour and starch, half of each, knead the starch and the flour in cold water until nothing thick remains. Heat water until it boils over and pour it on the flour mixture until it becomes thin. Take the paper and with your hand, paint it over and place it on a reed. When all the sheets of paper are painted and are dry, paint them on the other face. Return them to a plate and sprinkle them thinly with water. Collect the sheets of paper, stack them, then polish them as you polish cloth, if God wills.

The basic process just described by Ibn Badis was not the only one that was used. It seems that his book was addressed to the learned and to copyists to instruct them how to make ink and paper, and to bind books, thus saving themselves having to buy such materials or have the work done for them. Industrial methods utilised larger and more mechanised equipment.

According to the historian Dard Hunter, the main Islamic innovations in paper technology can be summarised as follows:

(1) *The invention of the bamboo mould* This was the mould from which the wet sheet of paper was placed to drain, and could be removed while still moist. Hunter says that this constituted '*the first real step in paper-making*, as it enabled the artisan to form sheets continually upon the same mould'. In other words, this invention changed paper-making from a craft into an industry. Hunter adds that 'even the most modern paper-machine employs precisely the same principles'.

Before this invention, the mould was a bamboo framework over which a piece of coarse-woven fabric was stretched. The wet sheet of paper could not be taken from the cloth and the sheet was dried in the mould before removal. The new invention provided a smooth and firm material from which the moist sheet would readily become free. Such a mould cover was made by placing thin strips of rounded bamboo side by side and stitching or lacing them together at regular intervals with silk, flax or horsehair. The bamboo strips and the stitches left marks that are known as 'laid lines' and 'chain lines'; in examining a sheet of paper from a manuscript of the *Qu'ran* dating from the sixth century AH (twelfth century AD), Hunter counted six and a half bamboo strips to every centimetre.

The laced bamboo mould cover resembled a piece of matting which could be rolled or folded. When a sheet of paper was to be made, the covering was placed loosely on the shallow wooden framework, which supported it firmly. The whole mould, both frame and cover, was then dipped in to the vat of macerated pulp and brought to the surface loaded with the wet fibrous material. The matting was then lifed from the framework and the wet layer deposited flat on a board, the workman rolling up the matting from the top edge to the bottom, leaving the moist, tender sheet firm and unwrinkled. This was the simplest and best method that could have been devised, and 'upon this form of mould the manner of making paper in all ages has depended'.

(2) *Flax and cotton, and linen rags in paper-making* The exact dates at which these materials were introduced are not yet certain. We have seen that Ibn Badis was using flax and it is reported that both flax and linen rags were both employed at an early date, but unwoven cotton and linen rags appeared only later. These were important innovations however, for the Chinese used the bark of mulberry trees and this was not available in Muslim lands, so substitutes had to be found.

(3) *The fermentation of rags* For making some kinds of paper the Muslims introduced the method of disintegrating linen rags by placing them in heaps, saturating them with water, and then letting fermentation occur; after this the mass was boiled with plant or wood ash. It was an alternative to the process using quicklime described by Ibn Badis.

(4) *Sizing the paper* Early Muslim paper-makers attempted to imitate parchment, and achieved this by sizing paper with wheat starch, an innovation that rendered the surface more suitable for writing upon with ink.

(5) *Using a trip-hammer to beat rags into pulp* The principle of the trip-hammer was known both in the Near East and in China. But Hunter says that 'later in the development of paper-making by the Arabs, a trip-hammer was put to use. The workers treading upon the end of the horizontal tilt-bar of this implement caused the hammer to fall heavily upon the substance to be beaten. This required far less labour than the Chinese process'.

(6) *First use of a water-wheel for driving trip-hammers in paper mills* This is a question of some historical importance and it seems appropriate at this stage to mention the views of some historians of technology. Robert Forbes states that 'in the tenth century [AD] floating paper-mills were found on the Tigris near Baghdad', whereas Hunter thinks that the water-powered

stamping mill used for beating was 'invented' in AD 1151 at
Jativa, the centre of the Islamic paper industry in Muslim Spain.
Again, the historian Glick claims there is documentation to
show that the Muslims of Jativa used a water-driven paper mill
and he also raises the general question whether the fulling mill
in Christian Spain (which also uses a trip-hammer) was inspired
by an Islamic model or a Northern European one.

Certainly, the trip-hammer was used in paper-making and in
rice husking (see Fig. 8.15, p. 218 below), both of which were
introduced into Spain by Muslims. Similarly, the vertical wheel
which drove the trip-hammers was related to the noria, and was
again a Muslim introduction into Spain. Moreover, though the
horizontal mill was in use in Christian Spain for non-industrial
purposes, the vertical wheel was unknown there before the
middle of the fourth century AH (tenth century AD). Another
clue is that in Spanish the vertical mill was sometimes
designated by the Arabism '*aceña*' derived from *saniya*, the
generic name for the vertical wheel. All this strongly suggests
that industrial water mills with vertical wheels were brought
into Christian Spain by Islam. It is true, of course, that the
vertical wheel had been known in France and Italy since Roman
times, but only for corn milling; it therefore seems that the
industrial uses of this kind of wheel were due to Muslims, who
transmitted them to Spain and thus to the rest of Europe.

7.2.2 Qualities and sizes of paper

Paper was used extensively in the Islamic world for all kinds of
documents and correspondence, for books and even for
wrapping. It was also an important export both from the
eastern and the western Muslim paper mills, and Arabic sources
contain information about the different grades and standard
sizes available, as well as their uses.

Al-Qalqashandi said that the paper of Baghdad (*al-Baghdadi*)
was the best quality, and was used for writing the Caliph's
documents and treaties. The *Shami* (Syrian) was of various
grades, one of which – the *Hamwi* (i.e. from Hama) – was used in
government departments. Among the remaining grades was a
lightweight type known as 'Birds' Paper', so-called because it
was thin enough to be sent by carrier pigeon; it was in effect the
equivalent of our air-mail paper. The varieties of Egyptian
paper were to a certain extent similar to those of Syria.

Paper was manufactured in shades of every colour. In more
than one manuscript we read recipes of how to produce paper
in such colours as red, green, blue, rose, yellow, onion, and

purple, while there are even instructions explaining how to make paper look old.

7.3 LEATHER

Skins were known to man before textiles and the transformation of skins into leather was developed throughout the ages in every civilisation. By the fifth century AH (eleventh century AD) the technique of manufacturing leather had been improved at the hand of Muslim craftsmen and there was a collection of established practices; these were transferred to the West and from then until the nineteenth century there were no changes in the basic principles of leather production.

7.3.1 Technology of making leather

There are three main stages in leather manufacture: preparation of the skins for tanning; the tanning process itself; and finally finishing the tanned material. Details of each stage differ according to the nature of the skin or hide and the type of goods to be made from it.

Salt was known early on as a preservative, the decay of hides being delayed by salting and then drying them in the sun. Once this had been done the dry, salted hides were taken to the tanner, who soaked them in water to remove dung, earth and albuminous matter. Next the hides were subjected to the action of lime to open their texture and soften the hair, which was then removed with special blunt-edged concave tools; any remaining flesh was taken off using a specially-designed two-handed fleshing knife. This last might require the prior application of a special treatment called 'swelling'. These preparatory techniques are only typical; they would differ according to the type of hide or skin.

After pre-treatment the raw material required further processing to turn it into leather. In brief, it required tanning to bring about chemical changes in the pelt to prevent decomposition and render it water-resistant, while still preserving the fibrous structure. The tanning process may be divided into three parts:

(*a*)   The oil process or 'chamoising';
(*b*)   A mineral process or 'tawing';
(*c*)   Vegetable tanning.

Muslim tanners used all three methods, either individually or in combination.

The oil process was an ancient one in which the skins were softened with fatty material. It became called 'chamoising' from the French *chamois*, a word once thought to be related to the chamois or mountain goat of the Alps. However, Robert Forbes has pointed out that 'this goat can never have been very common or accessible', and he suggests that it is much more probable that the word is derived from the Arabic *shahm* meaning 'fat'.

Mineral tanning with alum was important in Islam. Full instructions were available in Arabic manuscripts for the use of alum and salt, and for the addition of other ingredients such as barley, flour and yoghurt. Some Arab sources also mention tanning with alum and then impregnating with oil.

Significant though mineral tanning may have been, the most important tanning process was that which made use of vegetable tannins. In some of the manuals for the *muhtasib* we learn that *qaraz* (*Mimosa nilotica*) which came from the Yemen was much preferred over gallnuts for tanning goatskin, though several other vegetable sources were used, including sumac (*rhus*).

After tanning, leather was given various finishes to improve its appearance and impart specific properties. The method adopted depended on the final product and included dyeing, so that one could obtain goods in a wide range of colours that embraced red, brown, blue, olive green, yellow, and black.

7.13 A tannery in Marrakesh, Morocco.

One of the most renowned products of Arabic tanners was cordwain leather from Cordoba in Spain, which became famous all over Europe. Its manufacture started there in the eighth century AH (fourteenth century AD), using the skin of the mouflon, 'a haired sheep, horned like a ram and skinned like a stag', which now survives in Corsica and Sardinia. Different procedures were used by the Spanish Muslims to manufacture the leather, among them tanning with sumac and tawing with alum. A greatly esteemed variety, brilliant scarlet in colour, is thought to have been obtained by first tawing with alum and then dyeing with the insect dye kermes.

The cordwainers made all kinds of leather goods, but footwear was their most notable product, with the result that they became famous as shoemakers. From Cordoba the special techniques which included mineral tanning, tanning with sumac, and a combination of both, together with finishing with oil, migrated to Morocco. From these two centres the secrets of the craft later spread all over Europe; the descriptions 'cordovan' and 'morocco' used for some European leathers are symbols of the transfer of this technology, which remained in use until the nineteenth century.

7.3.2 Leather products

The leather industry flourished in several Islamic countries to such a degree that it formed a significant export. Yemen in particular was an important centre, as was al-Ta'if in Hijaz and, of course, Cordoba and Morocco. Cairo was noted for its trade as well as its manufacturing, but all the major Islamic cities had their own leather industry. Indeed, the leather trade was so extensive in the middle of the seventh century AH (thirteenth century AD) that in Aleppo for instance, taxes levied on its tanneries exceeded the total of those from the rest of its industries.

The range of products was very wide. It included garments, sandals, shoes and boots, bags and containers, water-skins, buckets, sieves, musical instruments, and a host of other items. Most of the crafts and trades for making these products were classified in the *muhtasib* manuals and were subject to quality control. In *Ma'alim al-Qurba* (*On the Duties of the Muhtasib*) for example, instructions were given on controlling the quality of footwear, the specifications requiring the use of well-tanned grained leather from al-Ta'if. They warn against hides insufficiently tanned or burned with excessive tanning, while the threads and even the needles to be used are specified. Warnings are given against fradulent practices, one of which was to stuff women's shoes with rags.

7.3.3 Bookbinding

This is a subject for which much mateiral is available, since in libraries all over the world there are leather-bound Islamic manuscripts that have been the subject of study by art historians; in addition manuscripts have been preserved that describe bookbinding techniques in detail. One such is *Sina'at tasfir al-Kutub Wa-hall al-dhahab* (*The Art of Bookbinding and of Gilding*) by al-Sufyani, another *Kitab 'Umdat al-Kuttab* (*Book of the Supports of the Scribes*) by Ibn Badis that we have met frequently earlier on. The descriptions are clear, a chapter of the book by Ibn Badis starting: 'Chapter twelve: On the art (*Sina'a*) of bookbinding and the use of all its tools so that one can dispense with resorting to bookbinders. With descriptions of the slab, the whetstone, the blade, the sword, the awl, the press, the mallet, the needles, the rulers and the compasses'. He then gives details of all the tools, describing in addition those needed for decorating leather covers.

Al-Sufyani's book is even more detailed, for he was himself a bookbinder. One chapter discusses how to make the cover boards, another how to tie the quires of a book and to press, yet another how to cover with leather, to design the centrepiece and the way to work the headband. Then he devotes a chapter to making a solution of gold, washing it, soaking it with glue and finally writing with it. The last chapter is on decorating the leather binding.

Bookbinding was a respected craft, and like instrument-making was sometimes practised by learned men. The geographer al-Muqaddasi, who wrote at the end of the fourth century AH (tenth century AD), was also a bookbinder and proud to practise his craft on some of his journeys, while in *Al-Fihrist*, the index to Arabic literature compiled in the same century by Ibn al-Nadim, mention was made of a number of well-known bookbinders.

The practice of impressing beautiful designs using metal stamps – 'blind stamping' – was influenced by the Islamic art of bookbinding (Fig. 7.14). As for using a hot iron and gold leaf, this is thought to have spread all over Europe from Muslim Spain. Gold tooling seems to have evolved in Persia, from whence it reached England by way of Venice; it was a technique later to be applied to all kinds of leather objects.

7.14 A craftsman in Fez tooling leather.

8 *Agriculture and food technology*

8.1 THE ISLAMIC AGRICULTURAL REVOLUTION

After the spread of Islam into three continents in the first and second centuries AH (seventh and eighth centuries AD) a remarkable revolution took place. It began in the eastern reaches of the early Muslim world but by the end of the fifth century AH (eleventh century AD) it had been transmitted across the whole Islamic empire from Spain and Sicily to Transoxiana. This revolution had very far-reaching consequences. It affected agricultural production, incomes, population levels, urban growth, distribution of the labour force, industries, clothing, cooking and diet, as well as other spheres of activity.

8.1.1 New crops

One important aspect of the revolution was the introduction and diffusion of new crops into Islam. These included rice, sorghum, hard wheat (*Triticum durum*, used for pasta), sugar cane, cotton, watermelons, egg plants (*Solanum melongena*), spinach and many other crops, fruits, vegetables and flowers. Diffusion was very wide, the new plants coming to be grown throughout almost the entire Islamic world, with not a few proving of great economic importance.

This was indeed remarkable, all the more so when we remember that the diffusion over this very large area was compressed into the first four centuries of Islam. Moreover, most of the plants were of tropical origin and not easy to grow in cooler and drier regions, so that their introduction had revolutionary effects on the whole agricultural system. Indeed, such an achievement was not to be equalled until the Renaissance and after, when whole new continents were discovered.

8.1 A harvest scene of the twelfth century AD. In the centre of the upper row a man is using a sickle; to the right of him two others are digging with spades. Below are shown winnowing, to the left, and threshing by means of a *nawraj* drawn by oxen, to the right. Bibliothèque Nationale, Paris.

درختهای انار هم هست کردا که در حوض تمام به برگزار

باغی عین باغ همین است در وقت زرد شدن انار بسیار

8.1.2 New farming practices

The introduction of the new plants was accompanied by changes in farming practice. The traditional growing season had always been winter, with land mostly lying fallow during the summer, but now a virtually new agricultural season was opened because many of the new crops required hot conditions to flourish. Rice, cotton, sugar cane, egg plants, watermelons, hard wheat, and sorghum all became Muslim summer crops, though rice and hard wheat were also winter crops in some of the very warm areas. With the introduction of summer crops, the rhythm of the agricultural year was radically altered; previously idle land and labour became more productive.

With the introduction of a summer season, crop rotation was introduced to make more intensive use of the land. Under the Roman and Byzantine systems the normal practice had been to crop the ground only once every two years, but with the Muslim agricultural revolution crop rotation made it possible to harvest the land four times or more instead of once during every twenty four month period.

8.1.3 Manure

Multiple harvesting reduced the fertility of the land. To combat this and actually to improve some soils, Arab manuals on agriculture recommended all kinds of manures, each with its own special qualities and applications, as well as the use of ashes, marl and various other materials.

8.1.4 New ploughing requirements

More ploughing, digging, hoeing and harrowing also became necessary. Al-Marqrizi (early ninth century AH/fifteenth century AD) mentioned that before sugar-cane was planted in Egypt, the land had to be ploughed six times using heavy ploughs, and Ibn al-Bassal recommended up to ten ploughings and manurings before cotton seed was sown (Fig. 8.3).

8.1.5 Revolution in irrigation

The new crops and their rotation around the seasons necessitated more water, especially since the new summer ones such as sugar, rice and cotton were particularly demanding in this respect. Before the rise of Islam the old irrigation systems had already fallen into decay and the areas that were watered had

8.2 (overleaf) The Mogul emperor Babur directing the planting of a garden of flowers and fruit trees in Kabul. Illustration from a manuscript of about AD 1600. Victoria and Albert Museum, London.

8.3 Illustration of ploughing from a manuscript of the sixteenth century AD. British Library, London.

shrunk; in any event, pre-Islamic methods were inadequate to meet the new agricultural revolution. Indeed, an important aspect of this revolution was that it was accompanied by a complete review of the whole system. As a result, old irrigation systems were everywhere repaired and extended, and new ones were built. The technology of water-raising devices and methods of storing, conveying and distributing water, were developed and diffused. Techniques for prospecting hidden sources and underground systems (*qanats*) for collecting and conveying such water were successfully devised (see Chapter 3). It has been said that 'So great was the progress made that it would only be a slight exaggeration to claim that by the eleventh century [AD] there was hardly a river, stream, oasis, spring, known aquifer or predictable flood that went unused'.

8.1.6 Extensive use of all agricultural land

The revolution was not confined to irrigated or fertile areas, for virtually all categories of land came to be farmed more intensively. Arabic farming manuals identified far more types of soil than the ancients had done, and by considering not only the type but also its moisture and temperature, Islamic agriculturists were able to see their potential much more clearly. Muslim manuals assumed that all soils would be used to full capacity, even the inferior lands which ancient writers had never thought of utilising. Thus the novel crops and the new specialised knowledge of rotation, land cultivation and soil expertise allowed the margins of farming to be pushed back into near desert lands which previously had been used only for sporadic grazing, if used at all.

8.1.7 Manuals on agriculture (*Kutub al-filaha*)

Such significant and new economic activity could not escape the attention of Muslim scientists, who set about developing a science of agriculture ('*Ilm al-filaha*). Important agricultural manuals were written, among them *Kitab al-filaha al-Nabatiyya* (*Book of Nabatean Agriculture*) of Ibn Wahshiyya. (The book purports to preserve the agricultural traditions of the Nabateans in Mesopotamia.) Important books on agricultural science were written in Muslim Spain during the eleventh and twelfth centuries AD, and among these were the works of Ibn al-Hassal an Ibn al-ᶜAwwan and several others. Some of these books were translated into Spanish and Latin, and so became a source of inspiration for writings that appeared later in the West.

During the fifth century AH (eleventh century AD) Arab agronomists in Spain carried out part of their research and some of their experiments in the royal botanical gardens in Toledo and Seville. These experimental gardens were the first of their kind and were not copied in the West until the sixteenth century, where they first appeared in the university cities of northern Italy (Fig. 8.4).

8.2 AGRICULTURAL IMPLEMENTS

8.2.1 The plough

During the passage of centuries, an intimate knowledge of Mediterranean climate and types of soil, techniques of ploughing, sowing, harvesting and threshing was built up. Among the agricultural implements that were developed, the chief was the plough. The design – the Mediterranean plough – proved its worth, cutting furrows only to a shallow depth, a technique that was ideally suited to the ground and to the prevailing climate and humidity. As a result, it continued to be used in the Near East and in all Mediterranean countries, Muslim and European, until modern times (Fig. 8.5).

The historian al-Maqrizi reported the use of heavier ploughs to prepare the land for sugar-cane cultivation in Egypt. It was also reported that in Iran different ploughs were used to suit different soil conditions. But in general the nature of the soil in Muslim countries did not require heavy ploughs. With the introduction of tractors in the Middle East, attempts were

8.4 A Moorish garden in Spain, the Generalife, Granada, elegantly laid out with pools and fountains amongst the luxuriant growth of trees, shrubs and flowers.

made at first to use the heavy mould-board plough in conditions where the Mediterranean plough had always been used, but the results were disappointing. For this reason, modern tractor-drawn implements still use either the Mediterranean plough with multiple shares, or the disc plough. Such present-day evidence as this has proved conclusively that Muslim peasants always made use of the best possible plough for their soil conditions.

In Arabic sources we find an extensive array of technical terms for all parts of the plough and for ploughing operations. Such terms clearly indicate that the technique of ploughing was based on extensive experience.

8.2.2 Harrows and rakes

Harrows were animal-drawn implements used after ploughing to break up clods and to cover the seeds (Fig. 8.6). One design

8.5 The shallow Mediterranean plough in use in Pakistan.

8.6 A simple spiked harrow drawn by oxen in Turkey.

8.7 A spade depicted in a Persian manuscript of the fourteenth century AD. Edinburgh University Library.

was known as *al-Mijarr*, another as *al-mislafah*. Both were beams with projecting teeth to engage with the soil. The *Mijarr* had two holes on the ends and two pairs of ropes attached, while at the top of the beam were two holes in which a bent hoop was fixed; in the middle there was a long handle for holding it. This design was attached to two oxen, and similar harrows are still in use in some Islamic lands.

Another type of harrow was *al-Maliq*, described as a 'broad wooden board drawn by oxen. It is weighted to make level the furrows left by the share of the plough and thus bury the seeds'. Again we find such an implement still in use.

There were also wooden rakes, which of course were hand implements. One type was *al-musht*, one purpose of which was to comb the ground to cover the seeds: 'It was a cross beam with teeth and a "handle-stick" in the centre'.

8.2.3 Digging and tilling implements

Various other hand implements were used for digging the land in places such as orchards and vegetable gardens where the plough was not necessary. The spade (*al-mishat*) took various shapes (Fig. 8.7), while the hoe (*al-mi'zaqah*) was also used for digging. The shovel (*al-mijnab* or *al-mijrafah*) was for lifting the soil after digging.

8.2.4 Harvesting

The prevailing harvesting implement was the balanced sickle in which the blade, toothed or smooth, was bent back at the handle end and then curved forward in a long sweep (see Fig.

8.1, p. 202 above). This enabled stems to be cut with less strain on the wrist, the stems being cut mostly near the base; reaping was done from a squatting position. Stalks were then tied into sheaves and transported to threshing sites in the villages.

8.2.5 Threshing and winnowing

Threshing was usually undertaken on threshing grounds (*bayadir*) at the edges of the villages. Wheat sheaves coming from the fields were laid down in circular heaps and three main threshing methods were used.

One was to allow oxen to tread the sheaves, but this was usually a preliminary operation to break the staw and flatten the heap. A second method was to use a threshing board or sledge (*lawh*). This was a thick, heavy, flint-studded board, slightly bent at the front (Figs. 8.8 (*a*) and (*b*)), which was dragged over the threshing floor (*baydar*) by animals. It was an efficient device and is still in use in some villages around the Mediterranean. The third technique used the *nawraj*, which consisted of two thick beams or skids held together by two cross-beams. Between the skids were two axles, each fitted with a set of toothed discs. The *nawraj* with its discs was driven over the wheat by a driver seated on what was essentially a cart-like vehicle (Fig. 8.9; cf. Fig. 8.1, p.202 above). This machine is also still in use in some villages in Syria, Iran and other Muslim countries.

Winnowing is the process whereby the chaff is blown away from the grain after threshing is completed. In a fair wind the peasant would throw the threshed wheat into the air using a wooden winnowing fork (*al-midrah*), the wind carrying the chaff away while the grain dropped to the ground (see again Fig. 8.1 above).

8.2.6 Controlling the quality of the implements

Steel was always used in ploughshares, spades, sickles, and the other implements of Muslim agriculture. In the manuals written for the guidance of the *muhtasib* there were special chapters on how he should control the products made by blacksmiths.

8.3 FLOUR AND BREAD

An outstanding feature of Islamic agriculture was the predominance of wheat, which was both a staple and major food. In

8.8(*a*) The underside of a Cypriot threshing board showing the flints set into it. Science Museum, London.

8.8(*b*) A horse-drawn threshing board in Turkey.

8.9 Threshing by *nawraj* in Egypt in the early twentieth century.

Northern Europe during the Middle Ages, even the upper classes ate mainly rye bread, and only at the end of the period did they begin to consume bread made from wheat.

However Arabic sources discussing state taxes and revenues (*kharaj*) abound with information on the extent of wheat growing; we find that some areas, such as Upper Mesopotamia (*Jazira*) and parts of Syria and Egypt, became granaries supplying neighbouring countries.

In some village households and among the nomads the hand rotary quern was used to *mill flour* (Fig. 8.10). Its grindstones were 45–50 centimetres in diameter, the lower being the stationary one. There was a wooden peg in the centre about

8.10 A woman milling grain with a hand quern. Sixteenth century AD. British Library, London.

which the upper stone revolved, and a wooden handle near the stone's outer edge by which it was rotated. The quern was fed with grain through a central space around the peg and flour left it at the edge of the stones, dropping on to a cloth placed under it.

By the fourth century AH (tenth century AD) such hand querns had largely fallen into disuse, even in villages. With the rise of the big Islamic cities and improvement in standards of living, the flour-milling industry flourished and soon increased to such a size that water mills were used everywhere, both in villages as well as near the cities themselves. There were floating mills and tidal mills, and in Baghdad one mill alone is reported to have had 100 pairs of stones with an annual turnover of 100 million dirhams (30 000 metric tons). Windmills were also used where there were favourable winds, as in Sistan, and there were also animal-driven mills.

Some of the water mills are still in operation in Islamic countries. For instance in Syria one can still see mills with horizontal water-wheels (norse type) (Fig. 8.11) and vertical ones (Vitruvian type) (Fig. 8.12), and until recently operating windmills were still to be found in Khurasan (Fig. 8. 13).

Whether it was a hand quern, a large water mill or windmill, the principles of operation were the same. Grinding was done by a rotating stone on top of a fixed one. The millstones themselves were made from special coarse sandstones, certain quarries being famous for supplying them; there was such a quarry at Amid on the upper Tigris, and another at Khollar, the latter supplying Persia until modern times.

Milling techniques were so highly developed in the Muslim world that all grades of flour could be produced, including white flour and semolina. Accordingly there was an elaborate technical terminology both for the parts of a milling installation as well as for its products.

Rice was second only to wheat in importance both as a food in itself and in the form of rice-bread. It was one of the crops developed during the Muslim agricultural revolution, when wheat-bread was expensive. Indeed, rice-bread alleviated the economic problems that arose in some areas.

Husking the rice was mainly done by pounding with pivoted pestles. The pestle was attached at right-angles to the end of a shaft, which was pivoted and counterbalanced so that it could be worked by hand or foot. From this developed the rice mill, which was in essence a water-driven trip-hammer. Both the man-operated pivoted pestle and the rice mill travelled with the spread of rice cultivation to the western lands of Islam. And

8.11 Horizontal water-wheel of a mill at Band-i Amir, Fars, Iran.

the spread of rice cultivation to the western lands of Islam. And as mentioned earlier, a similar water-driven trip-hammer mill was simultaneously in use in the paper industry. The water-driven trip-hammer mill is still to be found in Iran (Fig. 8.15).

Several varieties of *bread* were made in Muslim counties, an Arabic manuscript listing no less than twelve (Fig. 8.16). Most of the plain bread was flat and made from wheat flour. The simplest method of baking, still used in mobile Bedouin camps, is to place a convex steel plate on two or three stones and make a fire underneath (Fig. 8.17). The dough is flatened until very thin, then thrown on top of this hot plate; baking takes about

8.12 Vitruvian water-wheel near Isfahan, Iran.

8.13 Horizontal windmill at Nishtafun, Khurasan, Iran.

8.14(*a*) The millstone of a flour mill at Band-i Amır.

three minutes. Such bread is called *Khubz-il Saj* or '*Saj* bread' in Syria and Palestine, though it is also known simply as *khubz-ryuq* or thin bread.

Bread was also baked in an oven, the type known as a *tabun* being used in Palestine and described by al-Muqaddasi:

The *tabun* is for the villagers. This is a small oven (*tannur*) placed under the ground and the floor . . . is strewn with pebbles. Dung is set on fire around and above it. When it becomes red hot, loaves of dough are thrown down on the pebbles.

The *tabun* is essentially a household oven and is still in use in some Palestinian villages, though now its floor is usually strewn with broken pottery. *Tabun* bread (*khubz al-tabun*) is still well-known. There were other varieties of household oven of a similar size to be found in the villages of Islamic countries, and they too were usually called a *tannur* (Figs. 8.17, 8.18 and 8.19).

8.14(*b*) Preparing the surface of a millstone. Sixteenth century AD. British Library, London.

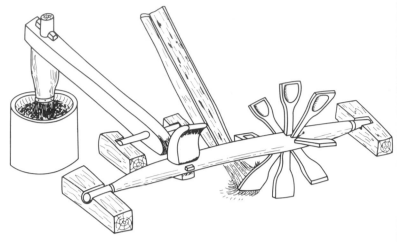

8.15 Water-driven trip mill for rice and other grain.

8.16 Kneading dough, Pakistan.

In most Islamic cities baking became a profession, though certainly in Muslim Spain and in Morocco most bread was still made in the home and only taken to the bakery for baking. None but travellers or the poorer classes with no home bought bread in the market.

8.17 Baking flat loaves on a metal plate placed immediately over the fire. Western Turkey.

8.18 A small underground oven for cooking bread. Eastern Turkey.

The professional bakers used large ovens, usually called a *furn*, and the baker was known as a *farran* or *khabbaz*; he was subject to the quality control of the *muhtasib*. The designs of large ovens varied. Some had a flat horizontal floor without pebbles; on one side of this floor inside the oven, a fire was kindled. Flattened dough was transferred to the oven by means of flat wooden shovels with long blades, and the baked loaves drawn out in the same way. In other cases the oven had an inclined brick wall covered with pebbles, the fire being in front of this inclined wall. The lumps of flattened dough were placed individually on the hot pebbles.

8.19 A larger bread oven in Turkey. A shovel is used to place the loaves in position near the glowing wood at the back of the oven.

8.20 Flat oval loaves, distinctively patterned on top, being prepared by a bakery team in Kabul, Afghanistan.

8.4 SUGAR

Sugar is a basic commodity that owes much of its development and spread to the Islamic civilisation. Sugar-cane was known in India, from whence it spread to neighbouring countries, though it did not become a foodstuff in pre-Islamic times. In Western literature it was seldom mentioned before the seventh century AD, and not many people were aware of it; honey was still used as a sweetening agent in Europe right through the Middle Ages.

The cultivation of sugar-cane was introduced into Persia soon after the Islamic conquest. Sugar-cane plantations and the sugar-refining industry then spread throughout the whole Islamic Mediterranean area, and sugar became a foodstuff as well as a medicinal material in all Muslim countries.

Of all the foods of the Middle Ages, sugar was the only one which required chemical processing; indeed, its manufacture necessitated high technological competence whether in the cultivation of the sugar-cane itself or in its refining. This was partly because growing sugar-cane required large irrigated areas, and partly due to the fact than in making sugar from the cane a series of separate processes is involved. The industry was therefore beyond the resources of small farmers or artisans, and from the start the State played a vital role in sugar-cane plantations and in the establishment of sugar factories.

8.4.1 Sugar technology

There is no lack of information on sugar-cane cultivation in Islam to be found in various Arabic sources and in Muslim books on agriculture, especially in *Nihayat al Arab fi Funun al-Adab* (*The Ultimate Goal* [*in the Literary Arts*]) by al-Nuwairi, who gave a particularly good account. It is interesting to see that as well as providing a detailed description of sugar manufacture, he also found room to remark on the use of heavy ploughs (*maharith kibar*) necessary before the sugar-cane could be planted.

In the manufacturing process, the sugar-cane was first broken and then peeled on a special area of the farm before being transported to the factory. The factory was divided into various sections. In the first of these workers cut off the upper unsweet parts of the cane and also the lower ends to free it from any remaining roots and mud. A second group then sliced the cane into small pieces which were then dropped to a second section of the factory, where they were divided into equal lots for pressing or crushing. This was carried out in two stages. In the first a rotating stone press was used, after which the cane was placed in netted baskets (*halfa*). It then moved on to a second stage in which it went under a platform wheel press (*doulab at-takht*) where 'the wheel rotates by means of a beam until it [the sugar-cane] is pressed sufficiently and the remaining water is extracted'. The juice from both presses flowed into one storage tank.

After extraction, the juice was filtered and passed into a calibrated tank which, when full, transferred the juice to the cooking plant (*al-matbakh*). Here it received a second filtration and was then poured into a large 'kettle' (*al-khabiya*). The liquid was now boiled for a considerable time until its volume was reduced to a specified amount. A third filtration followed next, after which the liquid was decanted into eight smaller 'kettles'. When sufficient 'cooking' had been done, the liquid (now called *mahlab*) was poured into wide-topped pottery vessels, which were narrow at the bottom where they were perforated with three holes. The holes were initially plugged with straw from the sugar-cane. A bucket was placed under each vessel and into this there dripped a thick liquid known as 'dripping honey' (*al-'Asal al Qatr*). The pots were frequently replenished, those removed being hung up in another section of the factory so that any remaining 'honey' could drain away and be collected.

All residues from the filtering were pressed and cooked separately to produce a lower-quality 'honey' (*khabiya*). There were therefore three products in all: the *qand*, the *qatr* ('honey') and the *khabiya*; all were under the control of the supervisor who made a report each day and night.

When the *qand* became dry and white it was transferred to the sugar refining section. Here it was first dissolved in water in which some milk had been mixed and then cooked; white refined sugar and drainings (*qutara*) were the result. Each *qintar* of *qand* produced five twelfths of white sugar; the remaining seven twelfths was *qutara*. Some sugar was refined twice to give an extremely white and pure product.

Other accounts of sugar refining can be found in Arabic sources, but the description just given indicates the general way sugar was produced in Islam. It was said, however, that the best quality came from Egypt, Syria and the Jordan Valley, the last being renowned not only for its products but also for its export trade in sugar. Recent discoveries in Jordan have revealed the existence of 32 water-driven sugar mills, while in Egypt and Syria wind-driven crushing mills were also used.

Sugar-cane plantations spread to North Africa and then to Spain and Sicily, but the West became acquainted with the industry only during the Crusades, when the Franks occupied the Syrian coast. The technology of sugar refining was also transferred from Islam to China. According to Marco Polo Egyptian technicians were called to China where they taught the people of 'Vuguen' (possibly Yen-p'ing in Fukien province) how to refine sugar using wood ash. It was also due to Muslims that sugar-plantations were first established in the West Indies.

8.5 EDIBLE VEGETABLE OILS

Edible vegetable oils were always an important part of the diet in Islam. These included olive oil and oils from sesame, cottonseed, poppy, and other similar substances. However, some, such as linseed oil and castor oil, were used only for industrial purposes.

Of the edible oils, olive oil was the most valued, so that the olive tree was highly esteemed in Islamic culture, being praised in the *Qur'an*. Due to the tree's very long life and the value of its fruit, it was always considered as important an asset as the land on which it grew. Olive trees were always widely cultivated in Mediterranean lands, and in Islam, Syria and the countries of the Maghrib, especially Tunisia, also became famous for their olive orchards.

In the accounts of Muslim geographers there is much information about the centres of olive oil production. In Syria (*bilad al-Sham*) Nablus was always famous for its olive oil, which was exported to other Muslim countries, particularly Egypt. In Tunisia production was permanently at a high level, al-Muqaddasi reporting that at Banunash there were no less than 360 olive presses.

Sesame was a summer crop and its edible oil *shiraj* or *sirij* was also highly esteemed. Its use was more widespread in those lands where olive oil was not produced.

8.5.1 Techniques of oil production

Methods of producing olive oil were developed mainly in Syria, the home of the olive tree since ancient times. Arabic sources give details of a variety of techniques as well as information about the different qualities of oil that were available. The principal method was summarised by Dawud al-Antaki, who explained how the olives were first crushed, then soaked in hot water and pressed. It was a method that lasted until modern times and the introduction of more sophisticated machinery.

Olives were crushed in a mill with vertical millstones. Design details varied but usually there were two cylindrical stones fixed on the same horizontal axle, which was itself fixed in the middle to a pivoted vertical axle. In Persia a similar edge-running mill was used, but with one grindstone only (Fig. 8.21). This basic design was in use long before Islam and was common in the Hellenistic world, for we now know that production of olive oil was a significant factor in stimulating the gradual evolution of mills with vertical grindstones.

8.21 An oil mill in Persia with a vertical edge-running stone being used to crush linseed.

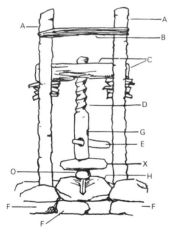

8.23 A simple wooden screw press still being used by Berbers in Siwa, Egypt in the 1920s. Uprights, A, about 8 to 9 feet high, held firmly in position by rope, B, at the top and large flat stones, F, above the lower ends, which were embedded in the ground, carried a cross-piece, C, through which a vertical screw, D, was fitted. The screw was turned by means of a bar, B, passing through a slot, G, and pressed down on two flat stones, X and H, between which was placed the olive cake, O. Oil from the cake then ran along a groove in H and poured out through a spout into a collecting pot.

From this first crushing a high quality oil was obtained, though there was still oil to be extracted. The pulp was often soaked in hot water before being subjected to a second pressing, this time using a beam or tackle and weight press (Fig. 8.22), or a screw press (Fig. 8.23). Such secondary pressing could be done in a number of stages by raising the pressure between one crushing and the next; indeed, a third stage was frequently used. The oil from later pressings was of lower quality than that from the first, so three qualities of oil were usually produced. In addition, the liquid that separated out from the pulp was stored in settling vats; later the water could be drawn off, leaving a low grade oil behind; this too was collected.

According to al-Antaki, oil was obtained from sesame by first soaking the seeds in water and then removing the skins. The peeled seeds were next roasted, ground and kneaded, and after this were soaked in hot water. However, the oil could also be obtained by pressing.

Oils from other seeds, whether for edible purposes or for industrial uses, were obtained by almost the same procedure as that adopted for olive oil.

8.6 FOOD AND DRINK

Food and drink differed from one Muslim country to another, for people continued to use those resources to which they had become accustomed before the days of Islam. It is true, of

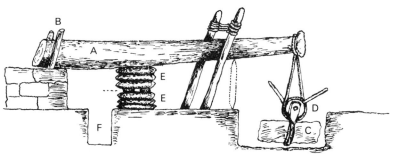

8.22(*a*) A beam press for obtaining olive oil in use in Algeria in about 1920. The heavy weight *C* was raised by means of the winch *D* and made the beam *A*, which was about 12 feet long and was held down at *B* by another beam across it (not shown), press down on the baskets *E* crushing the olives contained in them. Oil from the olives poured down into the trough *F*.

8.22(*b*) Detail of a similar beam press, in Morocco, showing the baskets in position under the beam, with the oil trough below.

course, that the cultural and political unity of Islamic lands had its effect on diet, but major differences always remained. In due course it should be possible for a study to be made to detail the variations between different Muslim countries, such a study beginning with pre-Islamic diets and then going on to examine Arabic sources to determine Muslim eating habits in each area. Such sources can be valuable; for instance, from al-Muqaddasi, who was a native of Palestine, we learn that some of the eating habits he met with in Egypt were unfamiliar to him. He observed that they did not eat much meat but consumed more fish, and found it strange how 'they prised open the shells of oysters and sipped the raw slimy material inside'. He noticed too that fruit was not abundant. As might perhaps be expected, this example implies that differences in diet were influenced mainly by the kind of food readily available in a particular country.

During the period between the fourth and tenth centuries AH (tenth to sixteenth centuries AD), many cookery books (*tabikh*) were written. Only one of them has been translated into European languages; most of the others are still in manuscript form. From such books it is possible to learn much about the main dishes served in Baghdad, Damascus, Cairo and other Muslim cities during this time. Thus *Kitab al-Tabikh* (*The Cookery Book*) by al-Baghdadi describes the recipes in Baghdad. The manuscript dates from 623 AH/AD 1226, though it may have been written earlier, and contains at least 153 recipes which can be categorised as follows: 22 sour dishes; 6 milk dishes; 18 plain dishes; 8 fried but dry dishes; 22 simple dishes; various chicken dishes; 9 pastry and baked dishes; 11 soused, turned dishes and pies; 5 fresh fish dishes; 4 salted fish dishes; 3 *tirrikh* (small salted fish) dishes; 4 sauces; 5 relishes; 5 savouries; 12 *judhab*, *khabis*, and other jellied dishes; 9 *halwa* or 'halva', or sweets; 10 *mutabbaq* (a type of pancake), *qataif* (doughnuts) and *khushknanaj* (dishes from Persia).

Another more comprehensive cookery book by Ibn Sayyar al-Warraq, also still in manuscript form, is concerned not only with all aspects of cooking and making drinks, but also begins by describing kitchen equipment and ends with table manners. It is interesting to note that many of the current dishes in the Islamic countries of the Middle East occur in these books.

8.6.1 Production of food supplies

The provision of food was the biggest undertaking in the daily life of the Muslim world, since for each food item that reached the consumer several operations were involved. For example, we have already seen how, in order to obtain loaves of bread, a whole series of large-scale technological stages were required, including ploughing, irrigation, reaping, threshing, storing, transporting, flour-milling and baking. Yet this was not exceptional; large-scale technological processes had to be used to provide rice, next only to wheat in importance. Sugar was

8.24 Churning butter, Wah, Pakistan

another big industry with specialised technology – in Fustat alone there were 58 cane sugar factories – though honey was also used extensively and there were even cheaper sweeteners, such as various kinds of treacle, dibbs and the rubb or must of grapes, as well as carob pulp and dates. Salt was produced and traded on a large scale, and was another major item in a grocer's merchandise.

The meat industry was also extensive. It commenced with the breeding of sheep and cattle, which then passed through the slaughter house and the butcher's shop. The consumer also had available various cooked and preserved meats as well as *naqaniq* (sausages) and *shara'ih* (sliced meat). There was also a fish-salting industry, while large-scale poultry production was practised in Egypt, where artificial incubators for chickens were well developed.

The oils and fats industry was on a large scale as we have already seen. Besides vegetable oils, animal fats were in common use, and still more important was *samn* or cooked butter. Naturally enough, the preparation of these fats had special technologies of their own, while cheeses of different kinds were widely available, being an efficient means of converting milk into a popular daily food (Figs. 8.24 and 8.25).

Vegetables and fruit were consumed when fresh, though they were also preserved and formed part of inter-regional trade. It was even found possible to preserve water-melons, though the major dried fruits were raisins, figs, nuts of various kinds, and dates.

8.25 Turkish women making yoghourt.

Vinegar was yet another important item among food supplies, and there was large-scale production of rose-water and other syrups. Wines and distilled *'araq* were also produced in some areas, such as Syria.

Each basic food commodity mentioned was traded through wholesalers and retailers, and in the large cities there were many shops that served cooked food. In the Middle Ages in Cairo it is said that there were no less than 10 000 to 12 000 vendors cooking food in the streets, and European visitors who reported this thought that the 'Saracens' seldom did any cooking at home.

8.6.2 Preserving food

As with most other subjects in this book, we can only touch lightly on the technology of preserving food. With the arrival of Islam old methods still continued to be used and developed, though new methods came to be introduced. Drying, salting and smoking were much favoured, in addition to pickling in vinegar and crystallising in sugar and honey. Curing with spices was yet another treatment, while cold storage was adopted too (see Fig. 8.26 below). Proper storage conditions were provided and there were other recommended methods for preventing decay.

Correct storage was important for wheat, flour and other cereals. Ibn al-Awwam and other authors of books on agriculture give information about this, as well as methods aimed not only at preventing decay but also for preserving these commodities from pests such as weevils and grubs.

Meat was preserved using drying, salting and smoking techniques, and in some cases spices were added. Methods for preparing dried meat (*qadid*) were described in various sources, al-Dimashqi giving one such process in his book on commerce, while manuals for the *muhtasib* gave details about the preparation of sausages (*naqaniq*). As previously mentioned, preservation by salting was always the preferred method for fish.

Fruit was stored from season to season in fresh condition; there were instructions on the proper storage of fresh apples, pomegranates and grapes among others, so that they could last without deterioration for several months until the next season. Cold storage was utilised, water-melons from Transoxiana being transported to Baghdad packed in lead ice-boxes. Indeed, the method was applied to ice itself, which was transported to Baghdad and Cairo and then stored to be used throughout the year by the wealthier classes.

A cheaper and more durable method for preserving fruit was drying, and dried fruits were used extensively. It was certainly an effective way of making use of surpluses and distributing them to distant regions, so was specially valuable in the case of grapes, figs and dates. Nuts such as chestnuts, pistachio, and almonds were also dried and widely distributed. Several kinds of vegetable were preserved in the same way and techniques for drying are found in some Arabic agricultural books. Crystallisation was a second favoured method for fruit preservation and is still one of the famous specialities of Damascus.

There was also the method of pickling in brine or vinegar. Products so preserved were known as *mukhallalat* and many kinds of fruit and vegetables were kept in this manner, among them olives, cucumbers and turnips. Dry cheeses were also preserved in brine.

There were even methods for prolonging the life of rose-water and other syrups, and for preventing the deterioration of vinegar and olive oil. Such methods are again to be found in Arabic agricultural books.

8.6.3 Adulteration and quality control

Adulteration was bound to occur, especially with important commodities, and this explains why the office of *muhtasib* was concerned with controlling the ingredients of foods.

A very interesting essay attributed to al-Kindi and called 'The chemistry of cooked foods' mentioned how to make adulterated dishes. He described meat dishes without meat, fried liver without liver, brain dishes using no brain, meatless sausages, omelettes without eggs, *Joudhab* (a rice dish) with no rice, *halawa* (sweets) without honey or sugar, and so on. And al-Jaubari in *Al-Mukhtar fi Kashf al Asrar* (*The Favourite Book on the Revelation of Secrets*) devotes one chapter to 'revealing the secrets of those who make foods', declaring that these people had innumerable tricks and left no food without some adulteration. He described a method of making artificial honey, another for artificial *samn* (cooked butter), one for artificial vinegar, methods for producing aritificial olive and sesame oils, and even a way of manufacturing artificial milk. These two authors were not alone; there are other similar Arabic sources that give adulteration recipes. The manuals for the *muhtasib* also discuss some of these methods and give directions on how to control the quality of sausages, cold meats, sweets and various other products.

8.6.4 Drinks

In the cookery book of al-Warraq we find fifteen recipes for various kinds of drinks. These range from iced water to fruit juices and wines. In Islamic countries, however, the prohibition on wine meant that most drinks were non-alcoholic. This restriction, coupled with the hot summers of the Muslim world, led to people devising various kinds of syrups for drinking. It was a development that was materially helped by an abundance of different kinds of fruit.

Iced water was very popular and ice was available throughout the summer, though, according to Ibn Sayyar, it was possible to make water cold by using only air. There were also perfumed waters (using rose-water or similar scented liquids), while other non-alcoholic drinks included those made from milk and

8.26 An ice house near Yazd in Iran. On cold nights ice formed on a shallow pool behind the wall beyond the dome (the wall being built to shade the water from the sun during the day and prevent it warming up). This ice was then collected and stored in a pit beneath the conical dome, to be used for preserving food and making cool drinks in hot weather.

yoghurt, grapes, carrots and lemons. Wines and beers were prepared in some localities, especially where there were concentrations of Christian communities; distillation of wine to make 'araq was also known.

Coffee (*qahwa*) was a rather late introduction which came from the Yemen. Its use spread early in the eighth century AH (fourteenth century AD) though it did not become known in Cairo until about 906 AH/AD 1500. In 951 AH/AD 1554 someone from Aleppo and someone else from Damascus opened the first coffee houses in Istanbul; it was to be another century before such places were established in Paris.

9 *Mining and metallurgy*

9.1 ISLAMIC MINES

In the vast Islamic empire ores and minerals played an important part. There was a great need for gold, silver and copper for minting coins and other uses. Iron ore was necessary for the manufacture of iron and steel for arms, some farm implements and other items. Minerals such as mercury, salt and alum had become indispensable for everyday life. Fortunately, the empire was richly endowed with these natural resources and the mining industry was an extensive one. *Ma'din* (plural *ma'adin*) denoted a 'mine' in Arabic sources, and *mu'addin* meant 'miner'; in modern Arabic the word *manjam* is used for 'mine', while *ma'din* or *ma'dan* is now used mostly for 'metal' or 'mineral'.

Information on Islamic mines occurs in geographical works, in alchemical treatises, in books on mineralogy, and in a variety of other sources. But these, as well as archaeological discoveries, have not yet been searched for the purpose of writing a history of mining technology, although some studies have appeared on the distribution of Islamic mines. We shall mention here only some of the minerals and a few of the mining centres, since it is not possible to list all the mines in a short review.

Gold mines were found in western Arabia, Egypt, Africa and in some eastern Muslim lands. But the first major gold mining area was at Wadi al-'Allaqi, which is a tributary on the eastern side of the Upper Nile, lying in the Buja country between Ethiopia and Nubia. The mines were in a desert area between the Nile and the Red Sea, the nearest towns being Aswan on the Nile and 'Aydhab on the Red Sea. The second gold mining area was called by al-Biruni the 'Maghrib Sudan'; it was the area south of the Sahara in Senegal and on the Upper Niger in Mali. According to al-Idrisi, Wanqara was the most important gold mining centre on the Upper Niger. Salt, cloth and other commodities were exchanged for gold.

Silver was either mined separately or in association with lead ores. The major silver mines were in the eastern Islamic

9.1 Syrian brass perfume burner inlaid with silver and gold. Thirteenth century AD. Victoria and Albert Museum, London.

provinces, prominent among them the mines of the Hindu
Kush at the towns of Panjhir and Jaruyana, both in the
neighbourhood of Balkh. According to one report, there were
about 10 000 miners working at Panjhir. Other important
silver mines were in Spain, the Maghrib, Iran and Central
Asia.

Lead (*usrub*, *rasas*) was obtained mostly from galena (lead
sulphide), which was of very common occurrence and is often
associated with small quantities of silver. Only two other lead
ores have any importance as raw materials, cerussite (lead
carbonate) and anglesite (lead sulphate); though the latter is
only of minor significance. Lead ores, especially galena, were
mined in Spain, Sicily, at the Maghrib, Egypt, Iran, Upper
Mesopotamia and Asia Minor.

Copper ore deposits were exploited in various mining areas,
including the important Spanish mines in the west. There were
also several deposits in the east, such as those of Sijistan,
Kirman, Farghana, Bukhara, Tus, and Harat, while the copper
mines in Cyprus were always a significant source.

The words 'calamine' or 'tutia' (Arabic *tutiya*) were used to
denote the natural ores of *zinc*, especially zinc carbonate and
white zinc oxide which was obtained during treatment of the
natural ores. The major mines for tutia were in Kirman
province in the east, though it was available also from various
mining areas in Spain.

Tin (*rasas qal'i*, *qasdir*) came from the Malaysian peninsula,
which was known as Kala; hence the name *qal'i* for the
metal.

Iron and steel were in great demand in Islam, and indeed iron
ore was utilised whenever feasible. It was distributed throughout most Muslim lands; there were five major iron mining areas
in Spain, including the mines near Toledo and Murcia, and in
the Maghrib ten mining areas were exploited in Morocco,
Algeria and Tunisia. These last included the mines in Jabal al-
Hadid in the Atlas Mountains, the Rif, Gawr al-Hadid in
Algeria, and Majjanat al-Ma'dan in Tunisia. Iron ore was also
produced and exported from Sicily, while in addition it was also
mined in the Libyan desert as well as in the Fezzan district in the
south-west of the country. Egypt exploited such ore as it had
available, for example at Nubia and on the Red Sea coast, while
Syria was famous for its iron and steel metallurgy (Damascus
steel), its iron ore being obtained in the south and in the
mountain ranges between Damascus and Beirut. However, the
Islamic countries of the east were better endowed with iron ore
than were Egypt, Syria and Iraq. The province of Fars in

southern Iran could boast of at least four important iron mining centres, while there were iron mines in Khurasan, Transoxiana, Adharbayjan and in Armenia.

Mercury came chiefly from Spain. Al-Idrisi mentions a mine to the north of Cordoba, where more than a thousand men worked at the various stages of mining ores and extracting mercury from them. Another source was Farghana in Transoxiana.

Salt was produced in numerous localities. It was an essential commodity and production in some areas was undertaken on a very large scale for export; an example was the Maghrib, where the salt mines were on the edge of the desert areas in the south. The salt produced here was carried by caravans to the south of the Sahara where it was exchanged for gold; thousands of men and camels were involved in these operations. Other important salt mines or production centres were in Khurasan, Arabia and Armenia.

The *alum* of Yemen was famous for its quality, but according to al-Idrisi the major source was Chad. It was exported to Egypt and to all the countries of North Africa. Egypt itself was also a major production centre for alum and for natron.

Among the many *other minerals* that were known and utilised in Islam was asbestos from Badhakhshan; this was used for wicks and fire-resistant cloth. Coal was also known and used in some areas, such as Farghana, where it was mined and sold as a fuel for ovens (*tananir*), while its ashes were utilised as a cleaning agent. As for petroleum deposits, their large-scale use has already been mentioned (Chapter 6).

Various kinds of *precious stones* were mined and Arabic works on the lapidary arts such as al-Biruni's book on mineralogy *al-Jamahir* are celebrated and deserve detailed study. Rubies were mined in Badhakhshan and were brought from Sarandib, diamonds came from Hindustan and Sarandib (Sri Lanka), agate and onyx from Yemen, emeralds and lapis lazuli from Egypt, and turquoise from Nishabur. Corundum was obtained from Nubia and Sarandib, and crystal was mined in Arabia and Badhakhshan. Diving for pearls was another flourishing occupation, while coral was obtained from the coasts of North Africa and Sicily.

9.2 MINING TECHNOLOGY

Although mining operations in Islamic civilisation were very extensive, as with most aspects of Muslim technology no attempt has yet been made to study them in detail. This is another field that requires extensive research. In consequence, there is a noticeable gap in the history of mining in general and whereas much information and archaeological evidence has been published on ancient mining and mining in the Roman empire, research is completely lacking for the period between the first and ninth centuries AH (seventh and fifteenth centuries AD). Not only should this gap be filled, but also there are academic reasons for re-examining much of the material that has been published on earlier mining technology,

It is therefore only possible here to give an outline of Islamic mining techniques using evidence gained by glancing into the brief accounts of geographers and into lapidary books. In Europe it was not until AD 1556 that the first book on mining – Agricola's *De re metallica* – made its appearance; before that time only a few books were available on lapidary techniques and these had mainly been translated from Arabic. The real development of European mining technology had, of course, not started during the period with which we are concerned.

There was not just one single form of mining technology in Islam because methods differed from mineral to mineral, from country to country, and from one style of ownership to another. In any one country there was, in fact, a range of technologies from the primitive to the highly developed.

As with modern mining there were two kinds of operation – underground and open-cast. Thus al-Biruni wrote: 'The search for *la'l* (a kind of ruby) is of two kinds; one is to dig the mine under the mountain, and the other is to search for it among the gravel and earth which result from the collapse of mountains by earthquakes or from their erosion by floods'.

In underground mining one method was to sink shafts vertically into the soil and then drive horizontal passages when the veins were reached. In Syria the shaft of the mine was called the *bir* (i.e. the well), and the horizontal tunnel the *darb* (i.e. the road). In the Lebanese mountains a typical shaft was only 6–7 metres deep, though the tunnels were 'very long'. But when al-Idrisi saw the mercury mines to the north of Cordoba in Spain, he was told that the depth from ground level to the bottom of the mine was not less than 250 fathoms (some 457 metres). Other mines of intermediate depth were reported. Thus in the silver mines of the Maghrib the depth was 20 cubits (*dhira'*) or about 10 metres. The techniques of drilling vertical shafts and horizontal tunnels were familiar in most Islamic countries from the great tradition of constructing *qanat* systems of underground water conduits for irrigation, with the exacting technical expertise they required.

However, in underground mining miners more often pre-ferred to dig additional adits or openings into the slopes of a mountain and then follow the veins, rather than sink shafts. This method was easier and less expensive for a miner who was working for himself and it is noticeable that reports of mines with vertical shafts usually apply to those owned by the State. A vivid description of silver mining activities in Panjhir in Khurasan, where 10 000 men were employed in the mining industry, was given by Ibn Hawqal. He wrote:

The people of Panjhir made the mountain and the market-place like a sieve because of the many pits. They only follow veins leading to silver, and if they find a vein they dig continuously until they reach the silver. A man may spend huge sums in digging, and he may find silver to such an extent that he and his descendants become rich, or his work may fail because he is overpowered by water or for other reasons. A man may pick a vein and it is possible that another man picks the same vein in another position. Both start digging. The custom is that the miner who arrives first and intercepts the passage of the other miner wins the vein and its results. Because of this competition they execute a work that devils cannot achieve. When one arrives first, the expenses of the other are wasted. If they arrive together they share the vein and then continue digging as long as the lamps are burning. If the lamps are extinguished and cannot be relit, they stop their progress because anyone who reaches that position would die immediately. [In this business] you will see a man start his day owning one million, and by nightfall he owns nothing. Or he may start poor in the morning and by evening become the owner of unaccountable wealth.

The main tool of the miner was the pick-axe (*minqar, saqur*) (Fig. 9.2). It had a sharp end to peck the stone and a flat end with which to hammer or drive wedges. There were also various hammers, chisels or wedges, crow-bars, hoes and shovels. Windlasses were used for hauling ore and materials out of the shafts. An efficient and simple form that was employed in the Syrian iron mines is still used in constructing *qanat* systems in Iran, for drawing water and in the building industry (Fig. 9.3). Here an assistant sits on a bench on one side of the mouth of the shaft or well, pulling the horizontal bars of the windlass towards him with his hands and pushing the opposite ones away with his feet at the same time. The ore was loaded into a small bucket about 30–35 centimetres in diameter, which had two handles to which the rope was attached by hooks fastened on its end. More sophisticated capstans were employed for heavier loads (Fig. 9.4).

Oil lamps were used for general illumination and for aligning the direction of digging; in addition they were good indicators of the adequacy of supplies of fresh air, as was the case in the silver mines of Panjhir. In Arabic technical literature there are

9.2 Islamic pickaxe illustrated in a manuscript from Tabriz. Fourteenth century AD. Edinburgh University Library.

various ingenious designs for lamps; one, protected against the wind and thus suitable for outdoor use, was described by the Banu Musa brothers (Fig. 9.5.)

Ventilation in mines was an important problem. In Panjhir, with thousands of miners working for themselves and feverishly hunting for silver, capital investment was kept to a minimum and usually no provision for ventilation was made. The miner simply abandoned digging if the lamps stopped burning. In more organised mining work, especially in the State mines, a means of ventilation was always provided, for here it was essential, particularly in the deep mercury workings. Either special ventilation shafts were dug or, when installing a drainage system where several shafts were required, these also served for ventilation; such special ventilation shafts have been found in Iran, some of them going back to pre-Islamic times. As might be expected, the problem of ventilating wells and mine shafts attracted the attention of Muslim engineers, who designed special ventilating machines. The Banu Musa brothers described a design for

a machine for use in wells which kill those who descend in them. If a man uses this machine in any well, it will neither kill nor harm him.

9.3 Windlass at the top of a shaft of a *qanat* in Iran.

This machine is suitable for wells that kill and for dangerous pits. If a man has this machine which we shall describe with him he can descend in any well immediately without fearing it and it will not harm him (Fig. 9.6).

The other important problem in mining was drainage. Small mines of silver could not, of course, afford to solve the problem as Panjhir showed, but on the other hand at the State silver mines at Zkandar in the Maghrib, drainage was carried out properly. As al-Qazwini reported:

Here are the silver mines. Anyone who wishes can undertake processing them. There are underground mines in which many people are always working. When they descend 20 *dhira'* [some 10 metres] water appears. The Sultan installs water-wheels and water is raised until mud appears. Workers bring this mud up to the surface of the ground and wash it. He does this in order to take the fifth [part]. Water is raised in three stages, since it is 20 *dhira'* from the ground level to the

9.4 Drawing of a capstan for raising heavy loads. From a manuscript of Taqi al-Din. Sixteenth century AD. Chester Beatty Library, Dublin.

surface of the water. He installs a wheel down in the mine on the water surface. Water is lifted and discharged into a large tank. Another wheel is installed on this tank. It lifts the water and pours it into another tank. On this tank a third wheel is installed. It lifts the water and discharges it on to the surface of the ground to irrigate farms and gardens. This operation cannot be undertaken except by a very rich person possessing thousands. He sits at the mouth of the mine and employs artisans and workers who bring out the mud and wash it in front of him. When the work is done the fifth of the Sultan is put aside and the rest given to him. It may come to be smaller than his expenditure, and it may be [more]. This depends on the man's efforts.

As we saw earlier (Chapter 2) the technique of raising water by water-wheel was highly developed in Islam, flourishing in

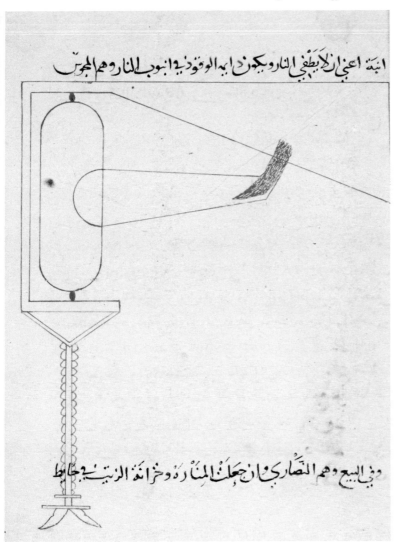

ابتة اعنى إنّ لا يطفئ النار ويكون دابه المؤدية إنبوب النار وهم المجوس

وفي السبع وهم النصارى إن جعلت المنارة وخزانة الزيت حائط

9.5 A miner's lamp with a pivoted shield, described by the Banu Musa brothers. The shield was designed so it would be turned by the wind to the position where it would protect the lamp. Ninth century AD. Staatsbibliothek Preussischer Kulturbesitz, Berlin.

North Africa and Spain. The passage by al-Qazwini just quoted is important because it should prompt a reconsideration of archaeological findings. For it is quite certain that other mines in Spain – in central and southern parts of the country around the areas of Cordoba, Almaden, Ovejo, Huelva, Murcia, Ilbira – and in North Africa, where the Muslims also carried out extensive mining operations, were being drained in a similar manner.

Water-raising devices of various types were used. These included the compartmented wheel, the chain-of-pots wheel, the Archimedean screw, the rag-and-chain pump, and the piston pump. Some of these were illustrated in Chapter 2, while

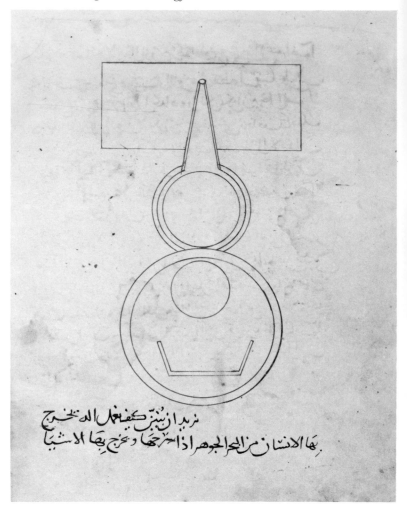

بزيد ان ببيّن كيفيعمل الدَّ بخرج
بها الانسان من البحرالجوهرا ذا اخرحها ويخرج بها الاشبا

9.6 A ventilation machine for use in pits and wells. It was made up of bellows and pipes and pumped in fresh air to replace poisonous gases. From a manuscript of the Banu Musa brothers. Ninth century AD. Staatsbibliothek Preussischer Kultur-besitz, Berlin.

Figs. 9.7(a) and 9.8 depict the Archimedean screw and the rag-and-chain pumps from the book of Taqi al-Din. Archae-ologists have found a screw pump in a mine near Cordoba; it has an oak screw and a barrel of sheet lead, but Robert Forbes has expressed doubts about whether this pump is really of Roman date as has been conjectured.

We come now to the dressing of ores. This includes crushing and milling, and sifting and washing, operations that were usually conducted at mining sites before the ores were transported to foundries and smelting works. Crushing and milling was carried out to reduce the size of the lumps of ore, gold ores being crushed or milled to a finer degree than any others. The use of a mill was more important with reef gold, which occurred in quartz veins. Milling ores was done with a quern, crushing by water-driven trip-hammers. In his book on

9.7(*a*) An Archimedean screw, illustrated in a manuscript of Taqi al-Din. Sixteenth century AD. Chester Beatty Library, Dublin.

9.7(*b*) An Archimedean screw being used to raise water in Egypt.

mineralogy, *al-Jamahir*, al-Biruni discussed the treatment of gold ores. He wrote: 'Gold may be united with stone as if it is cast with it, so that it needs pounding. Rotary mills (*tawahin*) can pulverize it, but pounding it by *mashajin* (a kind of trip-hammer) is more correct and is a much more refined treatment. It is even said that this pounding makes it redder which, if true, is rather strange and surprising. The *mashajin* are stones fitted to axles which are installed on running water for pounding, as is the case in the pounding of flax for paper in Samarqand'. This is an important text since it indicates that

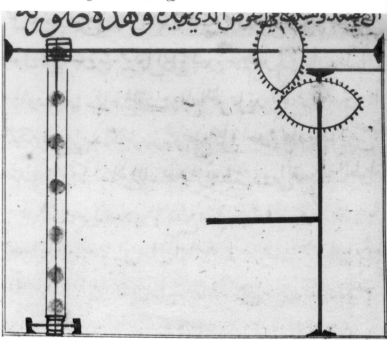

9.8 Illustration of a rag-and-chain pump for raising water. From a sixteenth century AD manuscript of Taqi al-Din. Chester Beatty Library, Dublin.

water-driven trip-hammers were already established for crushing ores before the fourth century AH (tenth century AD) (cf. Fig. 8.15, p. 218 above).

9.2.1 Pearls and underwater resources

The exploitation of corals and pearls became very large undertakings; pearls from the Gulf area were highly valued, the Chinese considering them to be the best (Fig. 9.9). Operations for obtaining them were organised by entrepreneurs, who would hire divers for two months and pay them regularly. Such enterprises were often highly profitable but also very perilous, and there are detailed descriptions of the great dangers that the divers faced.

In *al-Jamahir* al-Biruni provided details of the diving operation, and of particular interest is what he had to say about a new type of diving gear. He wrote:

I was told by a man from Baghdad that divers had invented in these days a method for diving by which the difficulty of holding the breath is eliminated. This enables them to frequent the sea from morning to afternoon as much as they wish, and as much as the employer favours them. It is a leather gear which they fit down on their chests and they tie it at the [edges?] very securely and then they dive. They breathe in it from the air inside it. This necessitates a very heavy weight to keep down the diver with this air. A more suitable arrangement would be to attach to the upper end of this gear opposite the forehead a leather tube similar to a sleeve, sealed at its seams by wax and bitumen, and its length will be equal to the depth of diving. The upper end of the tube will be fitted to a large dish at a hole in its bottom. To this dish are attached one or more inflated bags to keep it floating. The breath of the diver will flow in and out through the tube as long as he desires to stay in the water, even for days.

Another device was an ingenious dredging maching designed by the Banu Musa brothers and incuded in their *Book of Ingenious Devices*. They wrote: 'We wish to explain how to make a machine by which a person can bring out jewels from the sea if he lowers it, and by which he can extract things which fall into wells or are submerged in the rivers and seas'. Figure 9.10 illustrates their invention.

9.9 A pearl diver of Bahrain, with a clip on his nose to help him hold his breath while diving.

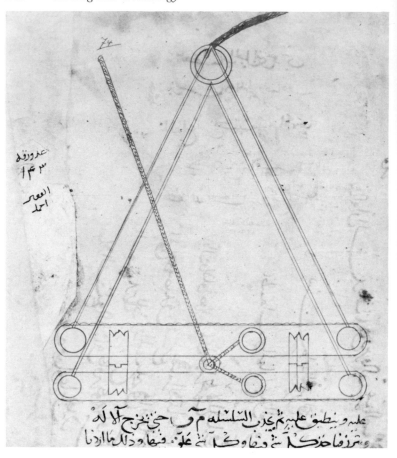

9.10 A dredging machine. Illustration from a manuscript of the Banu Musa brothers. Ninth century AD. Staatsbibliothek Preussischer Kulturbesitz, Berlin.

9.3. NON-FERROUS METALLURGY

Much information about Islamic knowledge of non-ferrous metals can be gained from alchemical and chemical treatises. There was a close relationship between the work of the metallurgist and the chemist, and Arabic sources reflect the experience gained in the laboratory and with the metallurgical furnace.

9.3.1 Gold

Speaking about native gold which was collected from gold mines al-Biruni said that it was usually not free from impurities and had therefore to be refined by smelting or other techniques. He also gave details of the amalgamation method that was used in the mines on a commercial scale:

After pounding the gold ore or milling it, it is washed out of its stones and the gold and mercury are combined and then squeezed in a piece of leather until the mercury exudes from the pores of the leather. The rest of the mercury is driven off by fire.

He also gives an interesting description of how gold is mined from the deep waters of the Sind river:

At its sources there are places in which they dig small pits under the water, which flows over them. They fill the pits with mercury and leave it for a while. Then they come back after the mercury has become gold. This is because at its start the water is rapid and it carries with it particles over the surface of the mercury which picks up the gold, leaving the sand to pass away.

Gold occurs mixed naturally with silver, and gold is sujected to a second purification process – cementation – to remove the silver. This process is called *tabkh* or *tas'îd*. According to al-Hamadâni, thin plates of gold were interleaved with the cementation compound, known as the *dawâ'*. This consisted of a mixture of vitriol, salt and ground brick. The whole was then strongly heated. The mixture evolved the vapours of sulphuric and hydrochloric acids. These did not attack gold but converted the surface silver and copper into chlorides which could be scraped off. Cementing could be done more than once if the gold was to be made really pure. Until recently, historians thought that this process was first described by Theophilus (c. 1150–1200 AD). But it is evident now that al-Hamadâni preceded him by about two centuries. Further, this process was the standard method for refining gold during the sixteenth century in Europe, namely six centuries after the detailed account of al-Hamadâni.

The use of aqua regia was first described by Jâbir, but its first use on an industrial scale is still an open question.

The purity of gold was tested by various methods. These included the touchstone (*al-mihakk*), measuring specific gravities, and noting the speed of solidification of gold after it had been removed from the furnace.

9.3.2 Silver and lead

Unlike gold, native silver was not found in alluvial deposits or in the sands and gravels of rivers, but was to be sought in mountainous regions, embedded in veins. In general however, native silver was not abundant and the main source was galena (lead sulphide), which was usually associated with small amounts of silver. The lead and silver ore, after being mined, was crushed and roasted in a special furnace equipped with double bellows and the lead run out through an outlet in the rear of the furnace into a tank. If lead in the silver ore was not significant, lead was introduced artificially, because it has an affinity for silver, and when it is fused with it, it acts as a solvent and extracts it from its union with baser metals. The lead was then placed in a dish, put back into the furnace and reduced into litharge. The silver ingot remained and could be removed. This ingot usually contained a large percentage of lead and this lead was removed by cupellation.

A cupel of crushed burnt bones was made which absorbed the lead and impurities, leaving pure silver. Another method used salt and pulverised brick instead. The amount of silver that could be extracted from lead ores varied from mine to mine. The report says that one *mann* of litharge from the lead ore produced half a *dâniq* of silver (about one gram of silver to every 3120 grams of litharge).

All these different sources of silver necessitated the application of a variety of techniques mastered by Muslim smelters and chemists, who therefore became experts in roasting, smelting, oxidation, liquation, leaching, cupellation and amalgamation. Details cannot be given in this brief discussion, but we can say that these methods fascinated the alchemists and were largely responsible, in our opinion, for the vast alchemical literature that resulted from their experiments with stones (*ahjar*) and metals (*ajsad*).

9.3.3 Tin, zinc, antimony, and arsenic

Tin (*rasas qal'i, qasdir*) was one of the seven malleable 'metals'. It was brought to the classical Muslim countries mainly from the Malaysian peninsula, though some came also from Spain and the West.

Zinc was not known as a distinct metal by early Islamic metallurgists and chemists. This is because they first came across it, and used it extensively, in the form of tutia (zinc oxide), which was classed as one of the 'stones' (*ahjar*). Later, as we shall see, they became aware of zinc (*ruh al-tutiya*) as a definite metal. Tutia (Arabic *tutiya*) is usually the pure zinc oxide obtained from natural zinc carbonate. Various authors described a method of extracting the pure product from the natural ore. They said that the ore was placed in furnaces that contained long ceramic rods. Al-Muqaddasi saw 'curious tall furnaces in the mountain villages' in Kirman, furnaces which later also attracted the attention of Marco Polo when he visited the same area. Before the tenth century AH (sixteenth century AD) *ruh al-tutiya* had become recognised as a metal and was alloyed with copper to form brass. It replaced *kharsini* (see below) as the seventh metal, and Abu al-Fadl in *'Ayn-i-Akhbari* (*Source of Information*) gave several compositions in which zinc was employed.

Antimony was obtained from antimony sulphide (Sb_2S_3). It was a constituent of copper alloys, and Arabic chemical books described its separation.

Arsenic was unimportant as a metal, though there is a description of the 'preparation of the mercury of arsenic sulphide', i.e. a preparation of metallic arsenic from its sulphides. In this connection, it is worth noting that those metals which were not among the original seven were given such 'combination' names as *ruh al-tutiya* or the 'mercury of arsenic sulphide' just quoted. The same applied to the mineral acids, which were not classified and hence were attributed to their salts.

9.3.4 Copper and its alloys

Copper was usually obtained from the sulphide ores because it seldom occurred in the form of oxides or carbonates. Yet these latter ores needed only the simple treatment of heating with charcoal, whereas the sulphides (*zajat*) required roasting, smelting with special fluxes, and partial oxidation. However, in Spain the interesting discovery took place that the sulphide ores, on exposure to air in the presence of water, became oxidised to form soluble sulphates. 'The Moors then found that if water containing copper sulphate is allowed to run over iron, pure copper is deposited and the iron dissolved.' As iron was cheap and abundant in Spain, this discovery yielded an efficient method of recovering copper from sulphide ore, and direct mining of copper ore became less necessary.

Bronze (*safr*, *isfidruy*) is an alloy of copper and tin. It was much used for plain kitchen ware and for cooking implements; it was also the alloy on which coppersmiths based most of their work (Fig. 9.11).

Brass (*shabah*, *birinj*) is an alloy of copper and zinc, the zinc adding a factor that renders the metal a stronger, harder and less malleable substance than pure copper alone. Various kinds of brass were obtained by varying the zinc content; copper with 20 per cent zinc gives a brass with a colour close to that of gold. Before zinc was known to be a metal, brass was made by heating copper in a mixture of powdered zinc ore and charcoal; as a result, a proportion of the zinc formed in the vicinity of the copper was diffused into it chemically by a process known as cementation. Later we read in '*Ayn-i-Akhbari* (*Source of Information*) about three qualities of brass containing increasing amounts of zinc; one was ductile in the cold state, the second ductile when

9.11 Bronze mosque lamp decorated with a kufic inscription on a pierced background. Arabian or Mesopotamian, tenth to eleventh century AD. Davids Samling, Copenhagen.

heated, but the third was not ductile at all, though it could be cast.

A cheaper alloy could be made from copper and lead. A kind of bronze, it was used for hardware and was called *bitruy* by al-Biruni, though some authors referred to it as *ruy*, and it also went by the name *shabah mufragh*.

Kharsini was a metal or alloy. Listed as one of the seven metals of early Islamic alchemy and supposedly originating from China, all later Muslim writers agreed that it was extinct and so no longer available. The time came when its place among the seven metals was taken by zinc and some historians now think that *kharsini* was in fact zinc, though others believe it to have been a cupro-nickel alloy. *Taliqun* was another metal or alloy of uncertain composition. Even in al-Biruni's time its nature was a mystery, though the general opinion now is that it was some sort of copper alloy.

9.4 IRON AND STEEL

The importance of iron (*hadid*) in Islamic civilisation is exemplified in the chapter on iron (chapter 57) of the *Qu'ran*: 'God sent iron down to earth, wherein is mighty power and many uses for mankind'. Indeed, iron was considered as essential as food and clothing, and was always a source of power. Even though the sword has ceased to be a major military weapon, the manufacture of iron and steel is still a basis for industrial civilisation and so for economic and military strength.

We have already seen that iron mines in the Islamic Empire spread from Spain in the west to Transoxiana in the east, with famous steel production centres at Harat, Bukhara, Damascus, Toledo and in the Yemen. Though iron and steel technology in the Middle East had a long history, its technology flourished and advanced under Islam. Until recently iron was considered glorious because of its association with swords, the excellent steel for which was epitomised by the name Damascus. As is the case with other major issues in the history of technology, that of iron and steel, and of Damascus steel in particular, has been a source of controversy. Yet Islamic iron technology has been largely ignored and important sources about it have not been given proper consideration. Indeed, some writers have even alleged that Damascus steel was alien to Damascus and to all Muslim lands.

The subject is so vast that we are unable to discuss it in detail here. We cannot, for instance, make any comparative study taking into account Chinese, Indian and European technology, and must therefore limit ourselves to extracts from some of the major Arabic sources. Even so, the conclusions will be obvious. More sources of information are now becoming known, but up to the present the best authorities on the subject have certainly been al-Kindi and al-Biruni. Both were great scientists and engineers who had critical minds that rejected legends and subjected scientific knowledge to actual observation and careful testing. The alchemical and chemical treatises of Jabir, al-Razi, al-Jildaki and others are also valuable, second in importance only to al-Biruni and al-Kindi. Furthermore, there are also military treatises which are significant for their discussions on the manufacture of steel for swords, its subsequent heat treatment, and the care taken over the *firind* or pattern on the blade. In addition to all these, there are other sources, all of which deserve attention.

9.4.1 Types of iron and steel

From a study of some of the sources just mentioned, we conclude that the following main kinds of iron and steel were used in Islam:

(*i*)   Wrought iron (*narmahin*);
(*ii*)   Cast iron (*dus*);
(*iii*) Meteoritic steel (*shaburqan*);
(*iv*)   Manufactured steel (*fuladh*).

Wrought iron has a very low carbon content; it is soft and malleable, and was considered 'female'. It could not be heat-treated and was used where strength was not important. Wrought iron was a significant component in the manufacture of steel.

Cast iron is iron that has a high carbon content. It is important to realise that the Muslims did indeed produce it, a fact not generally appreciated by historians of technology. Some details are therefore in order here. Al-Biruni in his book on mineralogy, *al-Jamahir*, said that *dus* (cast iron) was the 'water of iron' because it is the liquid which flows during smelting and in the extraction of the metal from 'iron stones'. Al-Razi also defined it as the 'water of iron'. And in a commentary by al-Jildaki on Jabir's *Kitab al-hadid* (*Book on Iron*) we read the following description of the production of cast iron:

Chapter: Learn, brother, that it is your comrades who cast literally, from *yaskubun* iron in foundries [especially] made for that purpose after they have extracted it [i.e. the ore] from its mine as yellow earth intermingled with barely visible veins of iron. They place it in the founding furnaces designed for melting it. They install powerful bellows on all sides of them after having kneaded (*yaluttun*) a little oil and alkali into the ore. Then the fire is applied to it [i.e. the ore] together with stones and fire-wood. They blow upon it until it is molten, and its entire substance (*jishmuhu wa jasaduhu*) is rid of that earth. Next, they cause it to drop through holes like [those of] strainers, [made in] the furnaces so that the molten iron is separated, and is made into bars out of that earth. Then they transport it to far lands and countries. People use it for making utilitarian things of which they have need.

The properties of this Muslim cast iron can be summarised from al-Biruni's book on metallurgy as follows:

(*i*)   It was quick to flow like water when iron ores were melted:

(*ii*) It was hard and whitish-silver in colour, though its powder sometimes gave a pinkish reflection;

(*iii*) It could not be forged to make swords;

(*iv*) It would not resist blows but shattered into pieces. 'Breakage and brittleness are characteristic of it';

(*v*) It was mixed in crucibles with wrought iron to make steel.

In the ninth century AH (fifteenth century AD) such cast iron was sold as a raw material, and we learn that there were two commercial brands, one from Iraq, the other from Istakhr (Persepolis).

Meteoritic steel was often mentioned in early Arabic literature, authors explaining that it was a rare material.

Essentially *manufactured steel* is iron having a carbon content between that of wrought iron and cast iron. In some cases it was made from wrought iron bars by 'cementation', a process whereby iron bars were packed with charcoal and heated until they had absorbed enough carbon from it. However, steel was usually made in the molten state, and at the centres where this was done, one or more of the following methods were adopted:

(*i*) By carbonisation of wrought iron (just described);

(*ii*) By decarbonisation of cast iron;

(*iii*) By fusion of a mixture of wrought iron and cast iron, which provided two qualities depending on the degree of fusion obtained.

We quoted earlier from al-Jildaki's commentary on Jabir's description of the production of cast iron. Let us now give the rest of the text to see how rods of cast iron were used to make steel by decarbonisation:

As for the steel workers, they take the iron bars and put them into the founding-ovens (*masabik*) which they have, suited to their objectives, in the steel works. They install hearths (*akwar*) in them [i.e. the ovens] and blow fire upon it [i.e. the iron] for a long while until it becomes like gurgling water. They nourish it with glass, oil and alkali until light appears from it in the fire and it is purified of much of its blackness by intensive founding, night and day. They keep watching while it whirls for indications until they are sure of its suitability, and its lamp emits light. Thereupon they pour it out through outlets so that it comes out like running water. They then allow it to solidify in the shape of bars or in holes made of clay fashioned like large crucibles. They take out of them refined steel in the shape of ostrich eggs, and they make swords from it, and helmets, lance heads, and all tools.

Such refining of iron according to its blackness is clearly a decarbonisation process; indeed, a classical Arabic dictionary *Lisan al-Arab* described steel as refined iron.

The other method of producing molten steel in crucibles by carbonising wrought iron was described by al-Biruni in his book on mineralogy:

Mazyad b. Ali, the Damascene blacksmith, [wrote] a book describing swords, specifications for which were included in al-Kindi's treatise. He commenced by dealing with the composition of steel and the construction of the furnace (*kur*) as well as with the construction and design of crucibles, the descriptions of [the varieties] of clay, and how to distinguish between them. Then he instructed that in each crucible five *ratls* [2.5 kilograms] of horseshoes should be placed, and their nails, which are made of *narmahan* (Persian for soft iron), as well as a weight of ten *dirhams* [31 grams] each of *rusukhtaj* [a golden coloured marcasite stone and so a form of iron pyrites], and brittle magnesia. The crucibles are plastered with clay and placed inside the furnace. They are filled with charcoal and they [i.e. the crucibles] are blown up with *rumi* bellows, each having two operators, until it [i.e. the iron] melts and whirls. Bundles are added containing *ihlilaj* [myrobalan, a vegetable astringent used in tanning], pomegranate rinds, salt [used in] dough, and oyster shells [*asdaf al-lu'lu'*, literally 'pearl shells'], in equal proportions, and crushed, each bundle weighing forty *dirhams* [125 grams]. One [bundle] is thrown into each crucible; then it [i.e. the crucible] is blown upon violently for an hour. Next, they [i.e. the crucibles] are left to cool and the eggs are taken from them.

The third method of producing molten steel in crucibles from a mixture of cast and wrought iron was also described by al-Biruni. This was the method used in Harat and gave two different qualities of steel. One was the result of melting components 'equally so that they become united in the mixing operation and no component can be differentiated or seen independently'. Al-Biruni says that 'such steel is suitable for files and similar tools'. The second quality was obtained if the degree of melting of the wrought and cast iron was different for each substance 'and thus the intermixture between both components is not complete, and their parts are shifted so that each of their two colours can be seen by the naked eye and it is called *firind* [pattern]'.

Some of these important texts have been confirmed in the reports of observers and travellers who described the making of crucible steel in Bukhara during the last century. In 1820 Anossoff, a Russian expert, was in Bukhara and found that crucible steel was made by carburising wrought iron with charcoal and other organic matter. Later, in 1841, Massalki, another Russian metallurgical expert who was also in Bukhara, wrote that Damascus steel was made there from a mixture of wrought iron and cast iron, just as al-Biruni had reported 900 years earlier from Harat, which is not far from Bukhara. Observers once thought that these reports were conflicting. But it is now clear that there is no contradiction; the steel, which differed in quality, was made from different materials and by different methods.

9.4.2 The Damascus sword and its *firind*

According to Cyril Stanley Smith, the noted historian of metallurgy, 'In comparison with the relative neglect of structure by the European metallurgist, the enjoyment and utilisation of it in the Orient is impressive. In the Orient, etching to display patterns depending on differences in composition was in use contemporaneously with the European pattern-welded blade, and was thereafter continually developed to a high artistic level'. The greatest achievement in this direction was the Damascus sword, which was made in all the Islamic centres and in India (Fig. 9.12). Because of its excellence the name was later given to all swords with a patterned blade. Islamic countries exported and imported steel and swords, and there were strong commercial links in this respect with India. Al-Biruni mentioned that steel eggs were cast in Harat and then sent to India, while al-Idrisi says that iron was exported from the Maghrib to India. In general it is no exaggeration to say that Islam and India formed one cultural area as far as Damascus steel was concerned.

Patterned swords (with a *firind* or a *jawhar*) were in use before Muslim times. Imru' al-Qays (d. about AD 450) described a *firind* of the sword as resembling the track of ants, while another poet, his contemporary Aws b. Hajar, said the blade of such a sword was like a pond with wavy streaks caused by the wind. In fact, in Arabic poetry the beauty of the sword with a *firind* was always a source of inspiration. However, the important observation we wish to make is that Damascus steel was a speciality of the Islamic world and of India for many centuries. Indeed, Cyril Smith has remarked that 'The geographical distribution of these swords seems to have been practically co-extensive with the Islamic faith and they continued to be made well into the nineteenth century'.

In Europe steel was produced in furnaces with an open hearth by the carburisation of wrought iron rods. To imitate the *firind* of the Damascus sword they resorted to placing together strips of iron and steel and then welding them

9.12 The *firind* or pattern of two Damascus steel sword blades made in Persia in the seventeenth century AD. Victoria and Albert Museum, London.

together, but such imitations never matched the quality of the true Damascene steel blades.

Cast iron was first produced in Europe in the fifteenth century and crucible steel in the eighteenth. But a steel of comparable quality to that of Damascus could not be made, and for more than 150 years a large number of metallurgists in European countries carried out extensive research to discover why this was so. Eminent scientists such as Faraday were involved in this research; Cyril Smith, in discussing European attempts to duplicate Damascus steel, observes that these attempts still failed; true Damascus steel could still not be reproduced. What happened later, Smith says, was that 'interest in the duplication of the blade declined as European steelmakers developed their own techniques and the introduction of the Bessemer and Siemens processes gave homogeneous steel more adaptable to large-scale production'.

There were, however, some benefits from this research, for it brought those engaged in it nearer to an understanding of the structure of Damascus steel. To quote Cyril Smith again: 'Damascus blades are made of a very high carbon steel (about 1.5 – 2.0 per cent) and owe their beauty and their cutting qualities alike to the inherent structure of the cakes of steel from which they are forged'. Figure 9.12 shows two such patterns. He continues: 'The light portion contains numerous particles of iron carbide (cementite), while the dark areas are steel of normal carbon content (approximately eutectoid [i.e. solidifying at a low temperature like steel with a small carbon content]). The structure is, of course, clearly visible only after etching, which was done with a solution of some mineral sulphate'. It is amazing how close this modern interpretation of the *firind* is to that of al-Biruni.

9.4.3 Welded 'Damascus' gun barrels and swords

Another beautiful technique which flourished in Islamic countries and in India in later centuries was a welding technique for gun barrels and swords. This was quite different from that of cast Damascus steel, though it was also called 'Damascus'. Cyril Smith suggests that 'the technique seems to have originated in the Near East in the sixteenth century, and such guns were a famous product of the Kashmiri smiths in the early nineteenth century'. Figure 9.13 shows the twisting mill for coiling steel strip as used by Hajji Mustafa, the celebrated Persian gunsmith of Istanbul, while Fig. 9.14(*a*) shows the pattern of a Persian barrel of a flintlock gun and Fig. 9.14(*b*) a Turkish one. The manufacture of barrels of this type began in Europe in the eighteenth century, and during this and the subsequent century great efforts were made to use this technique for both gun barrels and sword blades. In 1798 William Nicholson made a Damascus-textured metal by

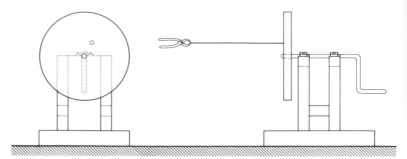

9.13 Twisting mill for coiling steel strip used by a gunsmith in Istanbul in the early nineteenth century AD, elevation (left) and section (right). The rotating millstone was about 19 cm in diameter.

compressing filings of steel and of wrought iron in a die, restriking the compacted material at welding heat and forging it into a plate. As Cyril Smith has remarked, this is an interesting anticipation of modern powder metallurgy. But let us read the following description of a somewhat-similar procedure that was practised in the fourth century AH (tenth century AD) in what is now Pakistan. Al-Biruni wrote:

I was told by somebody who was in the land of Sind that he sat by a smith who was making swords. He looked into them and found that their material was wrought iron [*narmahin*], on which he was sprinkling a finely pulverised drug [*dawa'*] whose colour gave a reddish shade. He sprinkles and welds by driving the powder deep then the takes it out and elongates it by forging and he sprinkles again and repeats the work several times. He said . . .; then I asked him what that was. He glanced at me derisively. Then I looked carefully into it and realised that it was cast iron [*dus*] which he mixes with wrought iron (*narmahin*) by forging to elongate [it] and hammering [to drive in] [to obtain a steel] similar to that of the eggs that are obtained in Harat by smelting.

9.14 Two examples of Damascus welded steel gun barrels.
Above A seventeenth-century flint-lock from Sind, the barrel probably made in Shiraz. Wallace Collection, London.
Below Turkish flintlock carbine. Nineteenth century AD. Victoria and Albert Museum, London.

9.4.4 Furnaces, crucibles and other equipment

We can learn much about Islamic metallurgical equipment from a study of the alchemical equipment previously mentioned (Chapter 6). The purifying operation or *istinzal* (p. 136) was mainly concerned with smelting ores to obtain metals, and according to al-Razi there was 'equipment for melting metals (*ajsad*) and stones', and also 'equipment for the further processing of these metals'. Iron smelting was given special attention in alchemy and we can safely assume that the alchemical equipment was a small pilot-plant of what was to become actual metallurgical equipment. Sometimes details of construction were identical, as we shall see in a moment.

Iron production from ores was effected using blast furnaces, but only further research will reveal how the design of these furnaces developed in Muslim lands. However we do know that cast iron was produced by this method before the fourth century AH (tenth century AD). And as we have already seen (p. 252), al-Jildaki gave a description of the smelting process while historians have reported experiments in Egypt on the casting of large cannon at the turn of the tenth century AH (sixteenth century AD). By the end of the twelfth century AH (eighteenth century AD), a typical blast furnace in the Lebanese mountains was 16 spans (3.84 metres) high by 7 spans (1.78 metres) wide. It was constructed of masonry and gave employment to 20 men. Layers of fresh wood and iron ore were stacked in the furnace, and two horizontal bellows with one combined outlet gave the necessary blast of air; each was operated by one man. Iron that accumulated at the bottom of the furnace was taken out in small amounts. It was then decarbonised in several open-hearth furnaces and forged on

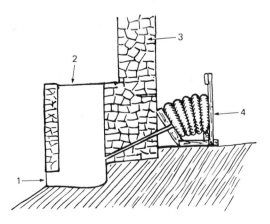

9.15 A small blast furnace seen in a village in the Atlas mountains of the Maghrib in the 1920s. The furnace had a small opening at the bottom (1) for removing the slag during the process and, afterwards, the iron; a larger opening on top (2) through which the mineral and charcoal were put into it and the smoke escaped; and a high wall at the back (3) which helped to draw the fire and also protected the man working the bellows (4) behind it.

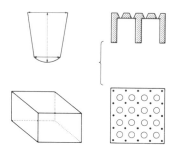

9.16 Components of a crucible steel furnace seen in use in Bokhara in AD 1840.

the same site to produce wrought iron. About 450 kilograms per day were produced from this furnace. Similar furnaces were in use in the Maghrib, one of which is illustrated in Fig. 9.15.

Crucible steel was melted in small crucibles. The text by al-Biruni quoted above describing the manufacture of this kind of steel by a smith in Damascus shows that several crucibles were put into one furnace and we know that several bellows were used, each operated by two men. Such a design was still in use in 1840 in Bukhara to make Damascus steel. Figure 9.16 shows the shape of this furnace and the support for the crucibles, as well as one crucible separately. Later though it is, the design is the same as that described by the alchemist Jabir ten centuries earlier (Fig. 9.17).

9.17 An illustration of a crucible steel furnace, from a book printed in the sixteenth century AD which was probably based on a thirteenth-century Arabic manuscript of Jabir.

10 *Engineers and artisans*

10.1 TECHNOLOGY AS A BRANCH OF SCIENCE

More than the Greeks, the Romans or the Byzantines, 'the Arabs recognised technology as a legitimate branch of science'. This is an important observation, which appeared in a recent history of medieval science in Europe; certainly Muslim scholars did pay due respect to all kinds of practical knowledge, classifying applied science and technological subjects alongside theoretical studies.

This is to be seen, for instance, in al-Khuwarizmi's work *Mafatih al-'Ulum* (*Keys of the Sciences*); in al-Farabi's *Ihsa' al-'Ulum* (*Enumeration of the Sciences*); the encyclopaedia of the 'Brethren of Purity' (an esoteric group of the sixth century AH/tenth century AD), *Rasa'il Ikhwan al-Safa* (*Epistles of the Brethren of Purity*); in *Kitab al-Najat* (*The Book of Salvation*) by Ibn Sina; in Ibn al-Nadim's famous biographical dictionary *al-Fihrist* (*Index*); in Ibn Khaldun's well-known introduction to his universal history *Muqaddima* (*Introduction*); in al-'Amiri's *al-I'lam bi-manaqib al-Islam* (*Introduction in the virtues of Islam*); in Tash Kubru Zadeh's *Miftah al-Sa'ada* (*The Key of Happiness*); and in al-Qalqashandi's *Subh al-A'sha* (*The Unveiling of the Blind*). Yet this list gives only some of the books in which such classifications appeared; it is by no means exhaustive.

Al-'Amiri's description of mechanics or engineering is worth quoting as an example of this approach:

Mechanics is a discipline that shares both in mathematics and natural science. It enables one to bring forth hidden water from the interior of the earth and also conduct water through water-wheels or fountains, to transport heavy objects with the application of little energy, to construct arched bridges over deep streams and to accomplish many other things, whose mention would take up too much room.

The science of mechanics is taken as a branch of mathematics and thus grouped together with arithmetic, geometry, astronomy and music; al-'Amiri (d. 381 AH/AD 991) concluded that 'from this survey of the mathematical sciences one can gather that there is no contradiction at all between them and the

10.1 Builders at work constructing a palace. Persian, fifteenth century AD. British Library, London.

263

religious sciences'. As described above engineering is no different from our modern conception of it, though by the time of later writers such as Ibn Khaldun (d. 749 AH/AD 1349), al-Qalqashandi (d. 821 AH/AD 1418) and Tash Kubru Zadeh (d. 968 AH/AD 1560), architecture (*al-handasa*) was also considered a mathematical science, for reasons soon to become evident. Together architecture and engineering could be divided into the following branches:

(*i*)   The science of all types of building;
(*ii*)   The science of optical technology;
(*iii*)   The science of burning mirrors;
(*iv*)   The science of centres of weights (centres of gravity);
(*v*)   The science of surveying;
(*vi*)   The science of rivers and canals;
(*vii*)   The science of bridges;
(*viii*) The science of prospecting for hidden waters;
(*ix*)   The science of pulleys;
(*x*)   The science of military machines;
(*xi*)   The science of navigation;
(*xii*)   The science of clocks;
(*xiii*) The science of weights and measures;
(*xiv*)   The science of ingenious machines.

All these sciences are technological, so that the word *handasa* just mentioned means, in this context, 'engineering and architecture', not just 'geometry'. And the word *muhandis* 'engineer' was used in this technological sense from the very early days of the Islamic civilisation; *handasa* or 'engineering and architecture' was an acknowledged and respected learned profession.

Mechanical and civil engineering, which were classified as mathematical sciences, were not the only technological subjects to be classed as science; there were non-mathematical technologies such as chemistry, industrial production and agriculture that were also thought of as 'sciences'. In addition, technological topics were to be found within purely scientific subjects; this was so in medicine, for example, where most books on pharmaceutical matters contain very useful information on the properties and manufacture of various organic and inorganic products. Again, arithmetic included technical calculations for engineers, while astronomy embraced treatises on the construction of measuring instruments, and so on.

10.2 THE ROLE OF ENGINEERS AND ARCHITECTS

Engineers and architects (*al-muhandisun*) enjoyed high social prestige in society and the title *muhandis* was usually added to the name of a person who practised this profession. We find the names of such people in Arabic sources such as *al-Fihrist* and other biographical and bibliographical reference books. Frequently, any scientists involved would concentrate on the physics of the profession, so that engineering might embrace mathematicians and astronomers as well as engineers, while some other scientific aspect of *handasa* might perhaps give openings for chemists or physicians. The distinction was not rigid however, as a few examples taken from among great Arabic scientists mentioned in Chapter 1 will make clear. Thus Jabir was a chemist and engineer, al-Kindi a physicist as well as a metallurgist and engineer, and al-Razi a chemist and engineer as well as a physician. Again, the Banu Musa brothers were mathematicians and astronomers in addition to being engineers, Ibn al-Haytham was a mathematician, physicist and engineer, and al-Biruni an astronomer, physicist and engineer. However, some like al-Jazari devoted themselves solely to engineering.

Most practising engineers did not write books and their names are in general not known to us, though some had their names inscribed on buildings that they constructed. An inscription dated 197 AH/AD 910 on a gate at Mardin in Diyar Bakr bears the name of the Caliph al-Muqtadir together with the names of the two engineers who erected the building. One of them was Ahmad b. Jamil al-Muhandiz. The term *al-mi'mar* was also used for 'architect' and we find this title on some Islamic buildings that still remain. Architects used to prepare general and detailed drawings for important buildings which they were designing, and also made scale models. For the engineering mathematicians the term *al-hasib* (literally, 'the one who calculates') was sometimes used, and the engineer himself could be a *hasib*. The *hasib* and the architect or engineer would always meet together for joint consultation.

Some engineers came from the ranks of the artisans. They started as builders, carpenters or mechanical craftsmen, then studied engineering and other sciences to become engineers and architects. Others were scientists who were highly skilled in various trades, which they sometimes practised.

Islamic engineers and architects were not only respected in society, as we have mentioned, but also could hold high positions in government. We know for instance that the Banu Musa

10.2 Architects with their instruments. Detail from a Persian decorated astrolabe disc. Seventeenth century AD. Victoria and Albert Museum, London.

brothers were favoured by the Caliph al-Mamun and his successors, and played an important role in the cultural and political life of Baghdad, while the Sultan al-Malik al-Zahir Barquq (d. 801 AH/AD 1399) married the daughter of his engineer al-Muhandis Shihab al-Din Ahmad al-Tuluni.

Sometimes high offices were created for engineers who, in addition to high salaries, were given rewards for specific achievements. For example, in the Mamluk kingdom among the Sultan's court there was the office of *Muhandis al-'Ama'ir* or 'The Architect of Buildings'; he was responsible for all buildings and building estimates, for town planning and for decisions regarding all those employed in the building trade. He was addressed by high official titles such as 'The Highly Dignified, the Respectable, the Trusty', and on occasions these titles could reach an even higher order. Other important offices for engineers lay in the construction and maintenance of irrigation systems; sometimes a tax was levied for the benefit of such officers. For very important works, committees of engineers were formed to design and supervise the complete project, as was the case when al-Mansur decided to build Baghdad. In some important ventures, joint missions were sent from one Islamic country to another.

Engineers sometimes acted as contractors. For example, the government would ask them to excavate a canal within a specified period and at a certain pre-determined cost. They in their turn would allocate sections of the work to sub-contractors, a system that is known to have existed in the third century AH (ninth century AD) in Baghdad.

10.3 ARTISANS

10.3.1 Artisans and the guilds

The study of artisans and industrial workers in the Islamic civilisation yields interesting results (Fig. 10.3). In the first chapter we discussed pre-Islamic civilisations in what became Muslim lands, and our conclusion was that while the older technical skills remained uninterrupted by Islam, they began a fresh lease of life with the new civilisation. This was because these skills were united into one culture with the help of the Arabic language and Islamic belief and outlook.

We have also seen how large cities were a characteristic of Islamic civilisation. Baghdad, for instance, was at one time the largest city in the world, with a population of about 1.5 million. Other Muslim cities competed in size with the larger cities of other contemporary civilisations, but no European city except Istanbul was comparable in extent to the great Islamic cities. Most of the inhabitants of these were artisans of various crafts and trades, which were numerous.

In Arabic the words for crafts, professions and industries are derived from the root *sn'*, which has the basic connotation of 'make' or 'manufacture'. Thus the word for craftsman is *sani'*, while *san'a* means 'manufacture' in one of its senses; and *sina'a*, is often used for any profession or trade. Thus medicine is a *sina'a*, as are literary activities and like subjects. A dry-dock for building ships was called a house of *sina'a* (*dar al-sina'a*); similarly a manufacturing industry was a *sina'a*. Thus in Islamic culture there is a feeling of respect for all professions, trades and crafts; skill in any one craft was – and still is – a source of pride. Among the present-day working classes of the cities the *sani'* or skilled worker is highly esteemed, and a father's ambition is always to see his son become skilled in one of the crafts.

In the Islamic cities of the East there were social organis-ations like the *futuwwa*; members were mostly young men from the working classes. It was natural that the *futuwwa* had strong representation from among artisans, and such organisations

10.3 An illustration from a Persian manuscript of the fifteenth century AD showing a group of craftsmen carrying out their trades round King Jamshed. They include a weaver, a woman with a spinning wheel, a carpenter and smiths. Chester Beatty Library, Dublin.

sometimes exercised a kind of opposition to class differences. They had high ideals, and reciprocal influences developed between them and the communities of Sufis (Muslim mystics).

From the beginning, each craft was located in one area or *suq*, and all the craftsmen of a certain profession were organised into a guild of their own. Such guilds and their relationships with the *futuwwa* have not been sufficiently studied, especially in the early periods of Islamic civilisation; nevertheless we do know that the relationship between the guilds, the *futuwwa* and the Sufi organisations became strong after the fifth century AH (eleventh century AD).

Membership of a guild gave the artisan a feeling of pride in his craft. But in addition to his professional objectives, the artisan had social and religious ideals; attainment of perfection in his craft became a spiritual ideal also. It could not take place except by hard work under skilful guidance of a master of that craft, so the first step was always to seek a master and be initiated into a guild. The guild had a chain (*silsila*) leading from the master to the patron saint of the craft, thence to the Prophets. Each guild had a *shaykh*, and all guilds were bound together by the office of *shaykh al-mashayikh* (sheik of sheiks). There were three professional grades in each craft; first the apprentice (*mubtadi'*), then the *sani'*, who had to pass a proficiency examination before becoming a master (*mu'allim*); proficiency certificates (*ijaza*) were sometimes given. These rituals and guild traditions became established in the Muslim lands of the East in the late Middle Ages, but they have developed from a combination of the rituals of the *futuwwa*, the Sufis and the guilds of earlier periods.

It is important to note here that the words *mu'allim* and *'ustadh* were both used to denote the master of a trade as well as to describe professors or teachers. This again reflects the social esteem of skill in trades and crafts, which is also confirmed by the fact that several Muslim men of learning used to practise certain crafts in order to earn a living. The family names of such men, and those of well-known families in Islamic cities, indicate the crafts that were practised most often by such people; these tended to be concerned with textiles and other basic industries.

Islamic regions and cities were also renowned for the skill of their craftsmen. Al-Muqaddasi, when describing the main assets of Bilad al-Sham (southern Greater Syria), said that 'it has marble quarries, drugs for all medicines, men of letters and writers, craftsmen and physicians'. When comparing Damietta and Tinnis in Egypt, he said that Damietta had 'better-skilled craftsmen than Tinnis'. Again, al-Qazwini, in speaking of Mosul, said: 'Its inhabitants are generous, manly and they are meticulous in their crafts'. Of Isfahan he wrote: 'Its craftsmen have surpassed others in every craft'. And of Jurjaniyya: 'Its people practise accurate and skilled crafts such as the blacksmith or the carpenter and they go to extremes in the accuracy of their workmanship'. Al-Zuhri described those who lived in Almeria in Spain and said 'all its inhabitants, men and women, are craftsmen working with their hands'.

So far we have covered the main trades and crafts in Islamic society and, of course, all were undertaken by craftsmen skilled in their arts. We shall now discuss briefly the three main types: the builder, the carpenter and the blacksmith.

10.3.2 The builder

The building trade comprised several crafts, the chief one among them being that of the builder (*banna'*, also called *mi'mar*). Sometimes his work included that of stonemason and sculpturing in stone. The outstanding examples of Islamic art and architecture are living testimony to the high level of craftsmanship which Muslim builders attained, and much has been written on this subject by historians of Islamic art and architecture.

In some cases the builder was also an architect. We find, for example, an inscription on an historic building dated 702 AH/ AD 1303 declares it to have been 'Executed by Abu Talib the Architect, the Builder'. In certain instances the builder was in fact an architect, preparing only the drawings and supervising the work, leaving the actual building to be done by others; several inscriptions on ancient buildings indicate this. One such runs: 'Builder: Mas'ud; Design drawings (*tarsim*) by Ustadh Ja'far b. Mahmud al-Halabi'. The designer or architect is here called *ustadh*, a title given to a person who is highly skilled, and in several buildings we even find the builder credited with the two titles *ustadh* and *banna'* together. In other cases he was called *mu'allim* and *banna'* at the same time. In addition, Arabic sources often pay tribute to the builders of famous Muslim buildings, giving their biographies, while the names of still other builders are known to us from archaeological inscriptions.

10.4(*a*) Carpenters sawing wood. Illustration from a thirteenth-century AD manuscript. Bibliothèque Nationale, Paris.

10.3.3 The carpenter

The craft of carpenter (*najjar*) is a basic one. It required a knowledge of geometry and measurement, and some Muslim notables were carpenters. In the woodworking trade there were, of course, several specialised crafts, such as sawing (Fig. 10.4 (*a*) and (*b*)), wood turning (Fig. 10.5), and combmaking; in addition there were the artistic crafts of wood inlay and wood carving. The museums of the world contain many fine examples of Islamic art in wood which have been the subject of several studies.

As with builders, Arabic sources mention the names and give biographies of some famous Muslim carpenters. It was also the practice for such men to leave their names on important works that they had made; some of these still exist.

10.4(*b*) Modern carpenters in Omdurman, Sudan using similar methods.

10.5 A turner in Pakistan using a bow to rotate the piece of wood on which he is working.

10.3.4 Techniques of the builder, carpenter and allied tradesmen

The basic tools of the builder and carpenter of today are not very different from those used in medieval times and can still be seen in use in many countries. Figure 10.4 gives an idea of the techniques and tools used in Islam (see p. 270 above), and it is striking to see how like present-day methods they are.

Ibn al-Ukhuwwa (who worked at the beginning of the eighth century AH/fourteenth century AD), included a chapter in his manual for the *muhtasib* on how to regulate, control and discover the fraudulent practices of carpenters, sawyers, and builders, and their labourers (*raqqasun*), as well as the gypsum burners (*jabbasun*) and lime burners (*jayyarun*). We shall give a summary of this chapter, since it conveys a good picture of the codes of practice and state of the art.

1. A trustworthy and honest man who is skilled in a trade (*'arif*) should be the one in charge under the *muhtasib*.
2. Most craftsmen are employed at a fixed daily hire. Provisions must be made to prevent them being late in the morning and leaving early in the evening; they should leave only at the proper time in the evening.
3. Some builders, carpenters and painters will give wrong estimates and make the customer understand that the work will not take long and also that it will be easy and inexpensive. The customer is encouraged, but once the artisan starts he will need more time and money than was

estimated. This is cheating and will harm the customer who may be made so poor or so much in debt that he may be obliged to sell the place before it is finished. This is a great wrong. Action should be taken to prevent this.

4. If a building craftsman neglects to use the necessary instruments such as squares, levels and strings to align his work so that it is out of true or not vertical or even oblique, then he is liable for correcting the faulty work.

5. If the builders spoil any of the hired wooden beams that are used as supports by cutting them, they should compensate for the damage and make apologies.

6. Labourers known as *raqqasun* (lit. 'dancers') should be made to wear special clothes (known as *tababin*) which cover their private parts when they ascend or descend. They should not leave before sunset.

7. Sawyers on each workshop site should not be less than three in number. One will sharpen (grind) the saws, another will work while the third is taking his rest. They should not leave before the evening. They should be prevented from conspiring against the customer.

8. Builders should make an oath by God that they do not accept any bribe or present from the lime burners or gypsum burners to persuade them to accept bad quality material. [Instructions are then given by al-Ukhuwwa on how to examine the quality of gypsum.] Lime burners should be controlled so that they do not sell any except best quality lime (*tawabiqi*). It should be sold by weight only. Builders should give good advice on these matters to their employers and clients.

9. Plasterers should not put too much lime with the gypsum. This is sometimes done to ease the work of spreading the mixture on the walls, but it will cause the gypsum to fall.

10. Carpenters making door locks should be controlled by a pious man who knows his craft very well. This is a serious matter and needs strict control for the protection of people's property and fortunes and for safeguarding women. They are not to be allowed to make two similar keys for two different persons. [Ibn al-Ukhuwwa then gives technical instructions on preventing bad workmanship for locks. Figure 10.6 shows such a door lock described in detail by al-Jazari.]

11. Painters should be prevented from cheating in their work. [There then follow instructions on the number of coats of paint and drying instructions.]

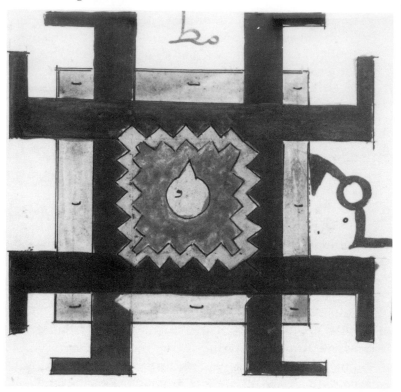

10.6 Al-Jazari's design for four connected bolts made of wood or iron
for locking a door. Thirteenth century AD. Bodleian Library, Oxford.

In another chapter on the quality control of combs, we gain
information on the kinds of wood that must be used and the
necessary manufacturing tools. Teeth are cut by the *makhraza*,
which is exact in its cutting stroke. Rounding the teeth is done
by a plane (*randak*).

10.3.5 The blacksmith and metal trades

Artisans working in metal were more numerous than those
engaged in building. In addition to the blacksmith, there were
foundry workers in bronze and iron. Among the artisans who
worked in non-ferrous metals, were coppersmiths, braziers,
tinsmiths, jewellers, gem-cutters, goldsmiths, gold-beaters,
gold lace spinners, silversmiths, embossers, engravers, wire
drawers (Fig. 10.7), and others. Among those who worked in
iron and steel mention may be made of nailsmiths, cutlers,
swordsmiths, scissors-makers, file cutters, gunsmiths, makers
of balances, locksmiths (cf. Fig. 10.3, Fig. 10.8 (*a*) and (*b*)), and
so on.

Though a blacksmith works with iron and steel, the title
could be applied also to makers of any of the special iron and

10.7 A craftsman drawing wire. Sixteenth century AD. British Library, London.

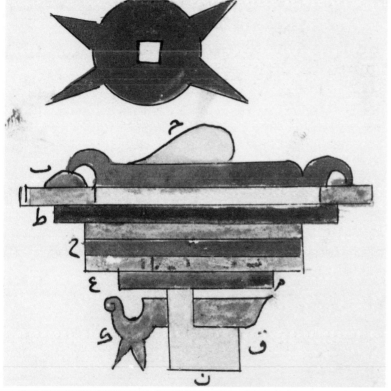

10.8 *centre and bottom*. Details of a lock for a chest designed by al-Jazari. The lock was operated by a combination of letters of the alphabet marked on rotating discs. Bodleian Library, Oxford.

steel products mentioned earlier. The art of the blacksmith was also another respected craft, and some of its practitioners were poets and men of letters as well, one file cutter being a noted debating jurist (*faqih*). Blacksmiths played a significant role in the art of Islamic ironworking, and many of their artistic products have survived. The names of these men are known because of the pride they took in their work.

Blacksmiths were indispensable in war, since they were the makers of arms and armour. There was, of course, some specialisation; there were blacksmiths for light products, others for heavy items. A decree issued by the Sultan al-Ashraf Qansuh al-Ghawri and dated 914 AH/AD 1509 conscripted all the metal founders and blacksmiths of both light and heavy work. But in times of peace, in addition to the products already mentioned, the blacksmith supplied society with its many needs; these included horseshoes, shovels, hoes, ploughshares, scythes, builders' tools, carpenters' tools and a variety of other iron and steel items. The tools of the blacksmith himself were hammers, tongs, chisels and cutters, while a forge was installed in every smithy, together with an anvil and a bellows (Fig. 10.9). The blacksmith's products were subject to quality control by the *muhtasib*

10.9 A blacksmith in his forge in Marrakesh, Morocco. In the background a boy pumps the bellows for the fire.

10.4 QUALITY CONTROL

Throughout this book examples have been given from the *hisba* manuals on quality control prepared for the guidance of the *muhtasib*. The system of *hisba* in Islam had an important role in the organisation of crafts and the quality of their products. We shall not discuss the religious aspects of *hisba* here; suffice it to say that it was the *Qadi* (Muslim judge in matters of canon law) who appointed the *muhtasib*, a government official whose duty was to look after public morals, to ensure conformity of religion in public, and to suppress seditious acts. He supervised weights and measures to ensure equity, and was responsible for complaints about scales and measurements; as well, he kept watch against fraud and cheating by manufacturers, and performed other municipal duties.

Such broad responsibility required wide knowledge, so it is not surprising that guide books and manuals were written on *hisba*, containing information on various goods to enable the *muhtasib* to carry out his duties. Among such books are the noted manuals of Ibn al-Ukhuwwa and al-Shayzari. Besides these texts there also appeared, as we have seen in an earlier chapter, some specialised writings which explained how to discover cheating in particular crafts, among them the famous *Kashf al-Asrar* (*Revealing the Secrets*) by al-Jawbari.

The *muhtasib* could not, however, be versed in all crafts and so he used to appoint several assistants for each speciality. Thus we read in Ibn al-Ukhuwwa that to supervise needle manufacturers the *muhtasib* must

appoint a supervisor who is trustworthy and honest from among their craft so that he can prevent them from mixing steel needles with soft iron ones, since these last ones if they are polished may look like Damascus steel needles, each type should be separated and he will exact an oath from them to do this.

The *muhtasib* was performing a duty similar in part to that of a modern-day specification and standards department and partly to those bodies which protect consumer interests.

11 *Epilogue*

11.1 THE NEED TO RE-EXAMINE CRITICAL HISTORICAL ISSUES

The story of Islamic technology is a fascinating one, and the authors have been thrilled to see new aspects emerge as a result of writing this book. In doing so, however, they have found it necessary to discuss some of these in general rather than in critical terms. This is because their purpose has been to stimulate an interest by re-examining issues which, until now, have been taken for granted.

In spite of its fascination, however, the story of Islamic technology is far from complete. Research in this area is still at an early stage and, notwithstanding what has been published so far, contributions by Islam to science and technology have yet to be fully revealed. During the nineteenth and the first quarter of the twentieth centuries, Western research into Islamic science yielded outstanding results, but only after a long period of silence has that interest now been revived. There is still a need for additional co-ordinated research if significant results are to be obtained. The field of alchemy, chemistry and chemical technology is a case in point. At present this is an almost totally neglected area, in which few seem to have taken even a slight interest since the admirable research several decades ago of Kraus, Ruska, Stapleton and Wiedemann.

Yet to pursue the subject means reading and examining the contents of most of the existing Arabic manuscripts in alchemy and chemistry. After all, comparative studies of the contributions of different civilisations to, say, the discovery and use of alcohol, simply cannot be made in the absence of such research.

There is a second factor which hinders the revelation of Islamic achievements in science and technology. We are constantly told that in Islam science came to a halt in the eleventh century AD, and it is customary to accept this claim without reservation. Yet it is simply untrue; Islamic science did not even go into decline at that time. All that happened was that the

279

pace of development slowed down during this period; indeed, Islamic science and technology continued to progress for several centuries.

We may, in fact, define three stages in the evolution of Islamic science and technology, an evolution which continued up to the advent of the Scientific Revolution in the West. The first is a period of transition and assimilation, leading to the emergence of Islamic science. The second is characterised by the prevalence of scientific innovation, and the third by innovation in both technology as well as science. This last may be said to have begun in the twelfth century and to have ended only in the sixteenth or seventeenth century.

We should like to draw attention to this last period, during which the hundreds of thousands of Arabic, Persian and Turkish manuscripts now to be found in libraries all over the world were written. Indeed, it is true to say that proportionately more technological manuscripts date from this stage than from the previous two. Very rich in scientific and technological accomplishments, it has nevertheless been a period largely neglected by historians of science and technology. Admittedly, such historians have acknowledged the progress achieved by Muslim scientists in mathematics, astronomy and the exact sciences, but they have for the most part been harsh in their judgement on Islamic technological innovation. Yet on closer examination it becomes clear that technology was directly involved in all material aspects of the civilisation of Islam; standards of living, the type and diversity of products used or consumed, the level and extension of agriculture, methods of irrigation, lines of communication, and the arms used in warfare, all depended on technology. When people speak of the splendour of Granada or Baghdad, they are referring in fact not only to their artistic grandeur but also to the high level of their technology. This is true, too, of the Crusades, where Islamic successes also depended to no small extent on technological achievements.

Underestimation or even denial of this aspect of Muslim culture may be attributed to a variety of causes. One is that Islamic technology has not been sufficiently studied. We are still largely ignorant of what it achieved. To rectify this is a worthwhile pursuit, though it requires historians not only able to read and understand Arabic but also to be familiar with Islamic civilisation in general. And just as there are many technological manuscripts in Arabic and other languages not yet translated or, if translated not yet published, in European languages, there is also a wealth of information dispersed in encyclopaedic works and in books on history, geography, literature and other fields. Nor have archaeological findings been sufficiently examined. Only after in-depth classification and analysis of such sources can there be an accurate appraisal of the technological achievement of Islam.

Another factor which may have influenced the judgement of some historians is that of personal prejudice. We shall not elaborate on this; it is a factor that is almost certain to arise when considering the developments of a different civilisation. Supporters of each culture are always eager to lay claim to the most important inventions, or at least to cast doubts on those of another. The scope for controversy widens, of course, when there is a lack of written documents, and it is well known that most discoveries were never committed to writing but were transmitted from one culture to another by travel, war and commerce. Furthermore, an invention or discovery which originates in one country may be developed considerably and be better exploited in another. Such occurrences can cause confusion and favour the emergence of prejudice.

There is a final factor which may have a psychological influence on the judgement of some specialists. This is the comparison between present scientific underdevelopment in the East and the high technological development of the West. However, evaluation of the earlier technology of Islam should in no way be influenced by the spectacular achievements of modern times.

Joseph Needham, for example, has dedicated much of his life to the study of science and civilisation in China. He has recalled that he did so when he discovered how little people in the West knew about China. Being passionately fond of the country, he began studying Chinese language and culture, gathering round him a group of scholars familiar with Chinese language and culture inspired by his fervour. A first-rate scientist himself, he led his team with the purpose of restoring the science and technology of China to its proper place. In this he has succeeded magnificently; his writings are considered the most authoritative works on the subject. The scientific civilisation of Islam, however, still waits for its Needham.

11.2 FACTORS OF DECLINE AND SOME OBSTACLES TO PROGRESS

In this book we have outlined the factors behind the innovations in Muslim technology. Study of these same factors can help us investigate the decline of Islamic science and technology in later centuries, and define the obstacles hindering the development in Islamic countries in our own times.

Just as political stability and economic prosperity were at the roots of the development of science and technology, so did the stunting of its growth come about, at least in part, as a result of political disintegration of the State and the deterioration of economic life. The rise of so many individual states, independent emirates and feudal systems was a manifestation of this decline.

The raids of barbaric tribes from central Asia helped precipitate this deterioration. One consequence of these assaults was the break-down of the established systems of irrigation and the deterioration of agriculture in both Iraq and the Jazira.

While Islamic religion was the main impulse behind the renaissance of science at the zenith of Muslim Arab civilisation, it was partly the post-sixteenth century rise of clerical faction which froze this same science and withered its progress. Western Christendom had similar religious set-backs, apostatic movements which tried to hinder the scientific revolution in the West. But the triumph of religious fanaticism over science in Muslim lands would not have succeeded had there been sufficient economic prosperity to generate a demand for science and technology. For Islam, as we have mentioned, was the driving force behind the Muslim scientific revolution when the Muslim state had reached its peak. In the ages of decadence, however, the movement of religious fanaticism against science was no other than an outstanding symptom of political and economic disintegration. The tragedy of the demolition of the last observatory in Islam, established in Constantinople by Taqi al-Din in 1580, exemplifies this victory of the clerical faction over science. And it is deplorable to note the inherent irony of the fact that the first observatory in the West was built around the same period, by Tycho Brahe.

In studying this period it must be noted that just before the Ottoman Conquest the distressing economic conditions were further aggravated by major world-wide events that eventually culminated in the rise of Western capitalism.

In 1497 the Portuguese Vasco da Gama sailed round the Cape of Good Hope, an event of lasting effect in the history of the countries of the Near East, even of the entire Islamic world. For thereafter the Indian trade shifted away from the Syrian and Egyptian ports, thus draining a rich source of revenue from Muslim lands. In addition, the subsequent rise of Western capitalism and Western colonialism, with its commercial and naval power, became a major factor in the economics of the Near East.

With the opening up of the route round the Cape of Good Hope in the first century of the Ottoman Empire, European traders began to encourage commercial ties with the Turks. In 1553, Sultan Soliman I granted British traders a charter of free trade with his Empire, and in the same year as the British set up the Levant Company, the Ottomans drastically reduced the customs duties on all British and European imports. In consequence the Ottoman economy gradually became subject to the European economy. In the beginning no one realised the danger of this policy, for the imported commodities were limited mostly to wool textiles, metals, and paper; not until the nineteenth century did local Muslim industry begin to feel its impact. The situation has worsened in the present century. In the wake of the Industrial Revolution, it is now evident that the dependence of Islamic countries on finished European products is having a detrimental effect on their economy and their industry. Moreover, the gap is increasing. During the nineteenth and twentieth centuries most Islamic lands were subjected to colonial rule by Western powers. As a result, whereas Western Europe witnessed an industrial revolution that started in the nineteenth century and gathered momentum in the twentieth, during the same period the colonially-dominated Islamic lands were calculatedly deterred from making similar progress.

After the Second World War most Islamic lands became independent once again, but the scars of long colonial rule remained. These are evident in the further fragmentation of Arabic and Islamic countries into smaller states, in the current sectarian feuds and devastating civil wars within various countries and the destructive wars between neighbouring ones, in economic dominance by foreign powers, and in the cultural domination exemplified in the use of foreign rather than national languages in higher education.

11.3 FUTURE OF ISLAMIC TECHNOLOGY

Despite all the adversities and obstacles facing Islamic lands, a number of them are already progressing along the road of scientific and technological development.

In discussing this further, we shall avoid reference to those highly-controversial theories of development that have been propounded in modern times and which have led only to despair among peoples of the Third World. All the same, it must be remembered that in the previous epoch many experts were to be found warning these peoples against the drawbacks of modern industrialisation. Much was said of the dangers of pollution, of the fear of imminent depletion of resources, and of the excessive harm to indigenous cultural values should they embark on modern industrial development. Some advocated instead milder doses of development, for instance by adopting the so-called intermediate technologies, epitomised in the slogan 'small is beautiful'. Others have called for merely the fulfilment of basic needs. Conviction that suggestions such as these are valid depends either on the acutely grim conditions of underdevelopment, or the abject poverty under which certain countries in the world are crushed.

In their investigation of problems of growth in developing countries, a common mistake made by some thinkers, in both the Third World and the industrial world alike, is to try to devise general and comprehensive solutions for problems which are individually different. This is mistaken because it must be recognised that there are various levels of development for countries of the Third World. Some have ancient civilisations, others are newly-born. Some are densely populated, others only sparsely so. Some enjoy abundant oil and mineral wealth, others suffer from a dearth of resources. To attempt comprehensive solutions to the diversified problems of those countries making up the Third World can only cause excessive harm, hampering the normal growth of developing countries and frustrating their peoples.

The lands of Islam have been the cradle of some of the richest civilisations ever known. Science appeared in the Nile valley, Syria and Mesopotamia. It continued uninterrupted over thousands of years, reaching its peak during the Islamic age. It flowed on incessantly, the wide gap of today opening only since the Industrial Revolution, less than 150 years ago. Thus there is a solid substratum to the civilisation of the Muslim world, which has indigenous and inherent cultural traditions and customs, deeply rooted in the peoples of the area. In addition, there are the crafts and industrial skills inherited over thousands of years. One example of the latter may be seen in Aleppo, where craftsmen manufacture the most delicate modern machinery, no whit inferior to imported and imitated versions. Plenty of other corroborative evidence may be found in the thousands of workshops and in the multitude of small industries, both traditional and modern, which are to be found in all Islamic cities of the Mediteranean. These countries, then, possess the fundamental ingredients of a modern industrial renaissance. The various classes of society have the necessary craft skills bred in them and handed down from generation to generation since time immemorial.

In approaching modern science and technology we must

remind ourselves of those lessons of history that help us look to the future. For history shows that there is nothing in the technical and substantive content of any part of science, or indeed of technologies high or low, that cannot be nurtured and developed by any people of any type of culture. Almost no society nor set of cultural conditions is hostile: on the contrary, almost all the great groups of mankind have throughout the ages made significant contributions to the common heritage of knowledge and techniques. Among the foremost of them we may count the peoples of Islam.

Once we realise that the substantive content of science and technology finds no cultural barriers, we arrive at another lesson of history. It has been said that 'in the past, as now, science and scientists flourish in large communities and linguistic groups rather than small, in affluent areas better than in poor'. During historic times science has indeed flourished only when an empire or a nation became mighty and rich, because it depends on the infrastructure provided by the existence of affluence. This is amply demonstrated throughout Islamic history.

The Islamic world is rich in natural and human resources, which is fortunate because the future of its science and technology depends upon the successful utilisation of a combination of these two ingredients. Development in all fields within a community depends significantly on the 'scientific size', which is itself proportional to the size of the population and the gross national product per head.

Individually, the oil-rich countries are all small in size. Each cannot by itself create an effective science and technology, or an independent industrial economy. Similarly, those Muslim countries which are endowed with human resources lack the capital essential for the development of science and technology and, indeed, for their general development.

Though most individual Islamic states now realise the importance of science and technology for their future development, and though some have achieved considerable success along this road, future progress in all Muslim countries, rich and poor, depends on the extent of economic co-operation and integration among them on a regional basis.

We can take the Arab States as an example of one large community having a cultural unity of language, religion and history. 'If the Arab States were to combine their human, capital and natural resources within the framework of an Arab Common Market, their ability to achieve rapid and diversified industrialisation would be unquestionably enhanced. At present the national markets are too small to enable important industries to be developed under competitive conditions. The collective demand of Arab countries for industrial products is substantial and it will continue to increase with the continuous process of socio-economic development. The creation of an Arab Common Market which can utilise the oil revenues and the surplus capital would make it possible for the Arab World to meet most of its individual requirements through domestic production.'

Wider regional economic co-operation and integration is quite feasible also among the various Islamic countries on a regional basis. To achieve this the countries of Islam require perception, determination and co-operative leadership.

Selected bibliography

1. INTRODUCTION

Anawati, G., 'Science' in *The Cambridge History of Islam*, ed. P. M. Holt, A. K. S. Lambton and Bernard Lewis, Vol. II, Cambridge, 1970, pp. 741–79.

Arnaldez, R. and Massignon, L., 'Arabic Science' in *A General History of the Sciences*, ed. R. Taton, *Ancient and Medieval Science*, London, 1964, pp. 385–421.

Daniel, N., *Islam and the West: The Making of an Image*, Edinburgh, 1960.

Forbes, R. J., *Studies in Ancient Technology*, 9 vols., Brill, Leiden, 1955–72.

al-Hassan, Ahmad Y., and Hill, Donald R., *Factors of Innovation in Islamic Technology*, UNU research report, 1981.

Mieli, Aldo, *La Science Arabe*, Leiden, 1966.

Nasr, S. H., *Islamic Science*, World of Islam Festival, 1976.

Needham, Joseph, *Science and Civilisation in China*, Cambridge University Press, 1954 onwards – in progress.

O'Leary, De L., *How Greek Science Passed to the Arabs*, London, 1948.

Sabra, A. J., 'The Scientific Enterprise' in *The World of Islam*, ed. B. Lewis, Thames & Hudson, London, 1976, pp. 181–200.

Sarton, George, *Introduction to the History of Science*, 3 vols., Baltimore, 1927–48.

Schacht, J. and Bosworth, C. E., (ed.), *The Legacy of Islam*, Oxford, 1974.

Sezgin, Fuat, *Geschichte des Arabischen Schrifftums*, Brill, Leiden, 1967 onwards.

Singer, Charles, *et al.*, *A History of Technology*, 8 vols., Oxford, 1954–8.

Wiedmann, E., *Aufsätze zur Arabischen Wissenschaftsgeschichte*, Olms, Hildesheim, 1970.

2. MECHANICAL ENGINEERING

Banu-Musa, *Kitab al-hiyal*, Arabic text, edited by Ahmad Y. al-Hassan, IHAS, Aleppo, 1981.

Banu-Musa, *The Book of Ingenious Devices*, an annotated translation of the Banu Musa's work by Donald R. Hill, Reidel, Dordrecht, 1979.

Carra de Vaux, 'Le Livre des Appareils Pneumatiques et des Machines Hydrauliques par Philon de Byzance', *Paris Académie des Inscriptions et Belles Lettres*, **38** (1903) Pt. 1.

Carra de Vaux, 'Les Mécaniques ou l'Elevateur de Héron d'Alexandrie sur la version Arabe de Qusta ibn Luqa', *Journal Asiatique*, 9ᵉ Série (1893), Tome I, 386–472, Tome II, 152–92, 193–269, 420–514. Reissued as facsimile in a single volume, with Introduction by D. R. Hill and Commentary by A. G. Drachmann (Les Belles Lettres, Paris, 1988).

al-Hassan, Ahmad Y., *Taqi al-Din and Arabic Mechanical Engineering*, Aleppo University, 1976.

Hill, Donald R., 'A treatise on machines', *Journal for the History of Arabic Science*, I, No. 1, May, 1977, 33–46.

Hill, Donald R., *Arabic Water-clocks*, Institute for the History of Arabic Science, Aleppo, 1981.

Hill, Donald R., *On the Construction of Water-clocks*, an annotated translation of the 'Archimedes' treatise, Occasional Paper No. 4, Turner and Devereaux, London, 1976.

Hill, Donald R., *A History of Engineering in Classical and Medieval Times*, Croom Helm, London, 1984.

al-Jazari, *Al-jami' bayn al'ilm wa l-'amal al-nafi' fi sina'at al-hiyal*, Arabic text edited by Ahmad Y. al-Hassan, Institute for the History of Arabic Science, Aleppo, 1979.

al-Jazari, *The Book of Knowledge of Ingenious Mechanical Devices*, an annotated translation of al-Jazari's work by Donald R. Hill, Reidel, Dordrecht, 1974.

Al-Khazini, Abu'l-Fath al-Rahman al Mansur, *Kitab Mizan al-Hikma*, Arabic text edited by Hashim al-Nadwa, Hyderabad, 1940.

Schiøler, Thorkild, *Roman and Islamic Water-lifting Wheels*, Odense University Press, 1973.

Schmeller, H., *Beitrage Z. Geschichte d. Technik in der Antike und bei der Arabern*, Mencke, Erlangen, 1922. (Abhdl. Z. Gesch, d. Naturwissen-schaften und die Med. No. 6.)

Tekeli, Sevim, *The Clocks in Ottoman Empire in 16th Century and Taqi al Din's: (The Brightest Stars for the Construction of the Mechanical Clocks)*, Ankara University, 1966.

Wiedemann, E., 'Über Vorrichtungen zum Heben von Wasser in der Islamischen Kultur', *Nova Acta Abh. der Kaiserl. Leop. Deutschen Akademie der Naturforscher*, **100** (Halle 1915), 1–272.

Wiedemann, E., 'Über die Uhren in Bereich der islamischen Kultur', Beiträge zur Geschichte der Technik und Industrie, *Jahrbuch des Vereins Deutscher Ingenieure*, **8** (1918), 121-54.

3. CIVIL ENGINEERING

Cahen, Claude, 'Le service de l'irrigation en Iraq au debut du XIe siècle', *Bulletin d'études orientales*, Vol. 13, (1949–51), 117–43.

Creswell, K. A. C., *Early Muslim Architecture*, 2 vols., 1932–40.

Glick, Thomas F., *Irrigation and Society in Medieval Valencia*, Harvard University Press, 1970.

Glick, Thomas F., *Islamic and Christian Spain in the Early Middle Ages*, Princeton University Press, 1979.

Goblot, Henri, *Les Qanats, une Technique d'Acquisition de l'Eau*, Mouton, Paris, 1979.

Hill, Donald R., *A History of Engineering in Classical and Medieval Times*, Croom Helm, London, 1984.

Ibn al-Ukhuwwa, *Ma'alim al-qurba fi ahkam al hisba*, translated by R. Levy, *Gibb Memorial Series*, **XII**, 1938.

Al-Karadji, Abu Bakr Muhammad b. al-Hassan al Hasib, *Inbat al-miyah al-khafiyya*, Hyderabad, Deccan, 1940.

Le Strange, Guy, *Lands of the Eastern Caliphate*, London, 1905, 3rd impression, 1966.

Al-Muqaddasi, Abu'Abd Allah Shams al-Din, *Ahsan al-Taqasim fi Ma'rifat at-Aqalim*, Vol. III of *Bibliotheca geographorum Arabicorum*, ed. M. J. de Goeje, Leiden, 1906.

Smith, Norman, *A History of Dams*, London, 1971.

Wulff, H., *Traditional Crafts of Persia*, MIT Press, 1966.

4. MILITARY TECHNOLOGY

Cahen, Claude, 'Un traite d'armurerie composé pour Saladin', Arabic text, French translation and notes, in *Bulletin d'études orientales*, **12** (1947–8)

Creswell, K. A. C., *A Bibliography of Arms and Armour in Islam*, London, 1956.

Mercier, Maurice, *Le Feu Grégois*, Geuthner, Paris, 1952.

Parry, V. J. and Yapp, M. E., (editors), *War Technology and Society in the Middle East*, Oxford University Press, London, 1975. (See in particular the article by Hassanein Rabie', pp. 125–63.)

Partington, J. R., *A History of Greek Fire and Gunpowder*, Heffer, Cambridge, 1960.

Reinaud and Fave, 'Du feu grégois, des feux de guerre et des origines de le poudre à canon chez les Arabes, les Persans et les Chinois', *Journal Asiatique*, 1849, 6ᵉ serie, **XIV**, 257–327.

Ritter, H., '*La Parure des Cavaliers* und die Literatur über di ritterlichen Künste', *Der Islam*, **XVIII** (1929), 116–54.

Scanlon, G., 'Source Material for a History of Medieval Muslim Warfare', *Proceedings of the Congress of Orientalists at Moscow, 1960*, **ii**, Moscow, 1963, 56.

5. SHIPS AND NAVIGATION

Adnan Adivar. *Sur le Tanksukname-i-Ilhani der ulum-U-Funun-i-Khatai.*, *Isis*, 1947, **32**, 44.

Bittner, M. *Die Topographischen Kapitel d. Indischen Seespiegels 'Mohit' ['Muhit' (The Ocean) of Sidi 'Ali Reis]; mit einer Einleitung sowie mit 30 Tafeln versehen, von W. Tomaschek*, K. K. Geographischen Gesellschaft, Vienna, 1897. (Festschrift z. Erinnerung an die Eroffnung des Seeweges nach Ostindien durch Vasco da Gama, 1497.)

Ferrand, G. *Relations de Voyages et Textes Géographiques Arabes, Persans et Turcs relatifs à l'Extrème Orient, du 8ᵉ au 18ᵉ Siècles, traduits, revus et annotés etc.*, 2 vols. Leroux, Paris, 1913.

Ferrand, G. (tr.). *Voyage du Marchand Sulayman en Inde et en Chine redigé en 851; suivi de remarques par Abu Zayd Hasan (vers 916)*. Bossard, Paris, 1922.

Ferrand, G. *Instructions Nautiques et Routiers Arabes et Portugais des 15ᵉ et 16ᵉ Siècles*. 2 vols. Geuthner, Paris, 1921–5. Vols. 1 and 2 *Le Pilote des Mers de l'Inde, de la Chine et de l'Indonesie*; facsimile texts of MSS. of Sihab al-Din Ahmad al-Majid (c. 1475) and of Sulaiman al-Mahri (c. 1511).

Ferrand, G. *Instructions Nautiques et Routiers Arabes et Portugais des 15ᵉ et 16ᵉ Siècles*. Geuthner, Paris, 1928. Vol. 3 *Introduction à l'Astronomie Nautique Arabe*. Consists of reprints of Prinsep; Congreve; de

Saussure, and excerpts from Reinaud & Guyard, etc., with biographies of Ibn Majid and al-Mahri by Ferrand.

Goodrich, L. Carrington. 'Query on the connection between the nautical charts of the Arabs and those of the Chinese before the days of the Portuguese navigators.' *Isis*, 1953, 44, 99.

von Hammer-Purgstall, J. 'Extracts from the *Mohit [Muhit]* (The Ocean), a Turkish work on navigation in the Indian Seas' [by Sidi 'Ali Reis, c. 1533]. *Journal of the Royal Asiatic Society Series B*, 1834, 3, 545; 1836, 5, 441; 1837, 6, 805, 1858, 7, 767; 1839, 8, 823; with notes by J. Prinsep.

Hourani, G. F. *Arab Seafaring in the Indian Ocean in Ancient and Early Medieval Times.* Princeton University Press, Princeton, New Jersey, 1951. (Princeton Oriental Studies, no. 13.)

Nadvi, Sulaiman S. 'Arab Navigation' in *Islamic Culture*, a series of articles 1941–2.

Needham, Joseph. *Science and Civilisation in China*, Cambridge University Press, Vol. IV.3, 1971.

Prinsep, J. 'Note on the nautical instruments of the Arabs.' *Journal of the Royal Asiatic Society, Series B*, 1836, 784. Reprinted in Ferrand.

Prinsep, J. 'Notes [on von Hammer-Purgstall's translation from the *Mohit [Muhit]* (The Ocean) of Sidi 'Ali Reis].' *Journal of the Royal Asiatic Society, Series B*, 1836, 5, 441; 1838, 7, 774. Reprinted in Ferrand, G., *op. cit.*

De Saussure, L. 'Commentaire des instructions nautique de Ibn Majid et Sulaiman al-Mahri.' In Ferrand, G., *op. cit.*

Szumowski, T. A. *Tres Roteiros Desconhecidos de Ahmad ibn Majid, o Piloto Arabe de Vasco da Gama*, Commisào Executiva das Comemoraçòes do Quinto Centenário da Morte do Infante Dom Henrique, Lisbon, 1960. Portuguese translation by M. Malkiel-Jirmunsky of *Tri Neisvestnych Lotsi Ahmada ibn Majida Arabskogo Lotsmana Vasco da Gamvi* [Three Unpublished Nautical Rutters of A. ibn M., the Arab pilot of Vasco da Gama], (in Russian) facsimile and translation, Academy of Sciences, Moscow and Leningrad, 1957.

Szumowski, T. A., 'An Arab nautical encyclopaedia of the 15th Century [*Book of Useful Chapters on the Basic Principles of Sea-faring*, by Ahmad ibn Majid, c. 1475].' In *Resumo das Comunicações do Congresso Internacional de História dos Descobrimentos*, Lisbon, 1960, p. 109. *Actas*, vol. 3, p. 43.

Tibbetts, G. R. *Arab Navigation in the Indian Ocean*, Luzac, London, 1971.

6. CHEMICAL TECHNOLOGY

Allan, J. W., *Abu'l-Qasim's Treatise on Ceramics*, Ashmolean Museum, Oxford, Reprinted from *Iran* XI, 1973.

Al-Antaki, Da'ud b., 'Umar, *Tadhkirat Uli al-Albab* etc., Cairo, 1308–9.

Berthelot, M. *Les Origines de l'Alchimie*, Steinheil, Paris, 1885. *Repr. Libr. Sci. et Arts*, Paris, 1938.

Burckhardt, T., *Alchémie*, Walter, Freiburg i/B, 1960. English translation by W. Stoddart: *Alchemy; Science of the Cosmos, Science of the Soul*, Stuart & Watkins, London, 1967.

Al-Dimashqi, Shams al-Din Abu'Abd Allan, *Nukhbat al-dahr fi aja'ib al-barr wa'l-bahr*, ed. by A. F. Mehren, St. Petersburg, 1866.

Forbes, R. J., *Bitumen and Petroleum in Antiquity*, Brill, Leiden, 1936.

Forbes, R. J., *A Short History of the Art of Distillation*, Brill, Leiden, 1948.

Forbes, R. J., *Studies in Ancient Technology*, Vol. IV, Leiden, 1964.

Garbers, K. (tr), *'Kitab Kimiya al-Itr wa'l-Tas'idat'; Buch über die Chemie des Parfüms und die Destillationen von Ya'qub ibn Ishaq al-Kindi; ein Beitrag zur Geschichte der arabischen Parfumchermie und Drogenkunde aus dem 9tr Jahrh. A. D., übersetzt . . . Brockhause, Leipzig, 1948. (Abhdl. f.d. Kunde des Morgenlandes, no. 30.)*

Hamarneh, Sami, K. and Sonnedecker, G., *A Pharmaceutical View of Albucasis (al-Zahrawi) in Moorish Spain*. Brill, Leiden, 1963.

Al Hasani, Mohammad Ibn Abi al-Khair, *al Nojum al-Shariqat*, Aleppo, 1928.

Hobson, R. L., *A Guide to Islamic Pottery of the Near East*, London, 1932.

Holmyard, E. J., *Alchemy*, Penguin, London 1957.

Holmyard, E. J., *The Arabic Works of Jabir ibn Hayyan*, vol. I, Paris, 1928.

Ibn Badis, *'Umdat al-Kuttab*, (see Levy, Martin).

Kraus, P., *Jabir ibn Hayyan, Contribution à l'histoire des idées scientifiques dans l'Islam*, 2 vols., Cairo, 1942–3.

Kuhn, H., 'Frühformen der Keramik', *Berichte der deutschen keramischen Gesellschaft*, Heft 4 (1958).

Lacam, J., 'La céramique musulmane des époques Omeyyade et Abbaside, VII au X siècle', *Cahiers de la céramique du verre et des arts du feu*, No. 20, Sèvres, 1960.

Lamm, C. J., *Das Glas von Samarra, Forschungen zur islamischen Kunst*, Vol. 4. Berlin, 1925.

Lane, A., *Early Islamic Pottery, Mesopotamia, Egypt, Persia*, London, 1947.

Lane, A., *Later Islamic Pottery*, London, 1957.

Levy, Martin, 'Medieval Arabic bookbinding and its relation to early chemistry and pharmacology', in *Transactions of the American Philosophical Society*, New Series, 52, Part 4 (1962), pp. 1–79.

Needham, J., *Science and Civilisation in China*, Vol. V:4. Cambridge, 1980.

Al-Rammah, Najm al Din Hasan al-Ahdab, MS. No. 2825 Bibliothèque Nationale, Paris (See Reinaud and Favé, *op. cit.*)

Al-Razi, *Kitab al-asrar wa sirr al-asrar*, edited by M. T. Danechepazhuh, Tehran, 1964.

Reinaud and Favé, 'Du feu grégois, des feux de guerre et des origines de la poudre à canon chez les Arabes, les Persans et les Chinois', *Journal Asiatique*, 1849, 6e Serie, XIV, 257–327.

Ruska, J., *Tabula Smaragdina*, Heidelberg, 1926.

Ruska, J., 'Der Zusammenbruch der Dschabir-Legende; I, die bisherigen Versuche das Dschabirproblem zu losen'. *Jahresbericht des Forschungs-Institut für Geschichte der Naturwissenschaft, Berlin*, 1930, 3, 9.

Ruska, J., 'Übersetzung und Bearbeitungen von al-Razi's Buch "Geheimnis der Geheimnisse" (*Kitab Sirr al-Asrar*).' *Quellen und Studien zur geschichte der Naturwissenschaft und Medizin*, 1935, 4, 153–238, 1937, 6, 1–246.

Sarre, F., *Die Keramik von Samarra* (Vol. 2, *Forschungen zur islamischen Kunst*). Berlin, 1925.

Sarre, F., 'Eine keramische Werkstatt aus Kaschan im 13.-14. Jahrhundert', *Instanbuler Mitteilungen des Archäologischen Instituts des Deutschen Reiches*, Heft 3 (1935), pp. 57–70.

Savage, G., *Pottery through the Ages*. Penguin Books, London, 1959.

Sezgin, F., *Geschichte des Arabischen Schrifftums*, Vol. IV, Leiden, 1971.

Singer, Charles *et al.*, *A History of Technology*, Vol. 2, Oxford, 1956.

Stapleton, H. E., Azo, R. F., and Hidayat Husain, M., 'Chemistry in Iraq and Persia in the tenth century AD', *Memoirs of the Royal Asiatic Society of Bengal*, **XII**, (6), 1927.

Stapleton, H. E., & Azo., R. F., 'Alchemical equipment in the 11th century.' MAS/B, 1905, I, 47 (*Account of the 'Ainu al-San'ah wa 'Aunu al-Sana'ah* (Essence of the Art and Aid to the Workers) by Abu-i Hakim al-Salihi al-Kathi, c. 1034.)

Wilkinson, C. K., 'The Kilns of Nishapur', *Bulletin*, Metropolitan Museum of Art, May, 1959, p. 235.

Wulff, Hans E., *The Traditional Crafts of Persia*, MIT Press, 1966.

7. TEXTILES, PAPER AND LEATHER

Beveridge, H., 'The Papermills of Samarkand', *Asiatic Quarterly Review*, 1910, pp. 160–4.

Bosch, K. G., 'Islamic Bookbinding: 12th–17th Centuries'. Unpublished PhD dissertation, University of Chicago, 1922.

Daumas, Maurice (ed.), *A History of Technology and Inventions*, John Murray, London, 1969.

Forbes, R. J., *Studies in Ancient Technology*, Vol. IV, Leiden, 1964.

Gille, Bertrand, 'The medieval age of the West', in Daumas, M., *op. cit.* pp. 422–573.

Hoernle, R., 'Who was the inventor of rag paper?' *Journal of the Royal Asiatic Society*, 1903, pp. 663–84.

Holt, P. M., Lambton, A. K. S., and Lewis, Bernard (eds.), *The Cambridge History of Islam*, Vol. 2B, Cambridge University Press, Cambridge, 1970.

Hunter, D., *Papermaking Through Eighteen Centuries*, New York, 1971.

Ibn Badis, *'umdat al-kuttab*. See Bosch, K. G. and Levy, Martin, *op. cit.*

Ibn Hawqal, Abu Il-Qasim Muhammad, *Kitab Surat al-Ard*, Biblioteca geographorum Arabicorum (BGA), Vol. II, 2nd edition, ed. J. H. Kramers, 1938.

Karabacek, J. von., 'Das arabische Papier', *Mitteilungen aus der Sammlung der Papyrus Erzherzog Rainer*, 5 vols. 1886–92, Vol. 2, pp. 87–178.

Karabacek, J. von., 'Zur orientalischen Altertumskunde: IV Muhamm. Kunststudien', *Sitzungsberichte der philosophisch-historischen Classe der Königlichen Akademie der Wissenschaften*, Vol. 172, Abn. 1, pp. 33–60.

Levy, Martin, 'Medieval Arabic bookbinding and its relation to early chemistry and pharmacology', in *Transactions of the American Philosophical Society*, New Series, **52**, Part 4 (1962), pp. 1–79.

Lewis, Bernard, *The Arabs in History*, Hutchinson, London, 1970.

Martin, F. R., *A History of Oriental Carpets before 1800*, 2 vols., Vienna, 1908.

Mez, Adam, *The Renaissance of Islam*, (Arabic edition), Cairo, 1957.

Al-Muqaddasi, Abu 'Abd Allah Shams al-Din, *Ahsan al-Taqasim fi Ma'rifat al-Aqalim*, Vol. III of *Bibliotheca geographorum Arabicorum*, ed. M. J. de Goeje, Leiden, 1906.

Al-Qalqashandi, Abu'l-'Abbas b. Ali, *Sobh al a'sha*, Cairo, 1963.

Al-Qazwini, Zakariyya b. Muhammad b. Mahmud, *Athar al-bilad wa akhbar al-'ibad*, Dar Sadir, Beirut, 1380/1960–1.

Sarre, F., and Trenkwald, H., *Old Oriental Carpets*, translated from German by A. J. Kendrick, 2 vols., Vienna, 1926–9.

Sarton, George, *Introduction to the History of Science*, Vol. III, Baltimore, 1947–1948.

Serjeant, R. B., *Islamic Textiles*, Beirut, 1972.

Singer, Charles *et at.*, *History of Technology*, Vol. II, Oxford, 1956.

Sufyani, *Sina'at tasfir al-kutub (The Technique of Bookbinding)*. See Bosch, K. G., *op. cit.*

Thomson, W. G., *A History of Tapestry*. London, 1906–30.

Von Falke, O., *Künstgeschichte der Seidenweberei*, Vols. I and II, Berlin, 1913.

Wulff, Hans E., *The Traditional Crafts of Persia*, MIT Press, 1966.

8. AGRICULTURE AND FOOD TECHNOLOGY

Al-Antaki, Da'ud b. 'Umar, *Tadhkirat Uli al-Albab* etc., Cairo, 1308–9.

Arberry, Arthur J., '*A Baghdad Cookery Book*', translated from the Arabic, *Islamic Culture*, Vol. XIII, Hyderabad, Deccan, 1939.

Colin, G. S., Article 'Filaha' (in the Muslim West) in *The Encyclopaedia of Islam*, Vol. II, 902.

Deerr, N. F., *The History of Sugar*, London, 1949–50.

Daumas, Maurice, (ed.), *A History of Technology and Inventions*, John Murray, London, 1969.

Forbes, R. J., *Studies in Ancient Technology*, Vol. II, Brill, Leiden, 1965.

Forbes, R. J., *Studies in Ancient Technology*, Vol. III, Leiden, 1965.

Holt, P. M., Lambton, A. K. S., and Lewis, Bernard (eds.), *The Cambridge History of Islam*, Vol. 2B, Cambridge University Press, Cambridge, 1970.

Ibn al-'Adim, Kamal al Din, *Al-wuslu ilu ul-Habib fi'wasf al-Tuyyibat wa al-tib*, IHAS, Aleppo University, 1986.

Ibn al'Awwam, Abu Zakariyya Yahya b. Muhammad, *Kitab al-filaha*, edited with French translation by Clement-Mullet, Paris, 1864–7.

Ibn Bassal, Muhammad b. Ibrahim, *Kitab al-Filaha*, edited Arabic text with Spanish translation by Jose M. Millar Vallicrosa and Mohamed Aziman, Tetuan, 1955.

Ibn al-Ukhuwwa, *Ma'alim al-qurba fi ahkam al-hisba*, translated by R. Levy, *Gibb Memorial Series*, XII, 1938.

Ibn Wahshiyya, *Kitab al-Filaha*, edited by Tawfic Fahd (in press). For a list of the manuscripts see Fuat Sezgin, *Geschichte des arabischen Schrifttums*, Vol. IV, 329.

Al-Jawbari, *al-Mukhtar fi kashf al-Asrar*, Damascus 1302 H.

Lambton, A. K. S., Article 'Filaha', in *The Encyclopedia of Islam*, Vol. II, 905.

Lambton, A. K. S., *Landlord and Peasant in Persia*, Oxford, 1953.

Lippman, E. O. von, *Geschichte des Zückers*, Leipzig, 1890.

Mez, Adam, *The Renaissance of Islam*, (Arabic edition), Cairo, 1957.

Müller-Wodarg, D., 'Die landwirtschaft Aegyptens in der frühen Abbasidzeit', *Der Islam*, XXXI–XXXIII, 1954–58.

Al-Nuwairi Shihab al-Din, *Nihayat al-Arab*, Cairo, 1954.

Rodinson, M., Article 'Ghidha' in *The Encyclopaedia of Islam*, Vol. II., Leiden.

Rodinson, M., 'Recherches sur les documents arabes relatifs à la cuisine'. *Revue des Etudes Islamiques*, 1949, pp. 96–162.

Watson, Andrew M., 'The Arab agricultural revolution and its diffusion, 700–1100'. *The Journal of Economic History*, XXXIV, March, 1974, No. 1.

Watson, Andrew M., *Agricultural Innovation in the Early Islamic World*, Cambridge University Press, 1983.

Wiedemann, E., *Aufsätze zur Arabischen Wissenschaftsgeschichte*, Olms, Hildesheim, 1970, Vol. 1, p. 18.

Wulff, Hans E., *The Traditional Crafts of Persia*, MIT Press, 1966.

Zayyat, Habib, 'Fann al-Tabkh al At'ima', *al-Mashriq*, Jan.–March, 1947.

Zayyat, Habib, 'Kitab al Tibakha', *al-Mashriq*, 1937, p. 370.

9. MINING AND METALLURGY

Abu-al-Fida, *Kitab Taqwim al-Buldan*, ed. Reinaud and De Slane, Paris, 1840.

Anossoff, P. A., 'On the Bulat', in *Gorny Journal*, Petersburg, 1841 (Russian); in *Annuaire du Journal des Mines en Russie 1843* (French); in *Archiv für wissenschaftliche Kunde von Russland*, Vol. 9, p. 510 (German). See Belaiew, N., 'On the Bulat'.

Banu Musa, *Kitab al Hiyal*, Arabic text ed. by A. Y. al-Hassan, Aleppo University, 1981.

Belaiew, N., 'Damascene steel', *The Journal of the Iron and Steel Institute*, Vol. 97 (1918), p. 417 ff.

Belaiew, N., 'On the Bulat' (Russian, O Bulatah), Petersburg, 1906, and 'über Damast'. *Metallurgie*, 1911.

al-Biruni, *Al-Jamahir fi ma'rifat at Jawahir*, Arabic text, Hydar Abad, 1355H.

Creswell, K. A. C., *A Bibliography of Arms and Armour in Islam*, London, 1956.

Forbes, R. J., *Studies in Ancient Technology*, Vol. VII, Brill, Leiden, 1966.

Hammar-Purgstall, J., 'Sur les lames des orientaux', *Journal Asiatique*, 3–4 (1854), p. 66.

al-Hassan, A. Y., 'Iron and steel technology in mediaeval Arabic Sources', *Journal for the History of Arabic Science*, 2, No. 1, 1978, pp. 31–43.

al-Idrisi, Abu 'Abd Allah Muhammad b. Muhammad. Part of his work was edited with Arabic text and French translation as *Description de l'Afrique et de l'Espagne*, R. Dozy and M. J. de Goeje, Leiden, 1866.

al-Muqaddasi, *Ashan al Taqasim fi Ma'rifat al Aqalim*, Brill, Leiden, 1906.

al-Qazwini, *Athar al-Bilad wa Akhbar al-'Ibad*, Arabic text, Dar Sadir, Beirut 1960–1.

Singer, C., *et al*, *A History of Technology*, vol. 2, Oxford, 1979.

Smith, Cyril Stanley, *A History of Metallurgy*, Chicago University Press, 1965.

Wiedmann, E., *Aufsätze Zür Arabischen Wissenschaftsgeschichte*, Vol. 1, Olms, Hildesheim, 1970, p. 706.

10. THE ENGINEERS AND ARTISANS

Cahen, C., Article 'Futuwwa' in *Encyclopaedia of Islam*, Vol. 2, Leiden, 1965.

Hourani, A. H., and Stern S. M., *The Islamic City* (see paper by C. Cahen), Bruno Cassirer, Oxford, 1970.

Ibn al-Ukhuwwa, *Ma'alim al'qurba fi ahkam al-hisba*, translated by R. Levy, *Gibb Memorial Series*, **XII**, 1938.

Ibish, Yusuf, 'Economic Institutions', in *The Islamic City*, ed. R. B. Serjeant, UNESCO, 1980, p. 114–25.

Al-Khuwarizmi, Abu'Abd Allah Muhammad b. Ahmad, *Liber Mafatih al-Olum*, Arabic text with critical apparatus in Latin, G. van Vloten, Leiden, 1895.

Lewis, B., 'The Islamic guilds', *Economic History Review*, **VIII**, I, Nov. 1937, 20–37.

Massignon, L., 'Les corps de métiers et la cité Islamique', *Revue Internationale de Sociologie*, **XXVIII**, 1920, 473–89.

al-Qalqashandi, Abu'l-'Abbas b. 'Ali, *Sobh al a'sha*, Cairo, 1963.

Qudsi, E., 'Notice sur les corporations de Damas', *Actes du Sixièeme Congrès International des Orientalistes*, 2nd part, Section 1: Semitique, 7–34, Leiden, 1885.

Rosenthal, Franz, *The Classical Heritage in Islam*, Routledge and Kegan Paul, London, 1975.

al-Shayzari, 'Abd al-Rahman b. Nasr, *Nihayat al-rutba fi talab al-hisba*, edited by al-'Arini, Cairo, 1946.

Taeschner, Fr., Article 'Futuwwa' in *The Encyclopaedia of Islam*, Vol. 2, Leiden, 1965.

Tashkpruzadeh, *Miftah al-Saada*, Cairo, 1968.

Credits for illustrations

Elisabeth Beazley 3.10, 8.26; Biblioteca Medicea Laurenziana, Florence 2.17; Bibliothèque Nationale, Paris 1.1, 2.13, 4.13(*a*), 4.14, 4.15, 4.18(*a*), 4.19, 5.2, 5.6, 5.9, 6.4(*b*), 6.8, 6.9, 6.10, 7.8, 7.9, 8.1, 10.4(*a*); Bildarchiv Preussischer Kulturbesitz, Berlin 9.5, 9.6, 9.10; Bodleian Library, Oxford 2.12(*a*), 2.14(*a*), 2.15, 2.18(*a*), 10.6, 10.8; P. G. Boxhall 5.5; British Library, London 4.1, 6.29, 7.4(*a*), 7.4(*b*), 8.3, 8.10, 8.14(*b*), 9.17, 10.1, 10.7; J. Allan Cash Photolibrary, London 1.3, 2.1, 2.2(*b*), 3.3, 3.4, 3.6, 5.3, 10.4(*b*); Maurice Chuzeville, Malakoff 4.13(*b*); A. C. Cooper, London 4.2, 4.11; Davids Samling, Copenhagen 9.11; Direction Générale des Antiquités et des Musées, Damascus 6.27; Edinburgh University Library 8.7, 9.2; Fine Art Photography, London 9.14(*b*); Werner Forman Archive, London 3.11; Forschungs-bibliothek Gotha 6.12, 6.25; Photographie Giraudon, Paris 7.5, 7.6; Michael Harverson 8.12, 8.13; A. Y. al-Hassan 6.13; D. R. Hill 2.7(*b*), 2.11(*b*), 2.14(*b*), 2.16(*b*), 2.18(*b*), 3.9(*a*), 3.12, 3.13; Hutchison Library, London, frontispiece, 5.1, 5.4, 9.9; Institute for the History of Arabic Science, Aleppo 6.14; A. F. Kersting, London 1.2, 2.3, 3.1(*a*), 3.1(*b*), 3.2, 3.7, 4.10, 8.4, 9.7(*b*); Olive Kitson 8.11, 8.14(*a*); Museum of the History of Science, Oxford 2.19, 2.20; Novosti Press Agency, London 1.4; Oriental Institute, Leningrad 4.20, 5.8; W. F. Paterson 4.5; Pieterse-Davison, Dublin 9.4, 9.7(*a*), 9.8, 10.3; J. Powell, Rome 1.5, 2.2(*a*), 4.3, 4.18(*b*), 6.5(*a*), 6.5(*b*), 6.19, 6.20, 6.21, 6.23, 7.2, 7.3, 7.10, 7.13, 7.14, 8.5, 8.6, 8.8(*b*), 8.16, 8.17, 8.18, 8.19, 8.20, 8.22(*b*), 8.24, 8.25, 10.5, 10.9; Rapho Agence Photographique, Paris 1.7, 7.11, 8.21; Science Museum, London 1.6, 6.2, 7.12, 8.8(*a*), 8.9, Anthony Smith 3.9(*b*), 9.3; Süleymaniye Kütüphanesi, Istanbul 2.5; Toledo Museum of Art, Ohio 6.16; Topkapi Sarayi Müzesi, Istanbul 2.4, 2.7(*a*), 2.16(*a*), 4.6, 4.7, 4.8, 4.9, 4.12, 4.16, 4.17; Victoria and Albert Museum, London 3.5, 4.4, 6.1, 6.3, 6.11, 6.15, 6.17, 6.18, 6.26, 6.28, 7.1, 8.2, 9.1, 9.12, 10.2; Wallace Collection, London 9.14(*a*); Zodiaque, la Pierre-qui-Vire, Saint Léger Vauban 7.7.

PHOTOGRAPHS AND DRAWINGS FROM PUBLICATIONS

Elisabeth Beazley and Michael Harverson, *Living with the desert*, Aris and Phillips, Warminster, 1982 / 8.11, 8.12, 8.13, 8.14(*a*), 8.26; M. Berthelot, *La chimie du moyen age*, Paris 1893 / 6.4(*c*), 6.6; H. J. Franken and J. Kalsbeck, *Potters of a medieval village in the Jordan valley*, North Holland Publishing Co, Amsterdam, 1975 / 6.22; A. Y. Hassan, *Taqi al Din and Arabic mechanical engineering*, Institute for the History of Arabic Science, University of Aleppo, 1976 / 2.6, 2.8, 2.9; A. Paris and F.

297

Ferriol 'L'industrie du fer chez les Berbères du Maroc', *Hespéris*, 1922, part 2 / 9.15; Hans Schmeller, *Beitrage zur Geschichte der Technik in der Antike und bei den Arabers*, 1922, volume 6 of *Abhandlungen zür Geschichte der Naturwissenschaften und der Medizin* / 2.21(*a*), 2.21(*b*), 2.21(*c*); M. W. Hilton-Simpson, *Arab medicine and surgery: a study of the healing art in Algeria*, Oxford, 1922 / 6.7(*a*), 6.7(*b*); M. W. Hilton-Simpson, 'Primitive Algerian oil mills', *Man*, August 1920 / 8.22(*a*); H. E. Stapleton and R. F. Azo, 'Alchemical equipment in the 11th century AD', *Memoirs of the Asiatic Society of Bengal*, I, 1905 / 6.4(*a*); John E. Volmer, E. J. Keall and E. Nagai-Berthrong, *Silk roads, China ships*, Royal Ontario Museum, Toronto, 1983 / 5.7; W. Seymour Walker, 'The olive press of Siwa', *Man*, April 1921 / 8.23;

ILLUSTRATIONS BASED ON DRAWINGS IN BOOKS

J. G. Landels *Engineering in the ancient world*, Chatto and Windus, London, 1978 / 2.10, 2.11;
Le Capitaine en Second Massalski, 'Préparation de l'acier damassé en Perse', *Annuaire du journal des mines de Russie, Année 1841*, 1843 / 9.13, 9.16;
Norman Smith, *A history of dams*, Peter Davies, London, 1971 / 3.8;
Hans E. Wulff, *The traditional crafts of Persia*, MIT Press, Cambridge, Massachusetts, 1966 / 6.24, 8.15

Index